Just Julia

In 1980 George Roberts took the biggest step of his life. He became Julia Grant.

Half the story, up to the operation, was first told in a BBC 'Inside Story' series at the time.

Now the full story is brought up to date. With no aftercare service for transexuals in the UK, many people go through surgery only to find it has not been the answer to all their problems. The success rate of male to female operations is not good, with many transexuals living as lesbians, turning to prostitution or, tragically, committing suicide within months of leaving hospital.

Julia's story is in many ways heartbreaking, but it is also a triumph. In her fortieth year she is Artistic Director of Wonderland Ceramics in Chesterfield and has a wildly popular stage show, 'The Bitch Is Back!' Fit and feisty, she is still fighting to become the woman she really is.

Just Julia

The Story of an Extraordinary Woman

Julia Grant

BXTREE

First published in Great Britain in 1994 by Boxtree Limited

Text © Julia Grant 1994

The right of Julia Grant to be identified as Author of this Work
has been asserted by her in accordance with the Copyright,
Designs and Patents Act 1988.

1 3 5 7 9 10 8 6 4 2

Typeset by SX Composing, Rayleigh, Essex
Printed and bound in Finland by WSOY for
Boxtree Limited
Broadwall House
21 Broadwall
London SE1 9PL

A CIP catalogue entry for this book is available from
the British Library.

ISBN 1 85283 481 1

Front cover photograph: Mike Prior
Design: Martin Lovelock

Contents

Dedication

To the memory of my mother, Jessica Agnes Roberts. After all these years, only now do I understand . . . Standing by my mother's coffin at her funeral, one of her neighbours tapped me on the shoulder and said, 'She was so proud of you. She talked about you all the time. She really loved you.' Perhaps things would be different today if we had learned to tell each other how we felt, before it was too late.

I would also like to dedicate this book to anyone out there who is confused or suffering, and feels lost in the wilderness. You are not alone, there are people out there who will be prepared to help you. All you need is the confidence to ask for that help. Do not bury your head in the sand – I tried it for years and believe me, it does not make your problems go away. You have to face up to reality sooner or later.

Finally, to those of you out there working on the voluntary help lines, keep up the good work: the system would crumble without you.

To you all, I dedicate this book. Thank you.

At the back of this book is a reference list of people who are prepared to listen and advise. The help they have given me over the years has been invaluable. If you need help seek it: total confidentiality is assured by all those listed.

Foreword

For the past forty years, my life has been a struggle and a challenge, but I am pleased to say that I have overcome the odds and beaten the system. It has not been easy for me to find my true identity, but in 1977 I finally made a stand: I admitted to myself and to the world that I had been born in the wrong body. In 1980, I did something about it by having gender surgery, but I found that the physical change, from George to Julia, was only the start of my transformation.

If you do not understand why men should want to be women, or women to be men, then read this book. I may not be a 'typical' transsexual (if such a person exists), and some of the things I have done and that have been done to me may shock and even disgust you, but many other transsexuals have faced the same problems and felt the same pain.

My childhood was certainly not pleasant: I was molested as a child, my rather raped me when I was fourteen years old, and in my youth other men were willing to pay for my services. I would not argue that this was responsible for my need to live as a woman but what it did do was develop my strength of character, which later enabled me to make the difficult decision to opt for surgery.

Many people think that transsexuals should be content to live as effeminate homosexuals or butch lesbians, but this completely misses the point for me. I had tried to conform – I even married and had children – but deep down I knew I wanted to be the woman I felt I was, and to love a man as a woman would. Often my pleas for help were ignored simply because people could not understand the inner pain caused by my conviction that I was living in the wrong body.

I realised some time before I opted for surgery that I was a transsexual, not a homosexual, and I had a dream that with the help of a skilful surgeon I could be freed from a living hell. I was not the first to undergo such surgery, or to face the problems that such a major step entails. Hundreds went before me and thousands have followed, but still society does not want to accept us fully. We can change our driving licences and even our passports, but we cannot marry and, as the law now stands, I still have to wait until the age of sixty-five to receive my state pension. In the UK, the gender we are born with is the gender we die with.

Having the surgery, at the age of twenty-five, was supposed to be the ultimate new beginning for me, but my euphoria was snatched away from me just six weeks later by a tragic accident. The media hype that had followed the television films covering the lead-up to my operation meant that I was forced to hide the fact that it had all gone wrong. Only now, fifteen years later, have I been able to tell the world what really happened, and to explain why I never told anyone before. I never regretted having the surgery, but now I have had to consider whether or not to do it all over again. This book tells how I reached my decision, and how the original producer and film crew got together to film the next chapter in the story they had told all those years ago.

I hope you will not feel sorry for me when you read this book, but I also hope that it will give you compassion towards other transexuals. If you meet one on your journey through life, show them some encouragement. If you are one, then follow your dream, but bear in mind that surgery is not always the answer. Seek help and find understanding, and you will discover the way.

Chapter 1
Childhood Memories

My earliest recollections of childhood go back to when I was about five years old. I was the oldest of eight children all born within a ten-year period. Following me were five girls: Shirley, the eldest, followed by Jeanne, Lesley, Julie and Beverley. Then at last my mother gave birth to my two brothers, Gary and Danny. Danny was the last child. I never really got on with Shirley. I think I must have been very jealous of her as a child, because I always blamed her if I had done anything wrong. She seemed to think herself 'above her station'. Jeanne and Lesley always tried to protect me. They were good kids at home when times got bad. Julie and Beverley were special. They were closer to my Uncle Ted, a man with whom my mother had had a very loving relationship. To Gary and Danny I was more of a mother than a brother in their first few years of life. The only thing I didn't do was give birth to them.

My mother was a wonderful woman. I remember feeling very proud of her when we walked down the street. Men would always turn and have a second look at her. She was a platinum blonde. The colour came out of a bottle, but it looked good. She was very tall and slim; she had a full figure and she always wore clothes that complemented it. Here eyes were always alive and shining, and her face was second to none – at least until Uncle Ted got killed. Then she changed dramatically.

My father? I never knew who he really was. I was told that I was a bastard, and that the name on my birth certificate didn't belong to my real father. A little indiscretion on my mother's part, I fear. I found out about this when I was about fourteen. The man who was my brothers' and sisters' father – well, the father of some of them – was a fisherman. He had come to our home town, Fleetwood, from Wales. A big man, slightly overweight but quite good-looking, he was vicious when he started. He had a violent temper that always seemed to come on when he had had a drink. He was rarely at home, thank God, as he spent fourteen out of every sixteen days at sea – a blessing to all the family. But then again, I must give credit where credit is due. He knew that my mother had two children by another man. He wasn't sure whether I was his or not. But he still supported the family and spent all his money on the children and my mother until things got too hot for him and he left home.

1

We all lived in Fleetwood. It had a large fishing port, the only industry that flourished in the town apart from I.C.I. It was also classed as a seaside resort, but we only got the overspill from Blackpool, seven miles away. The town had a pier and all forms of amusements on the sea-front. It boasted wonderful panoramic views of Morecambe Bay on a clear day – which wasn't all that often. In the winter it was like a ghost town. I think everyone who lived there had a husband, lover, father or son who sailed for one of the many prosperous fishing companies. It's not like that now – the big fleets of ships have dwindled and the large docks stand idle, employing only a handful of the men that they used to, but when I was a child everyone I knew had something to do with fishing. My grandfather was the manager of the dock-pool office, where the men signed on before they sailed. His father had been in the same job, and his father before him. Dockland ran through the family's veins.

On my frequent visits to dockland I used to get very excited at the prospect of becoming a fisherman. The only thing that put me off was the smell of the fish. On a windless day the smell would waft all the way down the main high street. Now it would take a gale to blow it that hundred yards. All the old fishermen are on the dole or work on the new industrial estate – a far cry from the open seas.

One thing that hasn't changed in Fleetwood is the friendliness of its inhabitants. They have had a hard time, yet they still keep on smiling. The public transport hasn't changed either; the large electric trams still thunder through the streets – up the main high street, around by the ferry and back out towards Blackpool. But all the little fish shops have gone. They have been replaced by novelty and fancy goods shops that have opened in the hope of attracting the few tourists. The old market has still survived, however, and the town comes to life on market days. The indoor market has always been busy, but the small outdoor market takes a bashing in the wind and rain.

The old fishermen's pubs have all gone now. The streets seem to be deserted, the soul has gone from the town. The little clubs where the girls used to entertain those single men who had money to waste have all closed down. The girls are still there, but business looks bad. Perhaps they think the town will jump back one day. Yet Dock Street with all its fine houses has been left to fall down. The ruins that still stand should be given a merciful end at the hands of a new bulldozer. They do little for the town's image.

The port is dying. The town is dying. If a large wave rolled in and swept it all away I don't think anyone would miss it – except those few fishermen who have fought a never-ending battle to keep their industry alive.

2

I was born in Blackpool Victoria Hospital at two a.m. on 21 September 1954. Mum had been in hospital for over six weeks, as she had toxaemia. I came out at a bouncing eight pounds twelve ounces, and was instantly nicknamed 'Billy Bunter' by the nursing staff. I was christened George William Roberts. Mum and Dad lived in rooms with Auntie Agnes in Hathaway Road, where I spent the first year of my life alone with Mum. I must have been a very loved child during that first year – and I must have noticed the difference when my sister was born, shortly after my first birthday. I was taken out of the limelight and didn't receive as much attention as I thought I should. I think this started the jealousy I felt for Shirley, which grew into hatred as the years passed. Thankfully, now we're friends.

The town was at its peak of prosperity, and its future looked good. The council must have thought so, anyway, because they started to develop the old Larkhome Farm, building the first of eight hundred houses that were to go up there in the next few years. When Mum was pregnant again with her third child in as many years, the council offered her one of the first houses to be completed. We moved in before any of the roads and gardens had been laid out. Jeanne was born within weeks of our arrival at 7 Medlock Place. Mum was by now used to giving birth and had her at home. I can remember the nurse who used to live just around the corner; she used to pop in every day to see if everything was all right. Nurse Ormerod also delivered Lesley the following year.

Family life was quite settled, although Dad arrived and disappeared for what seemed like weeks at a time. When I was five I started school in September at Chaucer Road, just round the corner. It was a rude awakening, and I decided on the first day that I didn't like it one little bit. It hadn't been too bad when we sat drawing and learning to spell, but the minute they had us outside running around the field and doing exercises I decided that school was not the life for me. I also missed my Mum.

Mum used to pick me up from school every lunchtime and also at four every afternoon. One day she turned up looking much happier than I had ever seen her before. With her was a very tall man. He was much taller than Dad, and better-looking as well. He had thick blond curly hair. I was introduced to Uncle Ted. He was going to live with us, but only while Dad was at sea. He always left just before Dad got home, and the picture of him and all us kids that Mum had taken on the beach one day was always removed from the sideboard and hidden at the bottom of the airing-cupboard.

At the tender age of six I remember bouncing up and down on Ted's knee one night. All the girls were in bed. Mum said to Ted that she wished I was his. I wished that he was my Dad, as well. He was always nice to me, not like my Dad, who used to frighten me when he shouted.

Mum was pregnant again and was kept very busy, so I started to go to the shops to buy what she needed for the following day. It was great running home from school and taking a pound note up to the Westview estate to do the shopping. The only thing I didn't like about the shopping was when we ran out of potatoes, because they were so heavy to carry all the way home. But I managed and never complained. Mum always used to treat me and give me sweets for helping her. She continually told me I was her 'number one'.

I came in from school one day to find Uncle Ted and Dad in the living-room with Mum. She had been crying. I ran up to her and asked what was wrong. She asked me if I would rather Uncle Ted lived with us or Daddy. I didn't know what to say to her. I liked Uncle Ted, but Dad would hit me if I didn't choose him. So I told her that I thought they should both stay. It must have been the answer to all their problems. Uncle Ted did not leave anymore: when Dad came in from sea, Dad slept on the couch.

Julie was soon born. She was very different from all of us. She had lots of freckles, and curly golden hair just like Uncle Ted's. No one seemed to understand why, or even care. Mum was so much happier when Ted was around. I remember the sunny weekends when we all used to help pack up a picnic. Julie and Lesley would ride in the big Silver Cross pram, with me and the other two girls dancing off with Ted up in front. Dad never came with us, even when he was in from the sea.

The girls all used to wear dresses the same colour, with matching shoes and socks. All of them wore ribbons in their hair. I used to have to wear my little sailor's uniform, but I didn't like the long trousers. When we got home and all the girls were asleep at night, I used to sneak into their bedroom and pinch Shirley's dress and ribbons. I could never get the dress to fasten up, as it was too small. The ribbons would never stay in my hair, either, because it was too short. Sometimes I would get into bed with the dress on and fall asleep. In the morning I used to have to hide it because it was so creased. Shirley used to go mad when she found it, always blaming me for doing it. Mum used to tell her not to be so stupid – I was a boy and didn't wear dresses. I would sit there laughing to myself.

Uncle Ted worked as a chef at the Norbreck Castle Hotel in Blackpool, so he left early every morning. The mornings were Mum's busiest times, so when I started crying and told her that I didn't want to go to school, she would always give in if I said I'd help with the housework. I liked cleaning upstairs, making all the beds and hoovering, then going over to finish off with a duster. It was a lot better than school. If I finished quickly enough I could always make it down into the kitchen to watch Mum prepare the lunch or do some baking. Sometimes I was even allowed to make my own cakes. Then I could take away the mixing-bowl and a spoon to finish off anything that was left.

Mum became pregnant yet again. When Beverley was born I don't think even my mother was sure who the father was. She definitely did not look like Julie had done as a child, not at first.

Things started to flare up at home very time that Dad was due in from sea. The atmosphere was terrible. The kids all got away with murder when Ted was around, but the minute Dad walked through the door no one said a word out of place. If they did, he would give them a thick ear. As the winter wore on, the friction between Ted and Dad got worse. On several occasions they nearly came to blows. One night, just before Dad was due in, the sea-walls broke. We lived only about two hundred yards from the wall. On the following day, when we woke up, there was almost four feet of water downstairs. The electricity had been cut off and everything downstairs had been ruined. We were all stranded upstairs. We did not see Nan and Grandad all that much, but the old boy got his rowing-boat out. He brought us the only food that we were to get that day. The water-level dropped slightly around lunchtime, but steadily rose as the tide turned.

All the kids in the area thought it was a big joke to go swimming in the living-room. Not so poor old Mum. All the carpets and furniture were ruined beyond repair. When Dad arrived home the following evening she had just about had enough. A full-scale battle between Dad and Ted raged for nearly an hour. Dad won, and Mum was given the choice of going with Ted and leaving us all behind or staying with Dad to patch things up for the sake of the children. For Mum it was a heartbreaking decision. If she had only known how things were going to turn out, she'd have left us. But she gave up her own happiness, knowing full well that she despised my father. She loved her children and only stayed to protect us.

Dad can't have trusted Mum, for he brought his mother down to stay with us. Nanny Davies was very strict. She used to go about the house giving orders to everyone and telling my mother how we should be brought up. She insisted that my mother should save money, and bought sheep's heads for her to cook with cabbage. I used to hate her; she was a miserable old bag with a lump on her back and a chip the size of Blackpool Tower on her shoulder. I used to play all kinds of tricks on her, and she would go mad with rage. Thank God, she only lasted with us for about two months; then

Mum packed all her gear up and threw her out. My father went berserk when he got home, and then things really started to change.

Mum was pregnant yet again. With six already, you would have thought that she had enough to cope with, but she was a natural breeder. I hoped that it would be a brother; mind you, it was a bit late, because by the time he'd be five I would be nearly fourteen. But I wasn't too worried, for I enjoyed playing with the girls. At Christmas-time I would always get one of them to swop a doll for a football, or a toy car for a dressing-table set. I couldn't stand all the boy's games that people used to buy me. I would much rather have been bought girl's toys.

Every week when the comics used to arrive from the newsagent I would always swop my copy of Valiant or Hurricane for one of the girls' *Judy*s or *Bunty*s. I used to like the stories in the girls' comics, all about horses, school or romance: much better than all the war stories that were bought for me. I always used to rip the back page off *Bunty* as soon as I got it, and later cut out the little doll and clothes that were on it. Over the years I built up quite a collection of little dolls. I used to number them and the dresses so that I knew which dress belonged to which doll, and I kept them all hidden in a big wooden box under my bed.

The other girls weren't allowed into my room, so they never found anything that I had hidden. And anyway when we were all playing in the living-room on a rainy day I was the only boy, with five sisters and my mother. If I played with dolls or knitted with the rest of the girls it didn't stand out. No one took any notice. It would have been different if I had had five brothers in the area.

I almost never went out to play with other boys in the area. When I did, I always ended up hurting myself. If it was for a game of football I always ended up in goal; it just wasn't worth it. If Mum forced me out to play, which was not all that often, I would go off walking by myself.

I was quite a lonely child, really. The other boys' dads used to play with there sons, but not mine. He just used to collapse into a chair and watch telly. If anyone interrupted one of the programmes that he was watching, he would go berserk, and big rows would always develop if Mum thought he was shouting unnecessarily. She was always quick to defend us; she protected us to the last, and the only thing that would stop the row was when she got a slap and he stormed off to the pub to meet the lads.

She used to sit crying for hours when he had gone. I always tried to comfort her, but she grieved for Ted and often she told me so. When Ted had left our home, he had gone to Grimsby and started fishing again. But only two months after leaving us he disappeared at sea. The police believed that he had jumped overboard. Whether it was for the love of my mother we'll never know. When Mum heard the news of his death, what was left of her love for men disappeared. Instead she learnt to use them.

Because her seventh child was due, the council gave us another house in Heathfield Road. It was a really rough area, but we had to take the house because we desperately needed the room. In Medlock Place the kids were all cramped. The very day we moved, everybody decided that they did not like the place – all the kids were so scruffy. They all used to swear badly, and we were soon to pick it up. We were all transferred to Flakefleet Junior school. It was terrible, and I spent most of my time at home. I was needed more at home anyway.

Gary, my first brother, was born as I approached my ninth birthday. Dad was at sea and Mum was very weak after Gary's birth. She had him at home. I stayed off school for ages and, with simple instructions from Mum, I cooked all the meals and kept the house clean. The shopping was my full responsibility by now, and I was a good little shopper. I knew that bargains were what counted, and special offers on regular foods kept the costs down. If getting corned beef cheaper meant a walk to town, then I went.

Mum started to drink Sanatogen wine to build up her strength. It was supposed to be a tonic and it certainly improved her mood. But she was still very unhappy, and I encouraged her to go out, like all the other mothers in the street. I was safe, left baby-minding, and once or twice wouldn't hurt her. I'll never forget the first night she went out and left me in charge. I was so excited. The children were all asleep in bed. The minute she had gone out of the door, I set to and cleaned the place up from top to bottom. Gary was left downstairs with me. I was quite capable of changing his nappy if necessary. Mum was home shortly after eleven p.m. and I was so proud because nothing had gone wrong. She looked as though the change had done her good. She was in high spirits, as she had met some of her old mates and had arranged to meet them the following week.

We became even closer, and when she had a problem we used to sit and talk about it. Money was always difficult. Mum said she could earn plenty if she went out every night. I was a big boy now, and told her that I would always look after the house. It was decided that a couple of nights a week would be O.K., and for a short time family life was restored. Mum popped out for her couple of nights a week, sometimes not getting home until two. I always stayed up and waited for her. The washing and ironing were always done if I saw them lying about.

Dad had quietened down a little, but he wasn't aware of Mum's drinking habits or her evenings out. Mum had started to drink during the day; she called it her 'medicine' when any of the kids saw her. I used to pick up a bottle of cheap wine every day when I went out to do the shopping. Within a couple of months it was two bottles a day. It built up steadily, and I ended up making two or three trips a day. But the drink was always well hidden, and when Dad was in from sea she never went out.

One night he came in roaring drunk at about midnight. I had only just gone to bed, as I had been keeping Mum company. He started hitting her and calling her a dirty old slag. I crept out of bed and stood at the top of the stairs crying my eyes out. I hated it when he hit her, but I dared not go down or say anything because I knew that he would start on me. I could hear Mum being thrown around the living-room and crying as he laid punch after punch on her. He had found out about her visiting a particular night club, the local whores' hangout. Mum ran out of the living-room and locked herself downstairs in the bathroom. I stood back against the landing wall, where I could just see the bathroom door. The tears were now stinging my face, but I was helpless, as I had been on many other occasions. Dad banged on the bathroom door and told her to open it. She didn't so he just kicked it in. He started to slap her about again. All the children were awake and crying for her. I ran back to bed and heard my father shout up the stairs that if they didn't shut up he would get the belt out. Within three seconds you could have heard a pin drop. They knew that he meant it.

I cried into my pillow; praying as hard as I could for God to stop him from hitting her. She had told me earlier that evening that she was pregnant yet again and she was going to surprise Dad when he got home. She never had a chance to say anything before he started on her. I despised and hated my father more and more. How could he beat her up like this? In the morning he would pretend that nothing ever happened. He'd go and put his arms around her to give her a cuddle and tell her how much he loved her, and she would cringe and turn away. I had seen it all so many times before.

But it wasn't going to be the same tonight. I had fallen off to sleep, and Mum woke me up as she climbed into the bottom of my bed. She had a black eye and her face was all swollen. I started to cry again when I saw her, and she tried to comfort me. The next thing I new, the bedroom door flew open and Dad came in, half-dressed. He told her, only once, to get into their bedroom. She told him to go away and leave her alone. He just grabbed her by the hair and dragged her out of the room. Their bedroom door slammed shut and all hell broke loose. My mother was taking a hell of a beating that night, the worst that I could ever remember. I lay on my bed with the pillow over my head, holding it against my tears, trying to drown out the noise.

All I could hear was my mother's screams, until I couldn't stand it any longer. I had to help her. I jumped out of bed and ran into their bedroom. Mum was lying naked on the bed, bleeding from where he had hit her, in the face. He was standing over her as I entered the room. I just hurled myself at him, kicking and throwing as many punches as I could. He just gave me one backhander that sent me flying across the room; but I wasn't going to give in that easily this time. I threw everything from the dressing table at him. Then I ran at him with Mum's hand-mirror and smashed it against the side of his head.

He grabbed hold of me by the hair and started to punch me all over. My mother screamed at him to leave me alone, but she was powerless to help me. He kept shouting that I was a no-good little bastard, and threw me towards my mother on the bed. It was an old-fashioned bed, and my shoulder-blade was ripped open as I hit the metal frame. He thought that I would give in then, but not I. He turned to start on my mother again, but as I ran out of the bedroom I shouted that I was going to get the police. He heard me, and as I went through the front door he was in hot pursuit. I didn't get very far down the street before he caught me. He threw me to the ground and kicked me several times, then dragged me home. My mother had barricaded herself in the children's bedroom with all their furniture. He tried to smash the door down but, seeing that he was beaten, he turned on me again. I ran like a frightened rabbit. He went back into his bedroom, got dressed and slammed his way out of the front door.

Once I was sure he had gone, I ran down and locked all the doors. Then I told Mum that everything was all right. It took a while to get the other kiddies back to sleep; they were petrified. She and I slept together that night, both praying that he wouldn't return and start again. The next morning I didn't really have any option; I couldn't go to school. In fact neither of us dared to go out. A couple of the neighbours came in to see how everything was, for they had heard the row the night before, but they weren't interested in helping – they were just bloody nosey, and I told them so.

Dad sent a taxi round for his clothes that afternoon. He was staying at the Fishermen's Mission, and sent the message that his wages would still come from the office every week. We all breathed a sigh of relief. But then Mum started to drink really heavily; and instead of the couple of nights a week, she went out every night. Dad still didn't know that she was pregnant, and he only heard when she was in her sixth month. The other children continually asked for him. They weren't aware of just what had been happening over the last few years. Yet, when he asked, she agreed to take him back in. She had been going out on the game to earn extra money, and now she was six months gone she couldn't do it.

Danny was born in Fleetwood Hospital. He was a Caesarean baby, and when Mum brought him home she told us that she couldn't have any more babies as the doctor had cut her Fallopian tubes. Dad had stayed at home while she was in hospital, but soon returned to sea when she came home. He had only been gone a few days when I walked into the parlour and found Mum in bed, bleeding badly. She had internal bleeding and was in one hell of a mess. I called the doctor and he in turn called an ambulance. Mum went into hospital and had a hysterectomy.

We went into a foster-home for the first time, until Mum returned home. When we arrived home after only three weeks away we were all like strangers to one another. Mum wasn't all that well, either. She stopped caring for herself. I now spent more of the daytime at home than ever. I had my evenings to myself, but was always home in time for her to go out. It did not take Dad long to go back to his old ways, and when Danny was only five months old Mum had a nervous breakdown. She was taken into hospital time and time again – sometimes for a couple of days, sometimes for a couple of weeks. If Dad was around, he used to look after us; if he was at sea, we just went into foster-homes. This really helped break the family up because we never knew whether we were coming or going.

During one of the many short periods at home I was woken up by my father one night at about two a.m. He was sailing on the 3.30 tide; he asked me to sit by the telephone and, dead on three o'clock, to ring the pool office and ask my grandad to send him home as Mum was not well. I fell asleep and did not wake until five. I telephoned grandad's office, but a strange man answered. My grandad had gone home. I asked for my father. The voice came back on the line and said that he had sailed with the ship. He asked if there was anything that he could do. I told him that my Mum was ill, but not to worry. It would be all right. Then I thought about what Dad had said, and I went upstairs to find out what was wrong.

I opened Mum's bedroom door and could hardly believe my eyes. The sheets were covered with blood. I remember the first time I had seen her like that; but this was different. I walked over to the bed and only then realised that she had cut her wrists. I started to panic, though I knew she needed to get to hospital. Nan was a nurse – I must get Nan. That's all that was going through my head. I ran into the street in just my pyjama pants with no shoes on, just as fast as my legs could carry me. I hadn't even thought of using the phone. I was soon soaked to the skin, but I was halfway to Nan's before I realised that it was raining. The wind and rain made it difficult for me to run; I was crying from sheer frustration. I tried to flag down a car, but it just drove straight past. I swore after it. Thank God Nan was in when I got there. I never thought that she could have been at work. I quickly told her the story, and she phoned for the police, then an ambulance.

A police car picked me and Nan up, and by the time we got home they were taking Mum away. As she passed me on the path with tears in her eyes she just looked at me and said, 'I'm sorry, love. I just can't take any more.'

I could not speak; I just watched them drive her away.

Dad was flown home to look after us. He went mad at me for not phoning him. I believe to this day that my mother had tried to commit suicide before he left home that night.

Mum was away for about three months this time. She had been taken into Lancaster Moor, a special hospital in Lancaster. She was under a special doctor there. Dad used to go and see her every fortnight. On his second visit I begged him to take me along. He didn't object, but he told me that I would not like what I saw. I now think he took me out of sheer spite, knowing how close Mum and I were to each other. The day we went he seemed in a cheerful mood. As we entered the hospital grounds he told me that he would not be seeing Mum this week because he was seeing her doctor. He took me over to ward 21 and rang a bell; a nurse came and unlocked the door. I thought that it was a strange hospital to keep all its doors locked.

Dad told the nurse that I was going to visit my mother while he went to see the doctor. She asked him if he thought that was a good idea. I remember his reply to this day. He said to her, 'It will do them both good.' Then he walked away and left me with the nurse.

She locked the door behind me and took me through a communal lounge. There were about twenty people in it, and they all looked absolutely nuts. An old lady stood in a nearby corridor laughing her head off; underneath her was a pool of water where she had peed herself.

At the end of a long passage the nurse stopped and opened another door. She stood back and let me go in. My mother was asleep in the cot that stood in the middle of the room. The nurse went across and woke her up. She sat up. I couldn't believe it: all her hair had been cut off and she was talking like a baby. The nurse just stood by me and told me to be brave. She asked me if I would like to feed my mother, as she hadn't eaten her dinner. I said that I would not mind. The nurse left, locking me in the room, and shortly returned with a bowl of jelly and ice-cream. I sat and fed my mother for about five minutes. She did not acknowledge that she knew me at any time while I was in the room. Then, when I offered her another spoonful of ice-cream, she just went berserk. I had never seen my mother so aggressive. The nurse grabbed me and took me outside. She could see that I was badly shaken.

In her office I asked her what was wrong with my Mum. She told me that she had had some electric-shock treatment to make her forget all the nasty things that had happened to her. But instead of just forgetting the nasty things, she had forgotten everything and was as far back as a three-year-old child. But she was getting better every day, the nurse told me, and in a few weeks she would be as good as new.

It wasn't long before Dad collected me. He just asked me what I thought of my precious mother now. I did not reply to his question; I just walked alone in a stunned silence.

In time Mum returned home. Dad then decided that we should all be given a new start in life. He arranged to get a mortgage on a big house in Hesketh Place. We were all glad that we were moving.

He soon returned back to sea, but Mum was not herself at all. She got annoyed with the children for the least little thing and just could not cope with them. I hardly ever went to school now. It just wasn't worth it: I would still have all the housework to do when I got home. Mum's drinking problem got worse every day. She made several more suicide attempts; some I didn't even report – just let her sleep them off. I was well versed in procedure now if anything ever went wrong, although some attempts led to our going into care again for short periods.

Dad left home and went to Grimsby to sail from there. He just sent the weekly money through. In his own words, he was pissed off with trying to help her.

Our final day at home as a family was soon to come.

Mum went out drinking every night. Bottles were bought every day to keep her going. She only went out on the game to earn money for the following day's booze. I started to hock things in the second-hand shop so that I could buy food for the kids' meals. I handled Dad's money every week. If Mum had ever got her hands on that, it would have all gone on booze too. I had replaced Dad for all the children, and for the young ones I was a mother too. I did all the cooking, cleaning and washing.

Mum started to bring her men-friends home. Some stayed a week or two, others only days. The minute that their money ran out, they were run out. It wasn't a nice environment for the kids to be in, but I shielded them from most of it. They were protected from the obscenity and degradation that went on. The older girls thought that I was plain bossy. If they had really known what I was up against they might have helped me.

Money ran out one day and there was just nowhere I could go to raise cash to pay for a bottle for her. I wouldn't ask any of my new-found friends – whom you will read about later – to lend me money. That would have been never-ending. We could not even go to the local off-sales shop and ask for credit, as Mum owed them over forty pounds already. Mum got more and more depressed as the day wore on. There was nothing I could do that would have helped. About 7.30 p.m. she disappeared off to bed. Once all the kids were in bed and I had cleaned up, I knocked at the parlour door. There was no reply, so I knocked louder. I tried the handle of the door, but it was locked from the inside. She had never done that before. There were three glass panels in the door, but I could not see a thing: the room was in darkness.

There was a strange smell. I couldn't place it at first; then I realised that it was gas. I ran into the kitchen, thinking I had left the cooker on, but as I went through the living-room I lost the smell. The gas had to be coming from the parlour. I went back and banged on the door yet again. I ran out into the street, then checked all the outside windows. They were all locked. There was only one thing I could do.

I ran into the kitchen and got the hammer out of Dad's old tool-box. I wrapped one of the tea-cloths off the sink around my hand, and just went and broke the first panel of glass. Most of the glass fell into the room and landed on the carpet, so I had not made too much noise. I stuck my hand in through the broken glass and undid the lock. The smell of gas was much stronger now. I pushed the door open and ran and turned the fire off. Then I ran to the bay and threw open the first window. Gasping for breath, I stuck my head out into the cool night air and inhaled deeply. Then I went to have a look at my mother. Straight away I noticed an empty bottle of tablets at the side of her bed.

I ran down to the phone-box and dialled 999. I was put through to the operator for the ambulance service. He said he'd not heard from me for ages and had thought we'd moved. He already knew the address, so I got home as quickly as I could. The smell of gas wasn't so bad now, but Mum was still out for the count. I sat on the bed holding her hand, waiting for the ambulance. A knocking started on the door – far sooner than I had expected. At the same time I noticed a letter on the floor addressed to me. I picked it up and stuck it in my back pocket.

It was the police; they were quick. They usually arrived after the ambulance. It was the same two cops that had come on numerous other occasions. The elder of the two just looked at me and smiled. He said, 'You've had it rough, kid. Boy, have you had it rough.'

The two cops stood by my mother's bedside, trying to revive her. I grabbed a suitcase and packed all the things I knew she would need. She did not regain consciousness until the following day, after they had given her a stomach-pump.

The young ploddy set off to bring my Nan to stay with us till tomorrow, when the welfare could sort us out. That same morning we were all placed under a court order and we would therefore all be placed in child custody until we reached our eighteenth birthdays.

I was to spend a fortnight with Nan before I went away, so I helped the welfare pack all the children's clothes and toys. Each child left home that day with his or her own individual black plastic sacks – full of rubbish. That's all we really had.

The children had been sent on a picnic to make the packing easier. When they returned I helped them with their goodbyes by being cheerful. It was harder to see the little ones go than it was the girls. But it didn't take long. Then I went around the house with a policeman and checked that all the doors were locked. As we passed the cellar door, he asked what was down there. I opened it and turned on the light. He just looked startled. About two thousand empty wine-bottles lay everywhere – some smashed, others just thrown in the corner. Mum never let me throw them out in the bin, in case any of the neighbours saw them.

That night, as I was undressing, I found the letter in my back pocket. I opened it. Inside was a short note in my mother's handwriting. She asked me to forgive her. She said that she had tried to be a good mother to us, but had decided to take the easy way out. She wanted me to tell the kids the truth about what had happened when they were older. Thank God she didn't die then, because I now know it was just a cry for help. She never had any serious intentions of killing herself – she loved us all too much – and although she tried all her life at regular intervals to end it all, it was usually under the influence of drink. Yet her drinking problems were to be her downfall, as she slowly killed herself with years of alcohol abuse.

One thing that I will remember to my dying day is turning the letter over in my hand. Written on the other side was a much shorter message, addressed to Ted. It just said: 'I LOVE YOU'.

Chapter 2
Young Love

Although until this stage my life had been quite protected, there was another side of it that walked along with me. Luckily this was kept out of public view; it would have outraged most people, as well as being most embarrassing for my family.

I should warn readers that this chapter describes my seduction at the age of ten by a middle-aged man. It is shocking, and perhaps the squeamish should pass over it. However, it is important to the story. I don't mean to sensationalise my life, but these next few pages deal with one of its turning-points.

Mother had gone out to do her usual round of pubs and clubs. This was becoming an everyday occurrence; she had left three sheets to the wind, so an early return was not guaranteed. I had been left up to babysit yet again.

It was a cold winter's night, and the howling of the wind and the banging of the gates in the back alley were a little frightening. I huddled up on the settee with a glass of pop and a bag of cheese-and-onion crisps. I had the television on; the volume was turned up quite loud to drown the noise from outside. The old western that was on the screen was as boring as I found all westerns to be. The only thing that brightened them up was the fashionable clothes the saloon girls wore. I only wished that women still wore dressed like that today, instead of the silly mini-skirts that all the girls seemed to like. They only showed bow-shaped legs and silly, thick panty-hose.

The film came to an end with the baddies being shot by the sheriff as per usual. I knew that the ironing had to be done, so while the news was on I dragged out the ironing-board and started to press the children's school clothes for the following day. I was happily ironing away when suddenly there was a loud knocking at the door. At first I started to panic. I had always been taught never to answer the door, especially late at night when Mum was out. Then I remembered that it could be my Uncle Malcolm; he had lived with us a few weeks and always seemed to forget his key.

He was a funny sort of man; small in stature and slightly balding, he had a very strong Scottish accent and always seemed to be smoking a pipe. He was approaching his fiftieth birthday. He had been a friend of Mum's for a few years and she had offered him accommodation when he had hit a bad patch. Besides, the money that he paid for the front parlour paid the rent for the rest of the house. He always appeared lonely; he had never married and had no close family. His main pastime was to pop down to the local pub for a game of darts. There he could get drunk with the rest of the lads.

I opened the door, and it was Malcolm. He seemed a little more drunk than usual, and slightly earlier. He half-walked, half-stumbled down the hall and into the living-room, where he collapsed into an armchair to watch the news. I carried on with the ironing, glad of company on such a foul night. Once I had finished it and laid out all the children's school clothes on the settee for the following day, I made a cup of coffee for Malcolm and poured another glass of pop for myself. I settled down to watch the next programme. The news had been full of horrors from all round the world as usual. I could never understand how we survived with so many wars always taking place. Surely the world would soon start to fall apart if it were continually bombed?

Malcolm invited me to sit on his knee, which he had often done on other occasions. I didn't really want to – I couldn't stand the smell of stale drink and smoke – but I didn't want to offend him either. We sat and watched the credits go by for the start of the next programme. He told me that I should not be watching this one, as it was for adults only. He whispered the words into my ear, and his tongue flicked just inside it, making me feel really funny all over. The programme was about the birth of a baby. I sat there absolutely fascinated, and continually plied him with questions. How? Why? He laughed and tried to answer all my questions, explaining exactly what was happening. I was still puzzled, and one question led to another.

I sat there, my legs straddling Malcolm's. I felt rather strange. There was a funny sensation running through my body. I sat still and tried to work it out. I could feel something moving below the cheeks of my bottom. I stuck my hand down and tried to move it away, as it was distracting me. I felt a huge swelling in Malcolm's trousers, which throbbed when I touched it.

I was even more puzzled when Malcolm pushed the swelling deeper into my hand. I looked up at Malcolm, but he just smiled and held me even tighter round the waist. I still felt strange, yet I was somehow warmed by the situation. The smell of beer on his breath did not matter at all now. He pecked me on the cheek once or twice; then he brushed his cheek against mine, and then his lips. I pulled away and looked at him. Should this be happening? I was thinking. Dad doesn't do this. But then again, he did not like me. I asked Malcolm. His answer was that Dad had my Mum and that was why he did not do it. Because Malcolm was alone, he did.

Malcolm stood me on the floor and ran his hands up and down the insides of my legs. I was astonished to find that I too had a lump in my trousers. I had had such a feeling before, but never in front of anyone. I felt deeply ashamed and tried to pull away. Malcolm just held me tight and told me to relax.

He slowly undid my trousers and let them fall to the ground. Then he took hold of me in his hand. He could see that I was terrified, and his soothing voice told me not to worry. I was amazed at the speed his hands moved; he seemed to be touching me all over at the same time, undressing me as he went.

Soon I was sitting on his knee again. He kissed my cheek once more and started to rub his hand across my body, telling me what a lovely boy I was and that some day I would make some woman happy.

He pressed my hand against him again. Then he unbuttoned his trousers and pulled them down. It was strange – he had on another pair of trousers, made of long prickly wool, which he called his 'long johns'. He unbuttoned these and took out his penis. I was shocked: I could just get hold of it with my two hands, and each time I tried to get hold of it it just jumped about.

Malcolm again started to rub my lower parts. After a short while he pulled off his long johns. He was very hairy; the hair went all the way up to his neck. He looked so funny – all that hair on his body, yet hardly any on his head.

He removed all the ironing from the couch and then lay down. He asked me to lie with him. I walked over and cuddled up to him. I played with the hair on his chest for ages while he caressed me. My erection had gone, but Malcolm's was as big as ever.

Casually glancing towards the television, I caught sight of a baby being born. The sight was disgusting. Malcolm jumped off the couch and told me that I shouldn't be watching such rubbish anyway. Then he turned on the radio and flicked off the centre light.

The fire in the hearth glowed and the flames flickered and threw shadows on the wall. Malcolm stood above me as I lay on the settee. He bent his head low, kissed me and tried to force his tongue into my mouth. I pulled away, gasping for air. He continued to do that for quite some time.

Then he lifted me up and lay in the centre of the settee; I lay on top. I started to sweat from head to foot. So did Malcolm. He asked me several times if I was all right, continually reminding me that what we were doing was to be our secret. I felt happy; I had no intention of telling anyone.

Suddenly the telephone started to ring. I ran down the hall, for I did not want it to wake up the other kids. It was Mum. She was well gone; God knows how she ever remembered the telephone number. I could hear people laughing and singing in the background. She was in the Blue Flamingo. I could hear someone calling her name, asking for her to sing another song, and I remember thinking she must have been absolutely pissed if she was singing for them. I told her everything was fine. She told me that she wouldn't be home for a while, so if I wanted to go off to bed I could. I knew there was no chance that she would leave the club before it closed at two o'clock. She was with Uncle Sam. He was a nice guy, in his sixties, but with money. He always seemed to be giving Mum presents.

I went back into the living-room, Malcolm was sitting in the chair by the window, pipe in one hand, rubbing himself with the other. I went over and sat on the floor between his legs. The hair on his chest was matted with sweat. I took hold of him with one hand and asked him if it had gone to sleep. He just burst out laughing and told me that if I kept hold of it it would soon wake up. Within two minutes it was big again. I was intrigued.

Malcolm asked me if he could make love to me. I asked him what he meant, and he explained. He did not lie to me; he told me that it would hurt at first but that after a short while it would be O.K. I agreed; what we had done earlier had not hurt me – surely what he wanted to do now would not be all that different? I climbed back upon his knee and he kissed me twice.

He placed his pipe in the ashtray, leaned back in the chair and turned me to face the fire. Then proceeded to massage my buttocks. His finger felt as though it were burning me.

He pulled me closer, inserted his penis between my legs and moved his body backwards and forwards. I relaxed – but it was then I received the shock of my life. All I felt was a sharp burst of pain as his huge weapon stabbed inside me. I let out a cry, but he covered my mouth with his hand. All the reassurance in the world was not going to calm me down. I tried to pull away; but Malcolm held me tight. There was no escape. I started to cry – the pain was too much to bear: it was crippling me. I tried to relax, but the more I tried the deeper the weapon slid inside me. I felt as if I were going to die.

Then Malcolm let me go. I felt very sore, and told him so. He told me that I had now lost my virginity. Sex would be a lot easier now, and should not hurt. He sat me on his knee again; I was still frightened, but he had promised that it would not hurt anymore. With hardly any pain this time, he re-entered me. He took his time this time, and I could feel the whole length of him stirring deep inside me.

The movement of Malcolm's body set my own in motion. I could smell our sweat. Our rhythm built up to quite a pace, and I tried to slow it down a little. Suddenly he tensed and let out a cry, pulling me even closer to him.

When I had pulled myself off him and washed myself, he stood and held me close to him for ages. He asked me if I was all right, and I assured him I was. Then he stuck £1 10s in my hand, with the advice that I should hide it so that no one could ask any awkward questions about it. We sat and talked for about ten minutes promising to keep our secret. Then I dressed, tidied up the lounge, sat in front of the fire and fell asleep.

The next thing I remember is Mum waking me up. She could hardly stand. Uncle Sam was with her; he must have had a guilty conscience, as he stuck a ten-shilling note into my hand before he ushered me off to bed.

As I climbed the stairs I remembered the thirty shillings Malcolm had given me earlier. It was still in my pocket. I started to undress, then dived into bed holding the money in my hand. I couldn't think where to hide it. I eventually slipped my socks back on and tucked the money into one of them. I started to think about what had happened earlier in the evening. I felt a little sore, yet somehow the banging of the gates and the howling of the wind outside did not really matter any more. I had a secret; and I had a friend whom I could trust. I felt happy and contented.

It would be dishonest of me to pretend that I didn't enjoy the experience. It awakened me sexually. But my pleasure has as much to do with the tenderness which this father-figure showed me. From an adult point of view that is deeply shocking, but at the time I thought I had obtained something which I could never find in my father: love and affection.

Chapter 3
Younger Men – More Action

My little secret with Malcolm was to last for only about three months. Then I was to find other ways of meeting men who would love to keep secrets with me.

While showering one day at school after an awful double period of games, I learnt something that was to change the course of my life. I was sharing a cubicle with a mate of mine called Geoff. He was telling me that on the previous Saturday he had been playing football on the Mount. This was a manmade hill in Fleetwood, right on the sea-front next to the Mount Hotel. It had a clock-tower on the top, and was a local landmark. It commanded a wonderful view of Morecambe Bay and the Irish Channel. On a clear day you could even see Barrow-in-Furness. It had wonderful flower gardens, and amusement areas for children. It was an attraction in the summer, providing a meeting-place for tourists in between the pier and the Marine Hall.

After the game Geoff had gone into the gents' toilet for a pee. There he had seen two men playing with each other. He thought this very funny and we made a big joke about it. But for me it was not a joke; it was something that I would have to look into – the sooner the better. It was not long till Saturday. I could wait; then I would go and spend the afternoon there, to see just what was really going on.

On Saturday I was up early and spent the morning doing the family shopping as usual. I think Mum was a little surprised when I was back in half the time it usually took me to get round the town. I rushed my dinner down and told Mum that I had arranged to meet some of the boys, and that I was going over to Knott End and would be back in time for tea. Mum looked even more puzzled. I very rarely went out on a Saturday afternoon. I usually stayed in and helped with the housework. and, as for going out with the boys, she could not normally get me out when she tried. After checking whether I was ill, she gave me six shillings and told me to be good and get home by six o'clock. So off I went.

I was really excited as I left home and went down to the bus stop. When I arrived at the gents' toilet I was disappointed; no one was there. But I stood at the stalls and pretended to have a pee, and it was not long before an old man came in. There were about twelve stalls, but he came straight over and stood in the one right next to me.

He was older than Malcolm and ugly. He was wrinkled to Hell and had that stench of old age and rotting flesh. You could not get it out of your nostrils. There was a limit, I did have some kind of standards. I just had to get away from him, no matter what the rewards might be. I buttoned myself up and walked outside. Just at the end of the path was a bench, where I squatted down so I could keep watch on the door and see who was coming and going. It was quite hot and the smell of blossom from the rosebeds filled the air. The green shrubbery all around was thick and full of life. I felt very happy, glad to be alive and enjoying my little adventure.

It was not very long before the old man left. Shortly afterwards, a vision of a man walked past. He turned up the path and headed towards the toilet. I was not into football at all, but I occasionally collected cigarette cards with footballers on them. I threw most of them away, only keeping the ones depicting players I considered good-looking. The man I had just seen go into the toilet was a match for any one of my old cards. It was the first time that I had ever seen anyone in the flesh who even came close to resembling one of my beauties.

He smiled as he passed the bench. I could hear bells ringing in my ears. That man was really lovely. I wondered what the chances were that he had not popped in to genuinely use the toilet. I waited for about two minutes; then I followed my vision into the toilet. He was standing in the far corner and turned to smile as I entered. I stood as far away as possible from him so that it would not be obvious what I had followed him in for. I undid my trousers and pretended to have a pee. I looked up and he just stood there smiling. I knew that he wanted to keep a secret with me. His arm moved slowly backwards and forwards; that could mean only one thing. I knew that he had an erection, and twisted around, hoping to get a better view. The young man just took a step backwards, revealing himself. He did have an erection, and it looked as hard as Malcolm's had done, if not as big.

He rubbed it with his hands, turning slightly so that I could see everything. We each took a step towards each other. Just then footsteps could be heard approaching the toilet entrance. We both returned to our original positions and pretended that nothing had happened.

It was the old man again. He took one look around, then went and stood right next to the man I had my eye on. The young man just smiled and shook his head, and as the old man strained to look over the stall, he just buttoned up and walked towards the door. My heart sank. That dirty old bastard had ruined my chances!

My eyes followed the young man. He paused in the doorway and the sunlight caught his blond hair. He inclined his head towards the outside – a signal to follow; all was not lost. He disappeared out of view. I was buttoning up my trousers, ready to make a move, when the old man moved towards me. I turned to make for the door. The old man made a grab at my arm. I was a little too fast for him, but he still asked me if I wanted to earn myself five bob. I told him to stuff it, and to come back when he could afford ten quid. He looked rather shocked. It had only been a ploy to get rid of him.

I shot out of the door. I thought that I would have lost sight of my vision – but no, there he was, waiting at the bottom of the path. As I appeared he moved off. I followed at an even pace, keeping an even distance between us both. We slowly walked up to the clock-tower. He went inside, so I followed. He was just disappearing through a gap in the wall as I entered. I walked over and came to a staircase that led to the platform above, where you could watch the clock innards working and the hammers for the bells preparing to strike the hour. It was near two o'clock; we were the only people up there.

'Hello, what's your name?' He spoke the first words of what was to be a beautiful two-year relationship. Simon was twenty-four years old, a partner in a local company. He was heavily tanned, having just returned from Spain. He had bright blue eyes that seemed to speak for themselves; he was very slim and about six foot tall. His trim blond moustache finished him off a treat.

We sat and talked for nearly an hour. Simon lived with his mother and father on the outskirts of Fleetwood; he was an only child. He had no intention whatsoever of getting married. Women terrified him, even his mother. He had spent most of his life in boarding-schools and at university. He visited the toilet about once every two months for relief. He was absolutely terrified of his mother's or father's finding out about his homosexuality.

I told him all about my family and my relationship with Malcolm. He seemed very upset to think that I had been corrupted by a dirty old man. He told me that he was worried about my age; he thought I was far too young. I told him that I liked him and would really like to see him again. After all, I would not be indulging in anything new. I was already corrupted. He was far too late to save me. Moreover, I would rather see him again than carry on my relationship with Malcolm. Now that I had met Simon, who needed Malcolm anyway? He had only used me. He was old, and he continually complained that I expected far too much from him. After all, he was over fifty.

Sex with him was no longer the same. I still allowed him to continue with our twice-weekly ritual – being screwed was one of the highlights of my week – but I had come to hate the smell of the stale tobacco on his breath, and his body colour was repulsive. I don't think he ever bathed, and he always seemed to be wearing the same long johns: they seemed to turn greyer and greyer with time. Now, when he came to kiss me, I always turned my head away in disgust.

Simon excused himself, as he had to go back to work before going home for tea with his mother. I arranged to meet him at six o'clock that evening at the bottom of Heathfield Road. We had only moved there six months earlier. He had his car, so we could go for a drive. Simon gave me a peck on the cheek, and away he went. I was by now really excited, and six could not come fast enough.

What I was to do with the rest of the afternoon was the next problem. I did not want to go home early. I walked back down the
Mount towards the gents' toilet. Nature was calling, so I answered
her. I was amazed to find the toilet was nearly full. I dug into my
pocket, came up with an old penny and went into the centre cubicle, the only one empty. I locked the door and hung my jacket on
the peg. I went about my business, just sitting there, not knowing
what to do with myself. I had an erection, still feeling excited about
meeting Simon at six.

I sat and read the writing on the wall, and a whole new world
opened up for me. For the next ten minutes I just sat there taking in
the advice about the best places to go in Fleetwood to pick up
'trade'. The quotes and notes written on the walls were most enlightening.

'YOUNG BOYS WANTED £2 A TIME MOST EVENINGS MEMORIAL PARK'
'TOILETS IN FRONT OF THE NORTH EUSTON HOTEL ARE GREAT AT
NIGHT'
'YOUNG MAN HAS 10″ WOULD ANYONE LIKE TO SHARE IT'
'BUSINESSMAN IN HIS EARLY THIRTIES WOULD LIKE TO MEET YOUNG
BOYS HERE ANY FRIDAY NIGHT. MONEY NO OBJECT'
'SLAVES WANTED BY 24-YEAR-OLD MASTER'

Christ I'd thought that I was the only one that was different!
According to the writings on this wall, everyone was as bad as me –
in fact, everyone was doing it. Suddenly I spotted a movement out
of the corner of my eye. I looked more closely and could hardly
believe what I saw. An eye was watching me. How long it had been
doing so I just did not know. The hole it was peering through was
about the size of a fifty-pence piece. I just stared at it in disbelief.
Someone had chipped a hole through four and a half inches of brick
and tile. I looked around. It was not the only hole in that wall, and
the opposite wall was just as bad. Even the door had holes in it at
all levels.

Interest overtook my disbelief, and I looked through the hole
where the eye had first appeared. An amazing sight met my eyes. I
changed to a different hole that commanded a better view. The man
was about thirty. He had on a red checked shirt and a pair of very
tight jeans. Even though he was casually dressed he looked very
smart. Now he was writing a note on a piece of toilet-paper. That
was not all that interesting to watch, so I moved to the opposite
wall and had a look through another hole. Into view came the same
thing that I had seen in the first toilet. I moved into another position
and looked through another hole: if it wasn't the old man that had

nearly ruined my chances earlier! He stopped and looked through the hole that I had been peeping through. I knew what was expected of me, but no way was I giving a free peepshow to that old bastard.

Age had suddenly got to me. Why should I have to mix with old men, now that I knew I could find men a lot younger if I visited toilets? Besides, the younger men were a lot fitter and more capable of fulfilling my needs and sexual desires.

I could hear a rustling of paper behind me. I turned just in time to see a piece of toilet-paper come through the first hole that I had looked through. On it, in very neat handwriting, were the following questions:

'My name is Paul. What is yours?'

'Do you come here often?'

'How old are you?'

'Would you like to come for a ride in my car? I have some photos that you can look at.'

A pencil came through the same hole. I ripped a piece of toilet-paper off the roll and replied to him.

'My name is George. I am 11 years old. This is the first time that I have visited this place. Yes, I would love to come for a ride. What kind of photos are they?'

As a footnote I added: 'It will cost you £2.'

The note came back through the hole in seconds with his reply. 'Sexy photos of me and the wife. O.K. Meet me outside.'

I heard Paul rip up the toilet-paper that I had replied on and flush it down the toilet. He opened the door and went out, and his place was taken immediately. I ripped up his note and flushed it away too, waiting to make sure it was gone. I looked through the hole again, and yet again someone was looking in. The old man was still in the other cubicle. He'd be there all day. I put my coat on and left.

As I opened the door several people turned to look at me. I just smiled and headed for the door. I hadn't realised just how dark it had been in the toilet. As I walked outside, the sunlight nearly blinded me and I walked straight into Paul.

He was very tall, over six foot, and very well-built, but he had a baby face. We walked together to his car. It was a sports job, bright red with all-white fur upholstery. He started it and drove on to the sea-front. He handed me a packet of photographs, all of himself and a lady in the nude making love on a couch. I asked if it was really his wife. He said that it was. She was very beautiful. Paul had turned the car off the sea-front and into Dock Street. He pulled up outside the general library, and told me to go through the main entrance and walk up the main stairs till I got to the first floor. Once there I was to go into the toilet and wait for him, but leave the door open.

I carried out his instructions, and within two minutes we were locked in a cubicle together. What a place to have sex! Paul was married and had three kids, so he could not take me back to his place. Anyway, he lived in Blackpool, and it would have taken too long to drive out into the country. My trousers were off in seconds. There was no petting or kissing – it was just not Paul's scene. He spat on his fingers and put it where it was needed. He unbuttoned his trousers and let them drop, and before they hit the floor he was in me. It was all over in a minute. No passion, just lust. No words, just action. He said that was his motto.

We both cleaned ourselves off. Two pounds were stuck in my hand; then Paul left, having made arrangements for the following Saturday. I later found out that Paul's wife was pregnant and he only participated in gay activities during the periods that he could not have sex with his wife. She knew all about it, and did not mind as long as he kept away from other women.

It was approaching 4.30 p.m. I walked back through the toilets in the Memorial Park as I headed for home. There were as many graffiti on the walls as there had been in the toilet in the Mount's grounds; but, alas, there were no men around. I found new information on the walls, though. Between twelve and one every weekday the students from the schools round about were regular visitors, and it seemed that plenty of men willing to pay for sex were around at that time. After school, at four o'clock, seemed to be a good time too. I would have to visit the place next week instead of having school dinners. They were lousy anyway.

I got home at about 5.15 p.m. Mum was up the wall feeding all the kids. My dinner was in the oven. Corned-beef hash again. We got that meal three times a week, just because corned beef and potatoes were cheap.

I asked Mum if it was all right if I went out to Geoff's place for a game of darts. It was as long as I was back home by nine o'clock so she could go out to the club. I put on my clean jeans and T-shirt; I wanted to look my best for meeting Simon. I half-walked, half-ran down Heathfield Road. I got there five minutes early, but six came and went and so did six-fifteen. My heart began to sink. I was feeling dejected. As my watch showed nearly six-thirty I turned to walk back home; I could give some excuse for coming home early.

A car horn started to beep behind me. It was Simon! I could hardly believe it. My heart lifted and a smile spread across my face as I ran across the road. Simon apologised for being late, but his mother had had to go to a party at the Marine Hall and he had given her a lift. It had taken longer than he thought for her to get ready. Anyway, we could now go back to Simon's place if we were quiet. Simon's dad was very ill in bed and must not be disturbed.

We went straight into the living-room. Simon closed the curtains and turned the television on. We just sat and kissed and cuddled each other for hours. Simon was very gentle and kind. He was different. He respected me and my body, for what it was worth.

When the screen flashed up the start of the nine o'clock news it was panic stations – we had both forgotten about the time. Simon drove me home so that I would not be too late. As I entered, Mum said she hoped that I had had a good game of darts, and left. Simon must have been watching her leave, because he knocked within two seconds. In the car I had dropped the two pounds that Paul had given me earlier, and Simon had thought I might need it. I invited him in, but he was very cautious. I told him that the other kids were in bed and the adults were all out getting drunk as usual. He eventually came in and kept me company until about ten-thirty. Then he left, making arrangements to see me the following day.

My relationship with Simon grew. We met most weekends. It was nearly three months before we had any serious sexual contact, but when we had reached that stage there was no turning back for either of us. And in that three months I had gained lots of experience from other quarters without Simon's knowing.

Malcolm continually made advances, but since the first day that I had met Simon I refused him his wishes, even though he started to offer me money again. One night he came in drunk and tried to force me to have sex with him. I turned on him and told him that if he persisted I would tell Mum the minute she returned home that evening. I told him to get it into his thick head that I didn't want to have sex with him any more. He was an old man. He couldn't keep up the pace. He was like all the other dirty old bastards that used the toilets. He had used me.

After my first meeting with Simon I was faithful to him for the first six weeks, meeting every Wednesday evening and Saturdays and Sundays; but, although our relationship had not yet developed into a sexual one, I lusted to be screwed. I tried to talk Simon into taking me; but he was not quite ready – and I badly needed screwing.

I got to the stage where I could not cope with it any longer, and I went back to the Mount toilet. I had not been there since the day I had met Paul and Simon. I walked straight into the centre cubicle. I had come prepared this time – I had my pencil in my pocket. For years I was always to carry one, and in time it became a joke. All the gays I was to meet who used toilets to pick up men always carried pencils so that they could write little notes and pass them under the walls or doors of cubicles. They were generally termed 'cottaging pencils'.

I did not have to wait too long before someone occupied the left-hand cubicle. I watched through one of the peepholes as the un-suspecting male unbuttoned his trousers, pulled them down and pulled down his underpants. He sat down, and I just caught sight of his private parts. I had a throbbing erection within seconds. I had another view of him dressing as he was preparing to leave. I could not see his face, but he did have a good body. What the hell! He was straight or he would have looked through one of the holes, or at least played with himself. I heard other people coming into the toilets, but no one came into the empty cubicles.

I looked through a low hole in the door, and there were two young men, both about twenty years old, playing with each other. It looked so inviting that I wanted to go out and join them; but I would have spoiled their fun. They both had erections and both took it in turn to bend down and suck each other. They could not have known I was there. I started to masturbate. The two boys were getting very excited. My poor arm pumped away. I had never come before; this was to be my first time. I suddenly felt very strange in-side and my knees started to give way. There was a surging and pumping deep within my body. My penis throbbed away; I thought it was going to burst. I very quickly sat down, feeling quite sick. Then I felt my whole body starting to shake from head to foot. The sensation was something I have never experienced since. I thought I was going to pass out – my heart was racing, I had started to sweat and I could hardly get my breath.

I looked down, and it had happened. I was a man. I'd done what Malcolm had done during my first sexual experience. I slowly got to my feet again; my knees felt weak and shaky. I leaned against the wall for a few minutes to get my breath back and till I felt a little more secure.

I looked through the hole in the door again – just in time to see the smaller of the two men ejaculate. The other man was mastur-bating himself with his free hand. They were passionately kissing each other, and the other man ejaculated within seconds of the first. I was fascinated.

What amazed me more than anything else was the fact that not one word had been spoken between the two men. They both cleaned themselves up standing well apart, and left the toilets in-dividually. This, I was to find out, was the way of the gay scene, full of casual insecure relationships. They could have been anyone and today it just can not be tolerated, even on the gay scene. The fear of

AIDS has made people more cautious, and at least when people do have casual sex, protection is normally used.

My relationship with Simon, now sexual, developed into a deep and meaningful one. I saw him every Wednesday and Saturday, and also on the occasional Sunday. But the time that we spent together just wasn't enough for me. Simon had replaced my father. I went to him with all my problems.

Mother was drinking more and more and had started to bring men home during the day. My life felt very crowded. I started to spend more time out, especially after Malcolm left home. Other lodgers appeared, but they were usually Mum's lovers. There were many, and none lasted long. Then a lodger a little different from the rest moved in. His name was Johnny.

He was only nineteen, but also one of her lovers. I thought that he was lovely – not in a beautiful but in a sexy kind of way. I started to resent my mother. How could a drunken old whore like her trap a young boy like that? It never ceased to amaze me. Just what special attributes did she have to offer him? I fancied Johnny something rotten and I occasionally made passes at him, but they were shrugged off as a big joke. Until we had to share the parlour.

Dad was sick and laid off sea for a trip, which meant that he would be home for a whole two weeks. No one looked forward to the prospect at all, especially not my mother. We also had a friend staying with us; she had my bed. Johnny used to go out drinking every night. He resented my father's sleeping with my mother, because my mother entranced him. He had told me that he loved her dearly; but I never believed that. I think the sex that she had with him fascinated him to such an extent that he thought it was love.

He used to come into the parlour late at night giving the impression that he was so drunk that he didn't know where he was or what was happening. He would always manage to wake me up with the noise he made. As soon as he was pretending to be asleep, I used to slip between the sheets and play with him, having oral sex and kissing him quite passionately. He always gave the impression that he was unaware of what was happening, but he managed to move his body in time with me, so I knew that he was awake. I didn't make a big show of it. I was quite happy to get my fill.

I suppose it was plain jealousy that made me do it. He was the first of mum's many lovers that I was to have sex with. She must have picked up a certain type of guy, because I had very few problems in getting them to screw me. I considered that all fishermen must be bisexual (they were nearly all fishermen). How can anyone possibly control his sex life in that way – having sex for two days and going without for the next fourteen? That is the life that most fishermen have to face.

Jealousy ruled the latter part of my period at home.

My sexual urges grew stronger and stronger. It was not long before I had made a lot of new friends. I had regular dates on Monday, Thursday and Friday, all with different men. I didn't love any of these guys; it was purely for sexual contact. The only person I loved was Simon. I still met him every Wednesday and Saturday, and he was unaware of my other sexual encounters.

I had started to go round to the Memorial Park most lunchtimes, also managing to make a few visits after school. I got over to the Mount on Tuesday evenings and sometimes on Sundays. If there was nothing going on at the Mount, it only took two minutes to walk down to the toilet in front of the North Euston. I met all kinds of people on these visits. One night I met my local vicar. Fishermen were plentiful, and being a young and eager queen I was always willing to please as many as possible.

On one of these many occasions I very narrowly escaped a run-in with the police. I had just left the North Euston toilets and was walking up Bold Street when several police cars surrounded the toilet and took away about ten people. I later read in the local paper that six men had been charged with indecency. I ran home thanking God that I had not been too greedy that evening. I was to have started work on my fourth client, but I had had a slight headache and been feeling hungry, so I had left in order to have time to stop at the fish-and-chip shop for something to eat.

The police often denied harassing homosexuals, but I can assure you that it is always taking place. I have stood and watched them beating people up outside gay pubs and then just turning round and saying that they are protecting the general public from a bunch of sick degenerates. Now, the scene has changed so much, that the gay underworld is out in the open. Pubs, clubs, shops and restaurants, many gay-owned, cater for the needs of the homosexual community. To be gay is more acceptable today and the media is more tolerant. Only child molesters, serial killers or gay members of Parliament seem worthy of note. But now some gay campaigners want to 'out' those they think should not be closeted: the campaigners stick up posters alleging the homosexuality of well-known people. Surely everyone is entitled to privacy, though? I feel it should be the individual's choice to come out. They are entitled to lead their own lives as they wish, as long as they do not affect the well-being of anyone else.

I was quite lucky; all my permanent boyfriends used to treat me to a pound or two every week, so I was never short of money.

Simon was the only one that never offered me money – nor did I expect him to. I was truly in love with him, and I suppose I still am. He was the first man ever to tell me that I should have been born a girl, and was the only one to have treated me as a woman in both a sexual and a much more loving way. He occasionally bought me little presents; one of which was a little pendant that I have to this day.

By now the family was being sent into foster-homes. It upset me, and when we were eventually sent home Simon was the first person I would contact. He used to take these breaks very badly. We never knew when we were going to be separated again. The reunions were sometimes very painful, with us both in tears, not wanting to separate at the end of the evening. When these splits became very frequent it affected us even more, because we both knew that one day I just would not return.

All types of other sexual encounters happened during my periodic returns home. I remember one evening playing in the back yard with a couple of the local lads when one of them asked me where I always got my money from. I told him, and he asked me if I could teach him how to do it. I said that if he was serious I would show him what it involved as long as he didn't tell anyone else. I would also introduce him to some of my friends.

We went back to his house and straight up in to his bedroom. He was a year older than me. We just stood and looked at each other; then he asked me what we had to do. I told him that we would have to get into bed together, and we did. I was feeling very randy. It was the first time I had gone to bed with anyone who didn't have any idea of what was to come. He had never even had sex with a girl, although he did masturbate.

We both lay there and played with each other for a long while; I got down and gave him a good blow-job, and told him to do the same to me. He did, although it took him a while before he got the hang of it. Then I showed him how to screw me. I told him that I wanted to do the same to him. He had seen that I had enjoyed it, so he agreed. I soon came, however, and we both lay talking about what we had done.

I gave him all the information about the toilets he should visit and how much he should ask from the punters. We had been there for about half an hour when suddenly his big brother walked into the room and asked us what the hell we had been up to. He had heard us come in and had been listening at the door. As he was talking, he started to get undressed, and then climbed into bed with both of us. He said that he had never done it before but we could show him what to do. He was about five years older than us. He ended up screwing the two of us. I found out years later that the two brothers still lived together in Manchester and had a loving relationship – a relationship which I had started. Most people will think that is disgusting. But, when we met years later, their relationship was one that most heterosexuals would have longed for.

People ask me if I was ever ashamed of the period of my life that was dedicated to prostitution, and I can honestly say that I wouldn't have changed a day of it. My encounters with men broadened my outlook on life. A lot of the men I met I grew to like – and, believe it or not, they did put a little security back into my life. I would have preferred any one as my father. But then, I was stuck with the one I'd got.

Anyway the fatal day came when we were taken into care. I had no warning and could not contact Simon or any of my other friends to say goodbye. I'm sure that they all read the headlines in the paper the following week. After all, in a small town like Fleetwood such a story was headline news; and if the boys hadn't read it in the paper, some of the local queens would have put it about. I never saw Simon again. He was my first love and I will always love him. I hope he did not take the split too badly. Perhaps it was for the best. I was jail bait. If we had ever been caught, he could have gone to prison for years.

I had been a male prostitute for two years when I moved to Preston. I was in a strange town. I was in a strange children's home that was quite strict. The fulfilling of my sexual needs and desires was to be a problem. Besides, not having the extra cash would take a lot of getting used to. I had been quite happy leading my sordid little life, even though it was degrading. The only thing that made the future at all promising was the fact that Preston was four times the size of Fleetwood, so somewhere in this black industrial hole I was sure to find a toilet that would at least give me directions as to where all the gay life was in Preston. It wasn't to take me long.

Chapter 4

I Want to Forget

The road to Preston seemed never-ending. I felt very lonely. My brothers and sisters were all over Lancashire in different foster-homes. As the eldest, I was the first to be transferred to the Harris Children's Home. It was to be the new home for us all, or so I was told. A stout middle-aged lady by the name of Green had picked me up in her old banger. The vague, encouraging murmurs forcing themselves between her lips didn't help me at all. I was scared; I was only twelve years old and I would never be allowed to live with my mother and father again until I was eighteen.

I had been in a foster-home in Kirkham for nearly two months and was already missing home. It was the longest time we had ever spent away. I was really missing my mother, even if I wasn't really bothered if I never saw my father again. The car swerved off the main Garstang-to-Preston road and in through the imposing entrance of the Harris.

It looked so big. A small cottage stood just to the left of the gate as we entered. It had a small weigh-bridge in front of it. Facing the gate over a huge bed of roses was the most beautiful house that I had ever seen, with lovely stained-glass windows. This connected to a schoolhouse, and a church with a large clock-tower. They were all built in deep-red Victorian brick. Although they looked rather splendid, I sensed hidden horrors behind the windows. We pulled up outside a building with a broken sign, swinging in the breeze above the door, announcing that it was the office and stores. I climbed out of the car, dragging with me a large plastic bag. It contained all my worldly possessions.

The home's supervisor and governor, Mr Brooks, was sitting at his desk smoking his pipe. He was in his early sixties, a huge man with a little moustache, slightly balding on top. We were introduced and my life was handed over to him in a file from the social services. The transaction was over – it had taken less than two minutes; my chauffeur disappeared, leaving me with this big man who frightened the life out of me. He looked strict and vicious, although I was to find out later that he was as gentle as a lamb.

He picked up the phone and spoke to the matron, his wife. Within minutes a lady in her late fifties, very tall and slim, arrived in the office. She smiled. It was very warming, she appeared very motherly and I took to her immediately. Mrs Brooks was responsible for reclothing the new children and settling them into their new homes. I was taken next door and the contents of my black plastic sack were emptied on to the floor. Everything that I possessed was there – old clothes that were falling to pieces, and the odd toy I had managed to rescue from Hesketh Place. After sorting out all the ripped clothes and rubbish there was very little left. Nearly everything ended up in the bin. I was amazed as Matron gave me two new pairs of shoes, slippers, socks, shirts, jumpers, underwear, trousers, a coat, and finally a new school uniform – the first that I had ever had. It was all black and had a lovely badge on the blazer and cap. I had new white shirts and the new school's black-and-white striped tie. I began to feel a lot better.

I was taken into the office again, as the doctor arrived. I quickly undressed, was examined in about two minutes flat, reported fit and taken off to my new home, the first of four large houses that I had seen on our arrived at the Harris: the Laurels (they were all named after trees). The back door led off a large verandah into a very big kitchen, where the biggest table that I had ever seen was laid for at least twenty people. We went into the living-room. Everything was clean and the smell of polish lingered in the air. A little old lady sat by the fireside and three children sat playing in the centre of the room. Miss O'Neill acted as a relief foster-mother and lived alone in the little cottage just by the main gate. Mr and Mrs Taylor, the home's foster-parents, were on their day off. Matron took me through the lounge into a great hall that had a carved oak staircase at one end. It all looked very grand.

I was to go to an outside school. The school in the grounds was for up to eleven-year-olds. Anyone above that age was sent out. After giving me that and various other information, Matron bade farewell. Mrs Taylor went back to her sitting-room and I returned to the living-room. All had gone quiet outside; the children that I had seen playing on my arrival had gone back into classes. Miss O'Neill said that she had better start on the tea, as all the gang would be home soon. I gave her a hand: she was amazed at just how quickly I worked and how willing I was.

At about four-fifteen you could hear groups of children running down the drive to their homes. Young boys and girls of all ages came into the Laurels. Mary and Sue were the first ones in. They were both a year older than myself. Everyone knew that a new boy was arriving, so they had hurried home. The two girls both had brothers, both called Thomas; these were two of the boys that I was to share 'the blue room' with. Beverley and Joanne, who were sisters, soon arrived, then little Stephen and Carol, who were seven-year-old twins. Stephen and one other child made up the foursome in our room. There were twelve children in all; each of the seven houses within the grounds accommodated the same number – plus, of course, the offspring of the foster-parents.

Once all the introductions were over I was besieged with questions. Everyone wanted to know why I was in a home. Was I beaten up by my mother and father? Did I play truant from school? Had I been in trouble with the police? Or was I just a parentless child.

None of these questions seemed to fit. Dad had left home and Mum just could not cope with us all any longer. Others' situations were far more tragic than ours. Some were orphans; one had been left on a doorstep as a child. A couple had lost their parents in a car crash. I was really one of the lucky ones – at least I would see my mother again.

It wasn't long before other members of my family started to arrive at the Harris, and within three months we were all there. Unfortunately we were not all in the same house. Luckily I was there to meet them all and calm them down as they arrived. I had asked the governor if we would be in the same house, but the chances of eight vacancies occurring in a single house was very remote. However, at least we could meet and talk to each other. If the others had problems they knew where to find me, and I was always willing to help them.

Life at the Harris followed a strict routine. The older children left for school every morning at eight-thirty after a brief discussion with the governor. The walk to Fulwood County Secondary took about ten minutes. We all stayed for school dinners and returned home about four o'clock. Then we all had individual jobs to do before tea. Shoes had to be cleaned, the outside areas had to be swept, the gardens had to be looked after. Once all the jobs were done we went in for tea. After the meal was over the older children had to go to the music-room and get on with their homework. Once that was completed we were allowed out into the grounds till about nine o'clock. On summer evenings I used to take a book over the back fields and lie in the bushes reading. I didn't like playing with the rest of the kids, even though I did get on with them all quite well. My younger sisters always knew where to find me and they would come over with the babies to keep me company. We all used to sit and talk about home. The future was always a topic of conversation. Would we ever go home? When would Mum come to visit us? I soothed the babies when they cried and tried my best to stand in for what they really needed: a mum and dad.

People who get their children sent into care do not realise just how much harm and distress they cause them. If they had known what we would have to go through then, they might not have given birth to us.

I couldn't stand being trapped in a room with a load of kids when the weather was bad, so I used to creep out to one of the outside toilets and sit, either reading my latest book or doing some knitting – one of the girls had taught me. Whenever I could I'd slide away and knit a few squares. I wouldn't do it in front of the lads, because I knew they would only laugh.

Mr and Mrs Taylor turned out to be a lovely couple, who did as much for the children in their care as any normal mother and father would have done. They had a son, who was very spoilt, but that was to be expected. He was their only son and perhaps he did not get all the love that he would have done if they hadn't taken their new job. So they bought him all kinds of unnecessary toys and games.

Thursdays were pocket-money days; the older children received 35p each, the youngsters only 15p. The stores converted into a little toffee shop for the afternoon, and Matron and one of the other girls sold sweets until five p.m. The governor sat in his office; if anyone wanted to save their money he or she would take it in to him and he would stick it in a post-office account. It was all very organised and speedy. After a while at the Harris I used to save all my money, for I found I could earn money again outside.

I took an entrance exam and was placed in the beta stream in the second year; I wasn't quite bright enough to make the alpha grade. But I soon caught up, and during the spring term I was transferred up into alpha. I only found the French lessons difficult to grasp, but then again I had missed the first eighteen months of study. Maths, English and science came quickly enough though. I was encouraged by my foster-parents to spend as much time as I could on my homework, which was to really help my future career. Mr Dunn, the music teacher, taught me the violin and the piano and helped me to train my voice.

At first everyone was cautious, for they knew of my family's past. They encouraged me to have a free hand at whatever I wanted to do, yet they kept me in hand and made sure that no responsibilities were put on my shoulders again. I actually looked forward to going to school, and I used to end up doing far more homework than I was supposed to do.

Gym still horrified me; I hated having to force my body to do things that it did not want to do; but I always cheered up towards the end of the lesson, knowing that I would have the secret pleasure of looking at all the boys in the shower. Some of them were very well developed for their ages; others were very small. Occasionally the teacher would shower with us, and for me that was an extra treat, although for the other boys it was disappointing because they couldn't mess around. I had a few sexual encounters with the boys in my class, but nothing serious. I did have a few more enlightening episodes with a couple of prefects. We used to meet round the back of the gym. One of them was spotty and horrible, but he had a big cock.

One of the guys in my class used to sneak home very lunchtime with his girlfriend for a kiss and a cuddle. One lunchtime he came over to me and asked me if I wanted to go back to his place with him, as one of the girl's friends fancied me. He wasn't aware that I was gay, and I didn't want to lose his friendship, so I agreed to go along with him.

His girlfriend's mate turned out to be a horror. She must have been fifteen stone if she was an ounce. We sat and talked in the lounge for about ten minutes, until he declared that he was taking his girl upstairs to bed. He told us to use the spare bedroom. We walked in and lay on the bed. We kissed each other once or twice; then she undid my flies and pulled me out of my pants. No way could I get an erection. I felt most embarrassed, but I felt I must do something to her. I slid my hand up her dress and rubbed her on the outside of her pants. She kissed me even harder and I could tell that she was enjoying it. She grabbed me again, but I was as limp as a used banana skin.

I told her that I hadn't known I was coming to see her, and had had a wank at break-time. That seemed to satisfy her curiosity. But I nearly died when she pulled her pants down and I put my hand back up her dress. Not really knowing what to expect, I slowly moved it higher and higher. When I reached her hairy little bush, I pulled it away as though I had received an electric shock. She opened her eyes and just looked at me. I replaced my hand, doing just what she expected me to do. I thought that it was disgusting, the way she moaned and wriggled on the bed. Thank God it was soon over. While she was putting her pants back on I went to the bathroom to wash my hands. I scrubbed and rescrubbed them, but I could still smell that disturbing odour.

I returned to the living-room. My mate and the two girls were sitting there. He called me a randy old sod and said they had both listened to us having it off. My young lady didn't deny it, so I just smiled. I was glad to retire back to school that afternoon. The following day I was invited back to my mate's place again, but I made the excuse that I had to complete a music lesson; I said the same every time, and after a few weeks he stopped asking me. I occasionally saw the young girl around the school; she always smiled and said that she looked forward to meeting me again one day. Not if I could help it, she wouldn't.

On most Sundays, if the weather was fine, there was church for the believers. I always went along, since it was a nice little walk and the governor made favourites of those who went with him. It was also crafty of me because those left behind had to clean the grounds and all the brasses on the outside door. The service was always long but quite cheerful. The ageing vicar conducted it with an energy that I had never seen before in anyone so old. Still, if it hadn't been for our crowd of about thirty, I'm quite sure that the old boy would have given up trying to save the other handful of congregation that came each week.

Two of the foster-parents in the Harris used to visit a Baptist church every Sunday evening and some of the older children used to go with them. I had behaved myself and was in favour, so, when I asked for permission to go along with them, it was granted. I soon joined the Baptist choir at Carey. This meant that I was allowed out on Friday nights and Sunday afternoons to go to choir practice. I also went choral singing with them in the market square after the evening service. But it was all a successful con-trick on my part. I had found toilets just like the ones in Fleetwood.

I had been shopping one Saturday afternoon in the town centre and had called into a public toilet to have a pee. I found out how to get around in Preston; if you were on the gay scene, Moor Park apparently had a toilet that was always in darkness. It seemed worth a visit, and I went there once or twice and made a few casual friends. The trouble was that you could never see whom you were picking up.

I remember going into the toilet one Sunday evening at around eight o'clock. In church I had seen a lovely guy who had made me feel quite randy. As soon as the service was over I had run down to the park, hoping that I would be able to find a decent bit of trade. As I went into the loo I saw two shadows in the far corner of the stalls. Eventually I was approached by a youthful man. He asked me to meet him outside, and I left the toilet.

To my horror I saw a police car outside. I turned and headed down Garstang Road, straight for the Harris. Behind the police car I noticed a police bike. A young man in a leather jacket and jeans left the toilet and started to follow me, but I wasn't to be fooled. The guy was a cop – I could smell it a mile off. He even looked like one. I tried to keep calm as, walking quickly, he gradually caught up with me. He asked me if I lived nearby. I just ignored him and carried on walking. He continually asked me if I wanted a lift on his bike. Did I go to the toilets often? Did I meet many men there? My heart was in my throat, and I just told him to go away. I looked back and saw that the police car was crawling at the kerbside about twenty yards behind.

I stopped and just stared at the guy, and told him that if he didn't piss off I was going to tell the policeman in that car that he was trying to pick me up. This turned out to be a very clever ploy, for he just didn't know what to do. He stopped and stared at me in amazement. I turned on my heel and walked off at a speedy pace. My heart was thumping away and my knees felt as though they were going to give way. I prayed that the ground would open up and swallow me. If the police were to arrest me and take me back to the Harris, the governor would go mad and I would never be allowed out again. I didn't know what the young man's reaction had been, so when I approached a bend in the road I looked back. I could see him stopping, talking to the driver of the police car. He was scratching his head. I disappeared round the bend and ran like hell down Garstang Road, slowing every time the police car passed me.

As I got nearer to the Harris I began to feel a little safer, so I jumped into a garden where I could not be seen from the road. It was only eight forty-five, and if I arrived early you can bet your life the Taylors would have been suspicious. I always arrived home dead on time, never late and never early. I sat on a pile of dead leaves for a long time, watching the police car patrol up and down. When I eventually made a move I climbed the remaining garden walls and got into the Harris over the side. I dusted myself down, but I only felt secure after a cup of tea and a biscuit with the Taylors, and after being tucked up in bed without having had to answer any awkward questions.

I realised that I had been lucky that night, and would have to watch myself in the future if I wasn't to spoil everything that I had set up. A lot of people would get into trouble if I was ever caught. I was under the age of twenty-one, so anyone that had sex with me had committed a criminal offence. I had made lots of new friends, and if I had ever been arrested I'm sure the police would have frightened their names and addresses out of me. It would have been the Playland scandal all over again; there would have been as many men involved, but instead of all the young boys who hung around Piccadilly Circus there would just have been me.

So the Moor Park toilet was out for a little while. That only left the Old Bus Station toilets. They had fascinated me ever since my first visit. I had gone into one of the cubicles and found the usual peepholes; but there was a special cubicle near the door, where you could remove five bricks out of the wall and it was as good as being together in the cubicle with the guy next door. No holds were barred!

When the money situation got really bad I would volunteer to take the collection up in the balcony at Carey Baptist. Once you had taken the collection, during the final hymn, the only way back was down some side stairs, out to the front of the building and in through the main entrance. A quick dip in the bag on the staircase always guaranteed a couple of quid to see me through the week. I was always careful not to take any of the little white envelopes, as they all had serial numbers on and I knew the verger kept the account books up to date. He would soon know if an envelope was missing, especially if he had seen the party in church that evening. I always tried to be careful. Luckily I was never caught, thank God. Some people will be disgusted by my behaviour, but I have a clear conscience now, for I returned to Carey a few years later and re-placed in the collection bag far more than I had ever taken.

I now considered the Harris to be my home. I had had far more love and understanding there in one year than I had had in the pre-vious ten. The governor turned out to be a really nice guy and I came to think of him as my father. Mrs Taylor had replaced my mother, although I did occasionally pine for her. Everything seemed to be going well. Even seeing my father had become more tolerable. I had refused at first, but when I was eventually forced into meeting him he had become a completely different person from the father I remembered. He started to come monthly, then every fortnight. His visits, however, were occasionally marred when my mother was brought into the discussions. She was a whore and an alcoholic in his eyes, and he blamed her for our being in care. The other children began to believe his stories. Only I knew the truth.

Mum's visits were about every four months. She usually came with a different man. They were enjoyable while they lasted, but ended in tears for me when she left. She had started to look better and to take pride in her appearance again. For her part, she still blamed Dad for our being there. The kids were torn: they just did not know who to believe. I dearly wanted to believe her, but I knew they were both to blame; they had both wanted to lead their own lives. We children were in the way. I relived my childhood memories with Mum's recollections of the beatings that my father used to give her and Dad's recollections of all her drinking and the strange men that used to visit her while he was away at sea. I des-perately wanted to get away from both of them. Each was trying to convince me that he or she was not the guilty partner; I knew dif-ferent. Thank God I would be old enough to get away soon. I was damned if I was going to stay at the Harris until I was eighteen, court order or not.

Finally something happened that shattered the happiness and peace which I had discovered at the Harris.

I was coming to the end of my third year at school. My reports had all been good, except for French and woodwork – I'd only managed to achieve a D grade in both. But I got As and Bs in every other subject. I had visions of becoming a journalist with *The Times*; so I put my name down to join the commercial class. It was a two-year course, which meant I would have to stay at school for a further year. With all my other subjects chosen, I was quite pre-pared to come back after the summer holidays and study hard. My father had been delighted when he had heard that I was to stay on at school, and he gave me ten pounds towards a typewriter.

I had been to sea with my father when I was ten as a birthday treat, and he wanted to take me again during the summer holidays. He had asked the governor if he could take me for a fortnight. The governor had checked with the authorities, and they had agreed that it would be good for me to go. I was not at all sure whether I would be able to cope with him for two whole weeks; it was a lot different from the usual day visits. But reluctantly I agreed to go.

After a fine camping holiday at Silverdale with the other children, I returned to the Harris for two days before being collected by my father and taken to Fleetwood. We weren't sailing until two a.m., so we visited some of the family, then went to the Regency Cinema to see the latest film. I returned to Nan's and Dad went off for a booze-up with some of the lads. The family had been pleased to see me and the film had been very funny. Dad had bought me all kinds of things during the day. He really did seem a different person.

When he returned after the pubs shut we packed our gear up and went in a taxi to the R.N.M.D.S.F. (the Royal National Mission to Deep-Sea Fishermen), by the dock gates. We had to wait there until the taxi came to pick us up again and take us down to the ship. Two of my Dad's mates arrived to wait for the taxi with us. We were all sailing on the *Boston Seaform* – quite a big trawler though not as big as the Icelandic boats. She had a crew of seventeen.

One of the guys, Danny, had red curly hair, and he appeared to me to be quite feminine. The other was a smashing coloured guy by the name of Jim. He was very jolly, laughing and joking all the time. They all sat drinking together in the mission until the taxi came to pick us up. After everyone had signed on in the pool office and my life insurance papers had been checked we all boarded the *Seaform*. I was to share a cabin with Danny and my Dad. There were only two bunks, they were on alternative shifts, so there'd always be an empty one.

I was looking forward to being the only boy among seventeen men, on the high seas for two weeks. As long as Dad didn't find out, I had every intention of having a good time. I suppose that was the main reason I had agreed to go in the first place.

I was surprised at the amount of alcohol being consumed below deck before we even set sail. The only people that appeared sober when we left port were the skipper and the chief engineer; everyone else was well gone. As the ship pulled out of the dock I stood and watched from the bow, and waved to all the fishermen's wives who had assembled on the quayside. Some of them shouted their fare-wells, some just waved, but they all looked relieved. They were getting shot of the old man for another fortnight.

It was a quiet night and the water was still calm. The only movement was our bow-waves. I made my way to the stern of the boat
and watched the lights of the Fleetwood and the buoys in Morecambe Bay drift away. We were soon in the open sea. The only
lights to be seen were those on the two trawlers that had sailed with
us. Dad was on the bridge doing the first watch, so I climbed up and
was greeted by the skipper. He congratulated my father on such a
fine strapping figure of a lad, who'd be good down in the ice-room,
chopping ice. He came over and gave me a hearty slap on the back,
then returned to his charts. I went over and stood by my father at
the wheel, and was taught how to alter the wheel to keep the boat
moving in the right direction with the aid of the compass set in the
ceiling.

It was interesting enough, but I felt very tired, so I went below to
get some shuteye in my dad's bunk. There wouldn't be much to do
for the next few days because it would take us a while to get to the
right fishing area. The ship had started to roll slightly and as I lay
flat the movement was very soothing. It wasn't long before I was
fast asleep.

My father sent one of his mates down to wake me up at about
nine a.m. as we were passing Radio Caroline. I rushed to the bridge,
and as we passed alongside we threw over a tobacco-tin with a message and weight inside. I had requested the D.J. to play a record for
all my relations, and later on we heard it over the air. I went down
to the galley for breakfast. The mess room was full of men drinking
and playing cards so I stood in the galley with the cook until he
made me a bacon sandwich. I climbed up on to the stern deck and
sat in the sunshine to eat it.

As lunchtime drew nearer an awful row broke out down below. I
went down to investigate what it was about. Jim – the coloured guy
– and another man were having a terrible argument. I think it was
about the card game they had been playing most of the morning.
No one even tried to calm them down; everyone was well drunk,
anyway. I had been given the job of peeling the potatoes for lunch
by the cook, so I did a disappearing act back on to the deck.

When I had finished I went to the bridge again. The skipper was
going mad with the mate. He wanted to know why so much drink
had been brought on board. The fact that everyone was falling
about the place made the matter worse. The skipper called to the
bridge the deckhand who had been ranting and raving at Jim. He
was just giving him a warning when Jim started shouting as he
made his way across the engine-room ramp, which led to a platform with a vertical ladder to the bridge. I was standing by the
bridge as Jim started to climb the ladder, shouting about 'that great

41

big honky bastard'. This proved too much for the decky; he pulled away from the skipper and started to scream about 'the stupid black bastard'. He leapt across the bridge and kicked Jim just as he appeared at the top of the ladder.

Jim fell down and the decky pursued him. I could hear him shouting for Jim to get up off the floor and fight. Then, suddenly, everything went quiet. The mate looked down the hole and just said, 'My God.' Then he turned round and sent me packing off the bridge. I climbed down by the outside ladder. The skipper shouted for me to wake up the chief engineer and tell him he was wanted on the bridge, then to get to my Dad's cabin and stay there.

Within minutes the engines had stopped. Everyone was moving around the ship, yet a deathly quiet hung in the air. Dad came into the cabin and said there had been an accident and we were going home. I went up into the galley; everyone was drinking coffee and sobering up a lot quicker than they had got drunk. Danny came into the galley a minute or two later and said that Jim was dead. The ship turned round and we started to steam back to Fleetwood. Apparently Jim had broken his neck in the fall.

We would be arriving back home about three a.m. The skipper had radioed the office, and the police were coming out to meet us. The decky who had kicked Jim had now become hysterical and was being held down in the skipper's berth. The atmosphere on board was frightening. Only the throb of the ships engines killed the silence. Most of the men had gone to their bunks after discreetly disposing of all their booze over the side of the ship. Full bottles of spirits and cases of beer went over. Evidence must not be found to prove that the men had been drinking at sea. There was bound to be an enquiry.

We arrived in Morecambe Bay at about one-thirty the following morning, and had to wait until three for the high tide. The police had come aboard about midnight and started to make their enquiries. When we eventually docked, the men's wives were all waiting on the quayside again. Gone were the smiling faces. They had all heard on the news that the ship was returning to port, and the office hadn't been able to tell them much more. Relief of a different kind spread across their faces as they saw their husbands and sons. Then they all wanted to know at once. Who was it? Who did it? How?

The men were completely different from the men who had set sail only twenty-four hours earlier. We were all taken down to the police station and asked to give statements. My father had told me to say that I had seen nothing and heard nothing. He had asked me on the bridge earlier if I had seen anything, and when I said that I had seen the decky kick Jim he went absolutely mad and told me that if I said anything he would give me a good hiding; it was better for the police to find out for themselves what happened. I mustn't get involved. He had looked really angry, and I knew what a foul temper he had. Anyway, I could not be sure that the blow I had seen Jim receive from the decky had been the final blow.

The office had said that the ship would sail the following evening, if the police would allow it. They didn't object. They had the statements they wanted and could always interview people again. Dad had telephoned Nan and told her what had happened. We would have to stay at her place for the rest of the night. She did not mind, although she had only moved in the day before and everything was in chaos. We would have to share a bed in the lounge – did we mind?

Once the police had finished with us we headed for Nan's. Dad still seemed slightly pissed and in a furious temper. Nan was waiting up for us; she had unpacked the bedding that we would need and had thrown a double mattress on to the lounge floor for us both. I was then approaching my fifteenth birthday.

That night I was to go through the most horrifying experience – one that I have relived many times. It was a painful and terrible thing: a homosexual rape by my father.

I climbed in bed, wearing my clothes as normal. My father sat on the settee and continued to drink. He told me that I would be too hot and that I should take my clothes off, as I pulled the blankets over me to go to sleep. I had seen how violent he could be when he had been drinking so I did as I was told and slipped off my jumper and trousers, leaving on my vest and underpants.

My mother had always warned me about being alone with my father when he was drinking and the warning nagged away at me. I pretended to go to sleep as he sat there, snorting and mumbling. I squeezed my eyes tight shut, and also tried to block out the sounds. The settee springs squeaked as he got up. I could hear him undressing. To this day, the sound of a zip sends a chill through my body. He flicked off the light and fell on to the mattress. He lay beside me for several minutes and I could smell the sickly fumes of beer and whisky. I moved towards the edge of the mattress to get away from him – I was literally hanging off the edge. My eyes had grown accustomed to the dark so I turned my head to sneak a look. My father had his back to me and the blankets moved up and down with the rhythm of his breathing. I relaxed as it looked as if he was asleep. The relief rushed through me and I stretched my legs. However, as I lay there I realised that something was wrong. The blankets were pulling towards him – he was masturbating. Fear

43

swept through me and I moved backwards towards the edge of the mattress, pulling myself into a ball. He turned over and was panting behind me. I pretended to be asleep. He was really giving himself some thrash but then he stopped and said 'Are you awake, bastard?' I ignored him; he spoke again and still I kept quiet until he punched me in the back of the head. Then I let out a cry and he pounced on me. I tried to call out and pull away, but he slammed his fist into my face. I could feel the blood welling up in my mouth. Then he thrust his hand under my chin, and covered my mouth. He moved his face close to my ear and said 'One peep out of you, bastard, and I will squeeze the life out of you.' I could hardly breathe. I struggled to get away but his grip was too tight. His free hand began ripping my underpants but I could not scream, and he then tried to penetrate me and I went to pull away, but he pulled me back. As he struggled to insert his penis into me I clenched my buttocks together. His grip around my mouth got tighter, and his free hand grabbed at my testicles. As he squeezed, the pain shot through my body and I immediately relaxed. He then forced himself into me.

I had made love with men before but it had been willingly. Now I was being plundered and I could not stop him, I could not fight and I could not stop the tears from flowing. Why was he doing this to me? I was his son, his flesh and blood.

I tried to bite his hand but he moved it from my mouth to around my throat, squeezing. As he thrust in and out of me the pain was unbearable, and it seemed to go on for hours but it must only have been a couple of minutes. Finally I felt him come inside me and the bile rose in my throat.

He still held me by the throat and with his other hand he grabbed my hair and yanked my head back. He spat in my face and told me that I was no son of his, 'You are a bastard and I know what you are up to. I have heard the lads talking at sea: you're a male slag who'll do anything for money . . . and if you think I am paying for it, you can thing again. I'll take it whenever I want it.'

His hand then yanked at my hair again and he forced my head down between his legs. He growled 'suck it'. I wanted to throw up but I feared for my life. Unless you have experienced a situation like this, you will never understand the fear that grips you. I did as I was told – I could do nothing else. He started to lose his erection and as he did, he started to punch me in the back of the head.

Suddenly he pulled me up by the hair and put both his hands round my throat. I thought I was going to die. Tears streamed down my face and my whole body trembled, but he just squeezed harder, laughing at me all the time. He pushed my head right back into the pillows and his face moved closer to mine. It was then that I honestly thought he was going to kiss me, but he just spat in my face and squeezed even harder. I closed my eyes so that I did not have to look at him. As I opened them, his eyes were level with mine and he spoke slowly. 'Did you enjoy that?' I did not reply so he asked me again. I nodded. He then told me that if I ever told anyone about that night he would kill me. He would kill me with his own hands. He then squeezed his hands even tighter and I could feel myself beginning to black out. But, he suddenly let go and I gasped for breath. He just pushed me away from him, turned over, and went to sleep.

I wanted to be sick. I could feel the vomit sticking in my throat but I just didn't dare move. I lay there terrified that he would wake up and rape me again. As his sleep became deeper I slid out of bed and into the bathroom. I had no sooner closed the door than I threw up clinging to the side of the pan for what seemed hours. I felt like someone had stuck a knife up my back passage and ripped me in two, and when I looked in the mirror, dried blood was spread across my face, my lower lip was split, and to my horror, I was bleeding from behind. Blood had dried on my legs. I started to clean myself up. Sitting in the cold bathroom I felt more dejected than I have ever felt. My Nan slept in the next bedroom. I should have gone to tell her what had happened, but would she have believed me? I felt so ashamed, I felt as though it was my fault. I knew how to come on to people, but I had never encouraged him. He was my father. I was the loneliest child in the world at that moment.

Finally, I heard my Nan's alarm clock ring, and I slipped back into the lounge. My underpants were in shreds, so I dressed as quickly as I could and sat on the couch until I heard my Nan pottering around in the kitchen. She was surprised that I was up so early. She looked at my face and asked how I had split my lip. I told her I had tripped and caught my head on the fireplace. Luckily my jumper covered most of the marks around my neck so she did not see them. When she went out to get the milk I slipped out of the back door and hid my underpants under some rubbish in the bin. When she returned to the kitchen she noticed that I looked pale. I said I had a headache so she gave me a couple of painkillers and told me to get into her bed for a couple of hours.

As I was lying in Nan's bed, I heard the bedroom door open and my father stood there. I went rigid with fear. He looked at me in disgust and snapped 'I warned you last night. You say anything to anyone and your days are numbered,' and he advanced towards the bed. He raised his fist and I thought he was going to lash out at me, but then he just smiled and walked out of the door. He wasn't my father any longer, he was a monster, a monster that I was going to have to spend two weeks at sea with. They were to be the most miserable weeks of my young life. I made sure that I was never alone with him. When he worked I slept, when he slept I worked: I was only safe if I could keep him at a distance.

The school holidays came to an end. I was going into the fourth year now – I was to be a senior as well as one of the oldest children at the Harris. With a sigh of relief everybody headed back to school; the seven-week break had been a long one, and we were all bored.

All the pupils congregated in the school playground. The fifth and sixth forms had started the previous day, so there were only the four main grades to sort out. Order was called and the different years were split up. The first-year pupils were allotted their classes and the second- and third-year soon followed. The fourth-year crowd had been greeting each other; for the last three years we had all shared the same classes. Now everyone was going to study different subjects with new teachers. There was a buzz of excitement – I suppose we were more uncontrollable than the first-year pupils, for we knew the systems of the school and knew just how far we could go.

I was as excited as everyone else. I was going to learn shorthand and typing as part of my commercial studies course. I also had to take up the other choices on the course, domestic science and needlework. I couldn't have wished for better. I was really happy at the prospect. I had hated doing woodwork and metalwork; thank God our stream weren't expected to do such things. Even gym lessons had been cut out of my curriculum. I was the only boy in the class and my doing gym would have made things awkward for everyone, so I had been given a free lesson instead.

The headmaster started to call out names for commercial studies, and girl after girl left the large group and started to assemble with their new teacher, Mrs Sullivan. She was a large tubby lady who wobbled around. About sixty girls had assembled around her. I was very excited. A lot of girls I liked were in the class – in fact I got on well with most of them. Then, suddenly, my name blared out over the megaphone.

The headmaster checked his list to make sure he had got it right. There was a deathly quiet all over the playground. Then the girls in my new class started to giggle, and soon the whole playground broke into an uproar of whistles and catcalls. I just could not move; I was paralysed. Then one of the boys behind me pushed me forward, and I went flying.

As I lay on the ground looking up at the hundreds of laughing faces all around me, a sudden realisation struck me. *I was different.*

I struggled to stop the tears that welled up inside me. I was helped up by a teacher, but I wasn't able to explain to him how I felt. My life changed on that day. As I walked towards my new class, dusting myself off, I knew that if I wanted to survive I must start to build up defences all around myself; and I knew that once they had been put up they would be very hard to take down. I knew that now I must face the truth about myself. Once I had the guts to admit to the rest of the world that something was wrong, I could start to take my defences down – but I would have to be well prepared first.

I didn't really give a damn what anyone thought at that time. After all, it was my life, I would live the life that I wanted to.

During a period of continual insults and abuse I tried to settle into my new course. I enjoyed it at first. Typing and shorthand came easily. I was given a further two free lessons when the girls started their sex-education lessons. The teacher thought that it would embarrass them if I were present. I ended up turning all my free lessons into music classes and plugged on with my violin training.

I found lessons with the girls far easier than I had ever found lessons before. I started to identify myself as one of them, even though at the time I did not understand why. I spent most of my lunchtimes with the girls, and the fact that I was a boy didn't really affect our relationships. If they had problems with their boyfriends they would ask me for my advice. They discussed their sexual fantasies quite openly, as well. If only they had known how much I envied them.

Teachers started to put pressure on me; they could see the reactions from the other boys. It was everyone's opinion that I was a poof. Sometimes I was openly discussed in class. I couldn't go into the playground, because I was branded a wanker. I started to stay in the classroom at breaktimes. Lunchtimes started to be lonely; I even took to staying away from the dining-room. Even the journey to and from school became embarrassing.

The other boys at the Harris didn't want to mix in my company, so I walked by myself. Life was getting lonelier. My father's visits posed a continual threat to me. Every time I knew that he was going to visit I used to make some excuse to stay at school; but he would always wait until I got home. What unnerved me was the way he used to smile at me and talk as though nothing had ever happened in the summer holidays. When I was alone in my bed at night I prayed that I would soon be able to get away from everyone. I wanted to be my own boss.

While looking through a careers leaflet at school one day I saw a recruitment ad for the Royal Navy, and I made a decision straight away. I was going to join up. That was one way of getting out of the Harris. I went to see the governor. I knew that my father would object, so I asked for the authorities' permission. I was told that I could apply, and that if I was accepted the court order that bound me would be lifted.

I went for an interview in the local recruiting office, and passed my entrance exam. The medical went all right and I was told that I would get my results and a starting date within twenty-one days.

I had to tell my headmaster that I was leaving that Easter. He was disgusted and thought that I had been wasting the staff's time. I had also filled a precious vacancy on the commercial course. I was disgraced and moved into the remove class on the same day.

My father went berserk when he found out that the authorities were releasing me. He tried his best to stop my release. Luckily I had signed on for twelve years and there wasn't a thing he could do about it.

After I had finished school I had six weeks to kill before I left the Harris, so the governor gave me a job. I worked all round the office and stores and gave as much help as I could. The governor and his wife had been good to me. I was sorry that I was leaving, but it was necessary. I couldn't have taken much more of the abuse that had been thrown at me.

A few days before I was due to leave the Harris a letter arrived with my travel permit and my first pass into H. M. S. *Ganges*, a shore base in Ipswich. I was to be free. At last I would be able to make my own decisions.

Chapter 5

In the Navy

As I climbed aboard the bus that was to take me to the central station in Preston, I glanced back at the entrance of the Harris. Tears welled up inside me. The governor and matron stood with all my brothers and sisters, waving goodbye. I ran upstairs and waved out of the back window until their images disappeared. I held back the tears. I was alone now, and a whole new world was opening up before me. I paid the fare and my thoughts began to drift. I had heard all kinds of stories about the Royal Navy. If only half of them were true, I was going to have a good time.

Several other guys had assembled at the local recruiting office by the time I arrived. We were all strangers to one another. Some looked more worried than others. Mums and dads stood with their offspring, murmuring the odd encouraging word and straightening ties. The office door opened and a deathly silence overtook the place. An impressive-looking officer in a blue serge uniform stepped out and checked all our names off. We collected our things together and made our way to the railway station. My journey to London was to be the furthest I had ever travelled.

Once assembled on the platform, the family groups broke up to say their final goodbyes. I felt slightly dejected as I stood there by myself. The officer in charge of the party came over and asked where my family were. He just smiled one of those knowing smiles and reassured me that everything was going to be fine. He ran his hand through my hair and patted me on the shoulder, he could sense that I was feeling slightly out of it. I glanced around all the little groups – they all looked so happy. All except one boy who was looking slightly harassed; our eyes caught each other's and he raised his in disgust as his mother fussed around with his jacket.

The train arrived and we all boarded very quickly. Everyone threw their luggage on to seats and then returned to the doors to wave goodbye to their families. I sat on one of the empty seats; the table was stacked with luggage. My own tatty little holdall looked very forlorn. Once the train had pulled out, the boys all came back to their seats and it was informal introductions all round. I had ended up sitting next to the poor guy that had been harassed by his mother. His name was Alan. We learnt a lot about each other on the four-hour journey. It was evident that he was not as confident as he tried to make out.

We arrived in London ten minutes later than had been planned. There was a mad rush, as we had to travel across London on the tube to catch our connection for Ipswich. As we headed for the 'Underground' sign I was beginning to wonder what I had let myself in for. There was a moving staircase that went downwards. It was only the second time I had ever seen one. One of the big stores in Blackpool had one, but I had never been on it. We took three of these staircases down. I must have looked puzzled as Alan explained to me that all the trains in London ran underground and were called tubes. I stuck by him after that, because he seemed to have done this all before. The tube arrived and we all climbed aboard; the doors slammed shut and we sped along the dark tunnels. I was getting ever so excited. Alan must have thought me a bit of an idiot, as I asked him all kinds of silly questions. How deep are we? Weren't there any buses in London? Did everyone travel like this?

We managed to stay together for the rest of the journey. When our second train pulled into Ipswich we were both bedraggled and tired. We had been travelling most of the day. A large blue naval bus was waiting in the forecourt of the station to meet us. We each in turn had to hand in our passes and give our names and dates of birth. Once we were all settled in the bus it was noticeable that we had all quietened down; and our numbers had grown considerably on the way as we had picked up other recruits at Crewe and in London.

The journey from the station to H. M. S. *Ganges* was comparatively short. The imposing mast that stood in the middle of the parade-ground was visible about five minutes before we even arrived. It was explained to us that for the first three weeks we would undergo training in a small camp opposite the main gates of the *Ganges*. It was this initial training that was to sort the men out from the boys. As the officer explained this he had a huge grin on his face.

We all had individual interviews as soon as we arrived. It all seemed irrelevant – we had been through the same question-and-answer routine twice before. I was allotted to Dreadnought Mess: bed and pack number thirteen. What a start for a superstitious new recruit. Alan ended up in the same mess. We were taken over to the mess and shown round, we then went for our first naval meal. It wasn't such a bad meal after all. By the time we had finished eating it was quite late. As we left the dining-hall we were given our first kit issues and our bedding-packs. Our clothes and shoe sizes had been taken on interview. I was then given a little tag with my name and number, Roberts D116849. I was no longer a civilian, I was naval personnel.

Forty of us were crammed into what was no more than a wooden hut, with a shower and toilet area attached. This was to be home for the next three weeks. We each had our own little area, with a bed and locker. Most of the lads just collapsed into bed, but I intended to start as I meant to go on. I made my bed up, then sorted out all my clothes and hung them in the locker. About six of us were showering an hour later. We were keeping everyone awake, but I just did not care. I was out of the children's home.

The next few days flew by, with more kit issues, medicals and lectures on VD and other sexual problems. Homosexuality was touched upon: the senior medical officer described it as a terrible disease. I laughed inwardly while everyone else jeered and called out obscenities, and thought to myself, would people never accept

that a homosexual love can be as loving and as tender as a heterosexual one?

The downer of the day proved to be the visit to the dentist. My
teeth were terrible at the best of times. He confirmed this by telling
me that I needed three extractions and two fillings. That terrified me.

We all spent every evening polishing boots and pressing trousers
and white vests. Alan ended up polishing my boots and I pressed
both our uniforms. We spent most of our spare time together. He
was not gay and wasn't even vaguely aware that I was. To him I
was just one of the boys. After lights out every night there was
trouble. The toughest of the guys wanted to prove that they were
the toughest, and fights were a regular occurrence. But order was
soon restored once everyone knew whom they could handle and
whom they couldn't. I had very little bother; I got on with everyone
except the mess bully, and I avoided him like the plague.

On the fourth day we were all assembled in the messes for our
first parade drills. They were quite exhausting at first. We had to
stand to attention whilst being inspected; then it was marching –
left-wheeling, right-wheeling, marking time; dressing to the left,
dressing to the right, then back to good old marching again. Two
hours on the parade ground were hell, but one got used to it.

After six o'clock each evening we had our leisure hours, and
everyone did their own thing. Alan used to go out with the rest of
the guys to play football. I was quite content to have a shower and
crawl into bed with a good book. I always meant to write to the
family, but never got round to it.

By the end of my first fortnight I was quite enjoying naval life.
The discipline was stricter than anything that I had been used to,
but I quite enjoyed being shouted at and marched around a parade-
ground. We had numerous lectures on all aspects of naval life. We
had to start making decisions as to what branch of the navy would
be most suitable for us. The drivers' and engineers' courses seemed
the most favoured. Myself, I opted for the TAS course. It was radar
work, and the main aim was to learn to operate torpedo anti-
submarine missile controls. My educational standard was quite
high, so I was accepted for that branch.

We had not been allowed out of the gates since we arrived, but
when the three weeks ended we were given four days' leave. After
that we were to move over to the main base. Most of the boys were
going home to see their families. Alan invited me to go and stay
with him and his family. I declined his offer. What I had seen of
London had whetted my appetite. The naval command centre
arranged for me to go and stay at a hostel there for the four days.
Everyone seemed very pleased that the first three weeks were over.

A couple of the officers had explained that they were the worst and when we moved to the main base things would be a lot easier.

I travelled with Alan as far as Euston station. We made arrangements to meet each other before catching the train back, so that we could have a drink together. The hostel that I had been allocated wasn't far from Euston, so I took my bag round and decided to get settled in. The place was a right dump. If I had been paying for it I would have gone mad. But then, it was only for four days; and it was also better than going back to the Harris. I had to share a room with five other guys, who ranged from drop-outs to alcoholics. I didn't have many civilian clothes, so I was not too worried about leaving them. I soon had everything sorted out, and I set off to see what London had to offer.

I had a look at Buckingham Palace, inspected the hotels in Park Lane and went window-shopping. But I soon reached Piccadilly Circus – a place I had heard many naughty stories about. I wondered what time all the prostitutes started work. Eros stood in the middle of the Circus, bow in hand, green and weathered, looking a right mess, and all around his pedestal, on the steps, were hundreds of people. Many were fast asleep and many looked the worse for wear. I crossed the road and headed for Shaftesbury Avenue. I stopped at a bookstall and looked at all the dirty books that were displayed. In Preston that kind of book was kept under the counter. Here they were displayed as boldly as anything.

I saw the odd one or two with men on the front cover. I picked one of them and started to flick through it. It was quite an experience. The guy who was working the stall came over and asked if there was anything he could do for me, I was so embarrassed I put the book back on the shelf, walked away and leant on a railing about twenty yards from the bookstall, occasionally glancing round.

I became aware that someone was watching me very closely. I turned and looked at him straight in the eye, and he just winked. I don't know whether I was more shocked or startled. I moved further on down the railing. The guy moved nearer to me.

I looked around again, and it suddenly struck me that there were hardly any women about. Young men stood all around, some dressed in very feminine clothing. I realised that I had stumbled on part of London's gay scene. I had never imagined that gay people would hang around on street-corners.

The guy who had winked at me had moved in even closer. I made it quite obvious that I was not interested by turning my back on him. I felt him move right to my side: then he said in a low voice, 'How much?'

I turned and said, 'For what mate?'

He just repeated, 'How much?'

'How much for what?'

He just nodded and said, 'Well, you know.'

I wanted to giggle, but I kept a straight face and told him to clear off because he couldn't afford it.

Again he asked me, 'How much.'

I told him, 'Twenty quid.'

He looked rather startled and moved away. I turned to view the rest of the scene. People were openly cruising and picking others up. Still others were prostituting themselves. I would never have got away with anything like that in Preston.

In two minutes my whole life had changed. I leant on the railing and felt a little more confident. A couple of queens came mincing over, both looking as if they had stepped out of a poodle parlour. After deciding that I was gay, we had a long chat about the scene. Once they had found out all there was to know about me, they drifted off. I had learnt that the going rate was five pounds for a quickie and ten pounds for the night. Roger, the slightly camper of the two boys, made his way over to the guy who had tried to pick me up. I saw the guy nod in my direction. No doubt Roger was telling him all about me.

A couple of guys boldly approached me and asked how much I charged. I stuck to my first rate: twenty quid. I did not need the money – I had been given three weeks' wages and the Navy was paying for my accommodation. Both the guys who had asked my rates just disappeared. Roger came mincing back over and told me that his friend fancied me and would like to take me out for dinner. I told Roger that I was not interested; I had already told the guy my price. Roger said, 'Come off it, love. Twenty quid's a bit steep, you know unless you have something special to offer, that is.'

I just raised my eyebrows. By this time the guy had made his way over yet again, and was standing by Roger. He just smiled. He was in his thirties, quite small and slim, with wavy brown hair. He then asked me himself if I would join him for dinner.

I was feeling quite peckish, so I agreed. He took me to a little Italian restaurant in Frith Street. We had a long talk over our meal. I found him very easy to get on with. Brian soon found out about my past. I asked him why he went to pick boys up at the Dilly so that he could pay them for sex. He was quite a good-looking guy – surely there was no need for it? He just shrugged his shoulders and said that he liked to have someone around to keep him company. He had been married, but that had ended in disaster. At the end of the meal, he asked me where I was staying. When I told him, he seemed quite upset.

He lived not far from the hostel, in Islington. He offered me a lift home, and because I was tired I accepted. As we arrived at the hostel front door Brian turned to me and said that he had a spare bedroom; he would rather I used that than stay at this dump. I declined his offer at first, but he promised that there would be no strings attached. I had heard that many times before, but I agreed. I didn't fancy sleeping in a room full of alcoholics.

We drove back to Brian's flat in silence. He kept reassuring me that everything would be all right. He had a lovely flat in a tall block. He made a couple of coffees then disappeared for a short while before returning to tell me that my room was ready. I had a quick bath, then went to bed. I expected Brian to make a play for me during the night. I suppose I was disappointed when he didn't. I didn't see him till the next morning when he brought me in a cup of coffee. He sat on the bed and held my hand; we just chatted. I decided that he was quite a nice guy.

He had a couple of days' holiday due to him, so he asked me if I would like to see the sights. I said I would, and we went along to the hostel to pick up my belongings.

The next few days passed very quickly. I was taken around all the famous sights, and at night we visited pubs and clubs that were only used by gay people. The atmosphere was great and I was able to let my hair down (not that I had much hair after the crop I had received when I reached H. M. S. *Ganges*). It felt really strange dancing with a guy to a slow record – but what the hell? Everyone was doing it. Each night we returned to the flat – I to the spare room, Brian to his. Each morning he brought my coffee in and we would have a long chat.

My final day with Brian was special. He took me on my first ever visit to the theatre, and afterwards we had a meal. We returned home and said our goodnights. I lay in bed thinking of the last few days. I had had a wonderful time and it was all thanks to Brian. I felt guilty because he hadn't let me pay my way while we were out together.

I got out of bed and went to his bedroom. The door was open and he was fast asleep. I crept across the floor, and climbed into his bed and cuddled up to him. It was some time before he realised I was there with him. He just opened his eyes and said, 'Hello.' I cuddled even deeper and thanked him for the last few days. He still did not make a play for me; he just held me tight all night. All he really wanted was someone to hold.

The next morning was hard to face. I hated goodbyes at the best of times. Brian had to get up for work, and I had to return to naval life. He dropped me off in Trafalgar Square on his way to work. I promised faithfully that I would drop him a line and see him next time I had a shore leave. But the last wave that I gave him was to last him a lifetime. We were never to meet again.

Alan arrived at Euston nearly an hour later, so we did not have as much time to mess around in London as we would have liked. He had asked me what I had been up to. I told him that I had had a great time, but had spent most of it alone. I couldn't have told Alan about Brian. He just would not have understood. Already I had done Brian an injustice by denying his existence. Such lies were to be one of my many defences.

Things were different when we returned to the *Ganges*. Alan ended up in Drake Division as he wanted to be a Steward. I ended up in Frobisher because of my T.A.S. training. There were six divisions, all leading off a long covered way. Each division had five billet huts; four were messes the other was a games room. Each mess contained about fifty beds. In between the messes was a divisional office, where the officers in charge of the division congregated.

My social services file must have found its way into naval hands, because on my first day back I was called in to see the divisional commander. All the officers seemed to know of my past, and Lieutenant Green was a marvel. He could not do enough for me. In many ways he replaced my father. He was the type of guy I wished my father had been. I soon settled into Frobisher and made lots of new friends.

I had only been back a few weeks when my homosexuality started to worry me. I could not go and talk to anyone about it, as that would surely lead to trouble; I knew full well that if I were to stay in the Navy I must keep it hidden. I was really enjoying Navy life, despite the fact that my intention had been to buy myself out at the first possible date. I had seen it as simply a means of escaping from the welfare. I continued training during the day, but kept myself to myself in the evening.

The other guys were always messing around in the shower. Often there was a wanking competition, to see who could come first. I always won, because the sight of the others always turned me on. But I don't think anyone realised that I was gay.

During our training periods I proved to be as capable as everyone else. There was only one day that I found a real struggle – it was the day we went over a five-mile assault course. It nearly killed me. I started off as well as the rest, swinging over holes that were filled with barbed wire, climbing net walls, struggling through mud pits, climbing trees and such like. It was when I had to face a twenty-foot wall that I started to worry. And, after that, one section in particular had me terrified. A series of four-inch-wide planks ran about eight foot high over a swamp area, which we had to cross. The stretch was about a hundred yards long, and what made things even worse was the fact that dummy ammunition was being exploded all around. It was no joke.

No sooner had I got over that than some brute of an officer pushed me towards a handle. Before I knew what had happened I was hurtling down a shaft about two hundred feet deep, holding on to a little wire handle attached to a cable. I nearly shat myself. Then some guy started shouting for me to let go. I did as I was told, a little late. Any later and I would have gone smashing into a wall. I could see all the senior officers standing about a hundred yards away, marking scores, so I knew the end was in sight.

My heart was nearly bursting as I headed for the thirty-foot wall, but there was worse to come before that. I would have given any-thing to have missed this part, but the sergeant in charge wasn't letting anyone get away. A piece of piping about forty yards long was set in the ground. It was half full of mud, topped up with water. There was a gap of about five inches between the water-line and the top of the pipe. It was just possible to breathe if you kept your head back. The first couple of yards weren't too bad, but once someone started pushing you from behind and you were bumping into people in front it became a struggle. The water-line kept rising as people struggled, and the higher it rose the harder it was to breathe. The mud did not help either, as our hands kept slipping. Our clothes pulled us back. Time stood still. It was impossible to stay calm, and I thought I was going to be sick on several occasions. Other people had been:the smell in that five-inch gap was terrible. I eventually struggled out of the other end and collapsed in a heap on the grass. I wasn't the only one; it looked as though we had all had a bad time. Our divisional officers kept shouting for us to press on and finish the course. I half-walked, half-crawled to the wall. Two pairs of hands lifted me up and two pairs of hands received me. The drop on the other side was worse than I'd expected – about thirty-five feet. I gulped and just let myself fall. I hit the ground with a ter-rible thud: I thought I had broken every bone in my body. I was dragged out of the way as other bodies were dropped from the wall, then dragged away too. I can laugh about it now, but that after-noon was a nightmare and I would not wish it on my worst enemy.

As if that had not been enough for one day, we were all taken to a hut, given clean overalls and gas-masks and told to form a queue. Everyone was wondering what was going on. Not being one for surprises, I stayed near the back of the queue. The first group of four went through the door and a green light came on; this was fol-lowed by a red, than an orange light. The door opened again. We expected the boys to return, but they didn't, so we were none the wiser. It was soon my turn. I walked in with the final group of four, and as the door closed behind us a voice from a speaker set in the wall told us that when the green light came on we were to put on our gas-masks, when the red light came on we were to take them off and when the orange light came on we could leave by the far door. The instructions seemed simple enough. As the red light came on we pulled off our gas-masks. The room was full of gas.

I struggled to put my mask back on, but a voice boomed that I should leave the thing off. Two of the boys were throwing up on the floor. I moved over to the far door, then threw up just as the orange light came on.

The door flew open and we all struggled to get out into the fresh air. We were greeted by a group of white, smiling faces on the other side. Even the strongest of us had thrown up. Some poor old naval rating turned the hose on the floor to clear up the mess and muttered to himself. 'Thank God that's it for another week.' I took great gulps as I collapsed by Alan. He was still feeling bad, and he had been in one of the first groups in.

We returned to our divisions that evening rather the worse for wear. I had decided that I had just about had enough. The following evening I called into the divisional office and asked for my discharge-by-purchase forms. I filled them in and returned them the same evening, much to the dismay of Lieutenant Green. He seemed to think I would have made a good career in the Navy, but I would not be dissuaded. However, about ten days before my discharge date I had a visit from the Preston social services. I was informed that if I bought myself out I would have to return to the Harris.

I felt trapped. I could return to the Harris and lose face; I had no alternative but to rip up my discharge papers and try to get out later. I knew full well, though, that after I had served six months I could always get out by walking into the medical centre and telling the senior MO that I was a homosexual. I would be out within forty-eight yours, and all it would say on my papers would be 'DISCHARGED FOR MEDICAL REASONS'.

Chapter 6
Love in the Navy

After a two-week shore leave I was glad to return to the security of the *Ganges*. Some of my friends had bought themselves out, Alan being one of them, and life was different. The training was more intensive: more was expected from the 120 of us that had returned out of the initial two hundred, even though another fifty were expected to drop out at the next purchase date. Another group of new recruits joined Frobisher, the fourth since I had been there. By then I was classed as one of the old boys.

My homosexuality had really started to worry me. I found that I was craving another man's love – not just sex: that did not mean as much any more. When I had occasional shore-passes I used to get the ferry over to Felixstowe and hang about in toilets all day.

One day I was out with a group of TAS guys at the rifle range when a bullet ricocheted off a wall and hit me in the ankle. I was rushed down to the hospital to have it removed. It was not until they cleaned the blood up that they realised it had travelled up my leg and come out again just below the calf. I can't stand blood at the best of times, so I felt even worse. I had a couple of X-rays and was stitched up. The senior MO signed me into the hospital for a week.

A week away from the drill and training suited me right down to the ground, and I made friends with a couple of the orderlies. One of them turned out to be gay. Through talking to him I found out that most of the gays in the Navy were either medics or stewards. As in civilian life, there were certain areas of employment that seemed to trap gays. On my second evening a very distinguished-looking officer came in to have a look around the ward. He looked great. I sat and tidied my sheets. He stopped and talked to the other guys in the ward. Then he came over, just as I was combing my hair. He smiled and said, 'You must be Roberts. I've heard quite a bit about you, young man.' Then he sat on my bed and asked how my family were getting on. He seemed to know quite a bit about me. The other guys in the ward were giving me a few strange looks, he noticed it too so he said goodbye and promptly left. For some unknown reason Chris – as I later found out he was called – really turned me on.

The gay orderly had a couple of days off and then reappeared on nights. The first night we had a long chat when everyone was asleep. The second night at around midnight I was asleep when he woke me up and told me that I had a visitor. He had made a cup of coffee and left it in the orderly office. He winked and told me that he would see me later.

I hobbled down the ward and into the orderly office, and who should be sitting there but Chris. I felt a mess – I had not combed my hair or anything. He apologised for waking me up and asked if I minded having a chat. What an evening it turned out to be! Chris was quite open, and told me that he was gay. He was also married and he fancied me. I was quite flattered. He had gone to a lot of trouble to find out about me before making his advances. There wasn't much he did not already know. He had been a lieutenant, and had just been upgraded to a lieutenant-commander. He had nothing to do with the hospital, really, but like all other officers he had to call round on his duty nights.

I was supposed to be discharged back to my division the following day, but we agreed that if I made a big fuss about the pain I was sure to get an extra few days in hospital. We sat talking for what seemed an age, just holding hands.

Suddenly there was a knocking at the door and the orderly stuck his head in to tell us that the duty officer was on his rounds. Chris had to disappear, so I hobbled back to my bed. The orderly was on all week, so Chris could pop in every night about midnight. Apparently they occasionally met at a gay club in Ipswich and for the past few weeks I had been the topic of Chris's conversation. I felt chuffed that he should show an interest in me; after all, I was just a junior rating and he was a fully fledged officer.

The next day when the duty doctor came round I must have put on a good act, because I was given another week in hospital. Chris came in every night, as he had promised he would, and had a couple of hours with me before the duty officer came round. The orderly always used to give us a knock once he saw the round progressing down the long covered way. Sometimes we were in some very peculiar positions and it used to take me all my time to hobble back to bed. Chris even visited on his night off – his wife must have thought he worked very odd hours.

I fell in love with Chris that week. He was so kind and gentle. When the day came for me to return to my division, it made life very difficult for the two of us. We arranged to meet on my shore leave and we used to go for drives, miles from anywhere. Occasionally, too, we would agree to meet late at night. He could always make his way round at night, but I was supposed to be in bed by ten. I used to climb out of the window by my bed and on to the roof; I then had about a dozen roofs to get over before I reached the hospital. I used to feel like a cat burglar: wore dark trousers and a jumper, gloves that I had bought one day in Ipswich, and a balaclava. Many was the time that I nearly fell off a roof, and several times I nearly got caught returning late.

Chris used to have a store-room down by the hospital. One night when we were in there the orderly officer from the gate did an extra round. I am sure that both our hearts stopped as he tried the door. The minute he was out of sight I had to dress and get back to the mess before he reached it. Once there, I did not even undress – I just dived under the covers as he came through the door. Two seconds later and I would have been caught red-handed. The minute he had gone out of the door a voice in the next bed said, 'That was close, mate. Where the hell do you go to anyway, every night?' I told him some story about meeting my bird round the back of the assault course every night. He believed me, and the story soon got around that I was a randy bastard who climbed out of the window for a screw every night. But from then on we had to be very careful.

Every evening in the mess someone would start something. We were supposed to be the seniors but we caused more problems than the proverbial soft Mick. We would occasionally carry a sleeping recruit along with his bed up to the parade ground when no one was in sight at the main gate. We would put down the bed and disappear back to the mess. God knows how each of those poor recruits must have felt when he woke up freezing cold an hour or so later with an orderly officer shouting down his ear-hole. Our favourite pastime was sending a new recruit up to the main gate for a long wait. The gate officers used to tell them to stand against a wall and, sure enough, they gave them a long wait. Another trick was to send someone up for a tin of paint to paint the last post. I know that once it sinks in the recruit feels a right idiot, because I got caught every time, and I did.

About once a week, too, someone would get a bucket of cold water thrown over him while he was asleep, and by the time the poor guy recovered from the shock we were all back under the covers. I could never hold back the giggles, and used to have the whole mess in stitches. Guess who always got the blame?

On one of our many meeting Chris asked me if I would go to Mount Snowdon with him for a week with a climbing party. I had to register my name on a list in the divisional office, and I got a few funny looks when I did so. Mountain-climbing wasn't something that I was expected to volunteer for. Knitting, maybe. But Chris was responsible for picking the lucky team, so I was sure of a place.

It was agreed with the group on the way down that I would be responsible for cooking and for looking after the cottage all day while everyone was off climbing. Chris had it all worked out; he was a crafty sod. But this time he had made one mistake. He had taken one more person than usual, and this was noted on the base. When we arrived at the cottage the mistake was quite apparent. There was a dormitory with sixteen beds in it, and an officers' room with two single beds. I ended up sharing the room with Chris. It was the silliest move we could have made.

On the fourth night two military policemen called at the cottage at about two a.m. to see if everything was O.K. We didn't hear them. We hadn't been asleep for long, for obvious reasons. The door to our room opened, and all hell broke loose when one of the MPs found us in bed together. Chris tried to talk his way out of it, but one of the MPs wasn't having it. For some reason he had had it in for Chris for a long time.

One MP stayed with us while the other went to get everyone packed up and dressed. We weren't even allowed out to the loo. The rest of the guys were eventually taken away. We sat there looking at each other. Chris told me not to worry, and that everything would work out O.K. Then we were taken away in separate cars. I was put in a cell at the main gate of the *Ganges* and left there for two days before anyone actually came to see me. I was very upset. After all, I had intended buying myself out in a few weeks' time. Chris had his whole future and his wife to consider.

My number one uniform was brought to me and I was told to prepare myself to meet a senior officer. It took me about an hour to get ready, then I was marched into the main block and upstairs into a small office. The MPs who had escorted me were dismissed at the door. Inside the room was a very old guy. He looked as if he were in his seventies. He wasn't in uniform, yet he stood erect before me. Military regulations were waved aside as he told me to sit down. I was told that my visit was unofficial and he was only there to see if he could sort the problem out quietly. I listened to what he had to say. Then he asked me several questions, and I was as honest as I could be. I wanted to protect Chris as much as possible.

The old man nodded as he listened. When I had finished speaking, he said, 'Well, you both think a lot of each other, of that there is no doubt.' He asked me just how far I was willing to go to protect Chris. I told him that I would do everything possible. He asked me if I would consider buying myself out. I told him that had been my intention anyway. He nodded his head in silent approval.

He excused himself and left the room. About half an hour later he returned, and with him was Chris. He seemed very flustered and could hardly look at me. The old man told us he intended to close the matter that day, and there were only two alternatives. I would purchase myself out of the Navy and Chris would move to another shore base, or we would both face a court martial. Chris tried to interrupt, but the old man held up his hand. He told Chris that I had already agreed to his proposals. Chris turned to me and said that I mustn't agree, but I told him that I thought it better in the long run. He just shook his head in disbelief. The old man stood up and excused himself. As he got to the door he asked us to finish our conversation, and said he would return in a short while. The minute he had gone out we fell into each other's arms. It was a terrible feeling.

Chris had to leave the base that evening, take a fortnight's leave and then move to his new base. We both promised each other that we would keep in touch. I gave him Brian's address so that he could write to me, and said that once I had a permanent address I would let him know it. The old man returned and we shook hands as Chris was asked to leave.

Then my discharge papers were brought in and signed. They were post-dated to forty-eight hours before my allotted time. The old man knew that it they went through immediately there would be problems with the welfare. He thanked me and we shook hands before I was marched out and returned to the mess. Even my divisional commander wasn't aware of what had gone on. It remained a mystery; everyone was asking me where had I been and what had happened, but I told them nothing.

The next few weeks were hell. I missed Chris a great deal. I knew I only had a few weeks to go, so I wasn't interested in my training or anything. I got hauled across the carpet in the divisional office twice. They weren't aware that my discharge papers were in, so they couldn't understand my attitude. During my last week I received a letter from Chris. It was long and sad. He pledged his love for me again, and stated that once I was out in Civvy Street he wanted to meet me. He implied that he was willing to lose his career and wife. But I was a nobody; I had nothing to offer him, and I knew that it just couldn't be. I read and re-read his letter, and the more I did so the more complications I saw.

The day of my discharge was the saddest of my life. I was called into the office the night before. No one could understand where my discharge papers had suddenly appeared from – I hadn't been through the discharge board or anything, yet there were my papers, all finished and signed. My divisional officer wanted to know when I had signed them, but I couldn't give him any explanation. I paid my twenty pounds that evening and prepared to leave. It came as a shock to all my friends. I walked through the gate the following morning, feeling very dejected. I had twelve pounds in my pocket and very few clothes. I thought of Brian. I hadn't written to him for months – in fact, not since my last home leave – but I thought that perhaps he might be able to help.

I travelled back to London and went straight round to Brian's flat. I rang the bell and a strange voice from inside asked who I was. I asked if Brian was at home. The door opened and a middle-aged lady stood there. She looked me up and down, her eyes lingered on the tatty holdall. She asked me who I was was, and I told her that I was a friend of Brian's. She nodded her head. 'One of his boy-friends, are you?'

I just looked at her. I didn't know what to say.

'Well, you'll have to clear off, love. I'm his sister. He don't live here any more.'

I asked where I could find him. It was important, I assured her.

'Impossible to see him, love. He's been dead nearly three months. He was killed in his car on holiday, and he's left me with a load of debts.'

I didn't hear much more. I turned and left. I went and booked into a small guest-house around the corner. It was only about eleven a.m., but I went straight to the room, undressed and got into bed with tears streaming down my face.

Chapter 7
Fleetwood Again

After getting over the shock of finding out that Brian was dead, I decided that I had better get myself sorted out, and the sooner the better. I had very little money, but I could not go and sign on the dole because I was obsessed with the idea that the welfare would be able to track me down if I did so. There was only one other alternative: returning to Piccadilly Circus to prostitute myself.

I went out the following morning determined to earn something. It took me nearly all day to earn forty pounds. It had been bloody hard work and some of the guys had been like animals. I went back to the hotel and booked in for a further week. I paid the cash in advance, which pleased the old girl who owned the place. My next job was to get myself some new clothes. The smarter I looked, the better my chances of picking up nice people. I had no intention of letting myself go like some of the 'rent boys' I had to work with.

It soon became obvious that there was far more money to be earned at night than during the day, so I started to sleep during the day and work all night. I used to rise about five-thirty, bathe and shave, then put on my smartest clothes. I used to buy lots of clothes.

I would take the tube straight down to Piccadilly Circus, arriving about seven-thirty. A visit to the gents' toilet, followed by a quick walk around upstairs, used to pay off. Once I had had my first client I used to go off and have a meal. While prostituting myself I would never let a guy take me home to bed. I used to just masturbate them in a toilet, or in their cars. I could never let any of them kiss me, either. I used to turn my head away. Most of the guys who were willing to pay were in their fifties or sixties, and old men really turned me off. It used to make me go cold, having their clammy fingers and mouths all over me. But then again, they were paying for it. The more they paid, the more they got – no matter how I felt.

After having quite an expensive meal I would visit a couple of the more notorious gay pubs in the West End. The Golden Lion in Dean Street was the worst in those days. I used to hang around there until around ten o'clock. If nothing had happened there, the Pink Elephant or the Le Foyer club was the next port of call before I went up to the Regency club. The Pink Elephant wasn't too bad, as it always had a good mix of people in. Le Foyer was completely gay, but the odd punter occasionally found his way in there by mistake.

The Regency – now that was a different matter. The dirty-mac brigade were always in there because it was always full of very young man.

I used the place for about a month, and during that period quite a few celebrities called in. If I were to mention some of their names here, the papers would be full of it. I would see more libel actions than *Private Eye*. Some celebrities have come out, and openly admitted that they have a different sexual preference than the norm, Freddie Mercury being just one of them. In this day and age I do not think a celebrity's sexuality is important to their fans. There is no disgrace in being gay, transexual or any other sexual preference, perhaps there really is a third sex? We are all different kinds of people and it takes all kinds to make up the real world.

These celebrities used to visit the club for the same reason as the dirty-mac brigade. They were guaranteed to pick up a nice young chicken. I often saw large backhanders being passed, along with the odd case of champagne.

It was always possible to pick up punters in the Regency – you just waited around until the offer was right. Quickies were the best, and I have seen a couple of the lads leave with as many as five different men each evening, being charged the full fee at the door each time they returned. I couldn't work like that. It was unclean. Tourists were my favourite. You could normally get more money from then, and they did not expect as much for it. I was always afraid of catching VD, so I started to visit the clinic once a week. When I was very busy I took to going every other day. I could not afford to upset anyone, as I had become quite popular with some of the villains who used the club. I always managed to do a couple of quickies every night, inside the loo or on the stairs outside.

When the Regency closed, at three o'clock, I used to nip down to Playland. It was an amusement arcade by Piccadilly Circus that was quite popular at that time of night. There were plenty of Greeks and Italians that used to pile in at around four o'clock to pick up all of us young boys. Most of the boys who used that place were being run by pimps. The odd pimp used to try and take me under his wing, but I wasn't having any of that. I always told them to get knotted. Some of the tougher ones became quite insistent that I should work for them, and I had a few close shaves in there, especially late at night.

I started carrying a carving-knife around with me. I only ever had to use that knife once, when one of the pimps pushed me against a wall and started to threaten me because I had picked up a guy that he had been working on for a young boy of his own. The pimp shat himself when he saw the knife. He shouted out, and everyone turned round. I had only pulled the thing out to frighten him. Everyone started moving away from me as if I were a madman. I shouted out that he was a dirty pimp and I wished he would leave me alone. Before I realised what was happening, someone grabbed the guy and pulled him to the floor. It all happened very fast. I just dropped the knife and ran like hell.

A guy shouted out that he was a copper and I must stop, but that only made me run even faster. At one stage there were four cops chasing me. I knew most of the back-streets and alleys in Soho, as I had walked them often enough, and I eventually lost the coppers around Soho Square. I hid in a doorway for what seemed ages. Then, after checking the street, I bolted like hell for the Le Duce club. Sandy, who ran the coffee-bar, asked me what was wrong. I asked him if I could hide in his store for a while because the police were looking for me.

He didn't ask any more questions but just locked me in the staff toilet. The police came down to the club about an hour later and asked Sandy if he had seen me. They did not know my name, but they had a description of me. Sandy said he recognised me from the description but hadn't seen me and did not know my name either. Once Sandy had closed the club up for the night at about five-thirty in the morning, he let me out and asked me what the hell I had been up to. I told him and he fell about laughing.

I stayed at Sandy's for the next three days. He was a man, but he dressed as a woman all the time, even though he looked like a man with women's clothes on. He did not seem to mind. It was really strange, but he said he enjoyed living like that. I thought that the police had my name and address, so I changed my hairstyle and colour with a little help from Sandy. I was planning to leave London. I dared not go back to the hotel in case the police were watching.

On the third night Sandy came home looking very worried. He told me that the police had been in the club the evening before with a mock-up photo of me that was a pretty good likeness. Apparently the police had been watching Playland for some time, and when I had pulled the knife out they had seen an opportunity to swoop and arrest a few people. In the end it turned into a big scandal. Sandy said it would be better if I could get out of London for a few weeks, but I didn't know what to do – my money had nearly run out. Sandy was in no position to help me, either.

I decided that I should head home to see my mother.

The journey to Blackpool seemed to take years. The coach stopped twice on the motorway. I could not even afford a cup of tea, so I stayed in my seat for the whole journey. I was sitting next to a young boy of about five; his parents were sitting in the seat behind. He was eating toffees and crisps all the way down, and he made me feel hungrier than I really was. The journey, however, proved too much for him, and the poor little mite fell asleep with half a Mars bar in his hand. It did not take long to work it out of his fingers; after all, it would fill a little gap in my stomach. When the little mite woke up, the first thing he missed was his Mars bar. He had his mum looking under all the seats for him. Then he asked me if I had eaten it. I just looked at him; his mother slapped him and told him not to be so cheeky. I told him that I thought he had dropped it on the floor. Sure enough, the paper was there – and sitting on the seat in front was an old girl with her dog. The dog got the blame, and the little boy started to cry. The little old woman felt so guilty that she slapped the dog and gave the little boy a two-shilling piece so that he could buy another bar later. I never did thank that old girl, so I'll take the opportunity now. Thank you.

Once we arrived in Blackpool, I had to walk the eight miles to Fleetwood. Even though I had no luggage it took me nearly three hours. At least I had stopped looking over my shoulder; but now I was praying that Mum still lived in the same house, as I hadn't written to her for ages. As I approached 16 Hesketh Place I could see smoke coming out of the chimney: at least someone lived there. The house looked terribly run-down and the odd window was smashed and boarded up with old cardboard that had sagged with the rain.

As I passed the entrance to the garage I noticed a pile of rotting rubbish, which stank. Surely Mum couldn't still live here?

I knocked on the front door. The glass was missing and two wooden boards had been roughly nailed up. A scruffy man in his late forties opened it. He had grey hair and a turned eye. I recognised him from somewhere, but could not place him. I asked him if my mother was in. He asked me my name. (In London I had been known as George – it was posher than Billy, the name I had been stuck with at home.) 'Oh, hello, Bill,' was his reply. 'Come in. Your Mum's having a sleep.'

I walked into what had been our parlour. An old wardrobe stood in the corner with its door hanging off. The curtains on both bay windows were closed. Once my eyes got used to the dark, I noticed that a mattress was laid against the far wall, and my mother was huddled there under some blankets. A coal fire had been lit in the hearth, but it was dying out.

The guy stood behind me and called my mother's name several times. 'Jessie, Jessie, your Billy's here to see you.'

My mother turned round. She was hardly recognisable. She had put on a great deal of weight and was wearing tinted glasses. She threw her hands in the air and cried out my name. I went over to where she was lying; it was good to see her. I'd missed her.

As she pulled me close to her, she asked me all kinds of questions, but I don't remember answering them. Only the smells of booze and body clung to my thoughts. Gradually I broke free and turned away. There was an old couch against the far wall, and I went over and sat on it. My mother got out of bed. We had both forgotten the guy who stood in the middle of the room. She turned to me and looked very guilty as she said, 'You remember Uncle Frank, don't you?' He had been living with my mother for quite some time.

I was asked if I would like a drink. Sherry was offered, but I asked for a cup of tea. I was deeply shocked when Mum went over to the wardrobe and got out a very burnt-looking pan. Then she pulled out a bucket half-full of water and filled the pan. I must have looked puzzled, for Mum explained that the gas and electricity had been cut off for the past six months and the water had been off nearly a month. Apparently my father had arranged that, to get my mother out of the house so that he could sell it; but she refused to move.

I asked her how on earth she had managed. Candles were used at night to light the place, when she could afford them. She had an occasional bath at Auntie Connie's, and collected the odd bucket of water from the neighbours.

The rest of the downstairs windows were covered with curtains, but the rooms stood empty. Dozens of empty wine-bottles stood around the old kitchen fireplace. Upstairs was even worse. There were four bedrooms there, and again all the furniture was missing. The windows were nearly all broken. The curtains were weathered and hadn't been washed for years. In two of the larger rooms stood piles of clothes that stank to high heaven. In the bathroom, you didn't have to look in the pan to realise that, although the water had been off nearly a month, the pan was still being used. The wooden floorboards all around it were yellow and rotting.

My disgust must have shown in my face as I re-entered the parlour. My mother had opened the curtains and tidied the bedding on the mattress. I asked if Dad's old tool-box was still down in the cellar. She hadn't been down there for years so did not know. I took a candle and went down into the stink-pit that had once been the cellar where we had all played as kids. The smell was worse than in the bathroom; old food and wine-bottles had been thrown down over a long period, and the food had rotted away.

Luckily I found our old tool-box in a corner. I soon had the panel off the front of the electricity box and was able to fiddle around and replace a few of the wires. Once it was all fixed I turned the power back on. I knew that I was committing a criminal offence, but who were the Electricity Council to let someone live in the conditions that my mother had endured? Of course, I admit most of it was brought on by herself; but social security did not offer much help either. More should be done for people with the problems that my mother faced – after all, she had brought eight children into the world.

On returning to the parlour. I tried the light but it did not work. I went quickly around the rest of the house and eventually found one light that was burning. All the other bulbs must have been dead. I returned to the parlour and fitted in the good bulb. There was a loud cheer from my mother as the light came on. It would save her a pound a week on candles – that meant she could buy another bottle of sherry. I could not do much about the gas, but the water was a different matter. I had a look around outside and found the water stop. I tried for an hour to get the thing back on without much success. The waterboard had made it foolproof. I wasn't going to give up that easily, though; and with the help of a pair of nutcrackers I had the water flowing back into number 16. Mum was very pleased that she would no longer have to go begging buckets of water from the neighbours. I took her down to the cellar and showed her how to reconnect the electricity if it was ever cut off again. She just did not seem to notice all the bottles down there, or the smell.

Dinner that evening was cooked on the fire – baked beans and fried eggs. They tasted ever so smoky. I managed to force the food down me. It was the most my mother had cooked for months. Frank sat about moaning all evening because he wanted to go out for a drink, but there was just no money till the following morning.

At about seven-thirty the front door flew open and banged against the hall wall. I wondered what the hell was happening, and my first thoughts went straight to the police and the happenings of the past few days. But Mum just said it would be the boys. About five guys staggered into the parlour with bottles of wine in their hands. I was later to find out that they slept on the floor upstairs and each paid two pounds a week rent. Drinks were offered all around. I declined, but my mother readily accepted their kind offer – she seemed quite at home in their company.

I decided to go for a walk on the sea-front for an hour. I called in at the old toilets I had used to visit, but the trade on offer did not interest me. I was not in a good mood. I had made a mistake by returning. The way that I had found my mother living distressed me, although I supposed she was happy.

I called into the Mount Hotel as I passed and asked if they had any vacancies. The manager came out and told me that he could not help, but if I tried again in a week or two . . . There was only one other hotel that I stood a chance in and that was the North Euston, the biggest hotel in Fleetwood. If they didn't have any vacancies, it looked as if Blackpool would have to be the answer.

I called in at the front entrance of the Euston. The young girl behind the reception desk looked familiar as I asked her if there were any vacancies. Carol recognised me straight away. We had been to school together before I was taken into care. After a short natter about the past, she rang the manager. He was off duty, so he could not see me until the following morning, but he might have a vacancy if I was willing to work as a junior in the restaurant. Carol passed his message back to me and asked me if I could return at ten the following morning.

When I arrived in the morning the manager had gone out, but I was interviewed by his assistant, who was not all that much older than myself. I managed to convince him that I was the man for the job. After he had taken all the details he sat and looked for a minute or two at his notes, then said, 'O.K., we'll give you a trial period of a month.' He told me that I could move in the following morning and start work that evening. I had not expected the job to have accommodation, but that sorted out another of my problems. I shook hands with him and made for the door. Just as I pushed the door to leave he called me back and asked me if I had the uniform that was needed. I assured him that I had the white shirts and trousers and bow-tie.

But I hadn't. What on earth was I going to do? If I'd been in London I would have soon been able to knock up the cash that I needed – but in Fleetwood it would take me a week. I returned home to number 16. From the look on my face my mother automatically assumed that I had not got the job. When I told her what had happened she went mad. The money she had collected from the dole had already been spent on the week's supply of booze, but she stood up and said that no son of hers was going to be beaten for the sake of a couple of quid. With that she put on her coat and told me that she would be back in a couple of hours.

At about four p.m. she returned. She had £25 in her hand. She gave me twenty and told me to go out and get what I needed. I asked her where she had got the money from. She just shook her head and said that there was only one way for a girl to get money in this hell-hole of a town, and to pull my finger out and get round to John's, the menswear shop, before he closed.

I felt guilty that my mother had gone out and prostituted herself on my behalf. I could not complain about her life-style now; I felt like a pimp. But I caught the shop open and bought myself two pairs of black trousers and two white shirts along with a black bow-tie. The bill was only fourteen pounds. I stuck two quid in my pocket, and when I got home I offered Mum four pounds back. She told me to keep it in my pocket, as I would need it until I got my first week's wages.

I arrived at the hotel the following morning and was shown to a lovely room in the back, above the kitchens. It was very small, but it was clean. I was told that I had to start at six in the evening. I was ready to go at four. I went down to reception and bumped into the assistant manager. He told me that I looked very smart, showed me around the kitchen and restaurant areas, and told me to get myself a cup of coffee and to wait for the rest of the staff to come in.

I had noticed that only half the tables in the restaurant had been laid, so I set about laying the rest up. I looked at those already laid and just copied them. The restaurant was all in gold and red, with Roman signs and plaques on the walls, and attached to it was a cocktail bar. It all looked very grand. I had just finished laying all the tables when Bella came in. She introduced herself as the head-waitress. She had a look around the restaurant and congratulated me on my work. For the next few weeks I always turned up an hour or two before everyone else so that I could lay everything up, and it wasn't until I realised I could never get the room finished that it dawned on me that people were leaving earlier every day and expecting me to do their work.

I did not receive any wages for two weeks, and my first wage-packet soon disappeared after treating Mum to a fiver. However, depending on which chef was on duty at night, I was able to steal some of the leftover meat and run it round to Mum. Over a four-month period I nicked all kinds of glasses and odd plates and things so that Mum had some decent crockery. I even managed to nick some decent bedding from the linen room to replace the tatty old sheets that were rotting on Mum's bed. She was always grateful, but warned me about getting caught. I knew I was doing wrong – it was becoming part of my life.

I occasionally visited the Sporting Club with Mum. She'd bucked her ideas up and had got rid of Frank. She bought herself a few new clothes, washed her hair and put on some make-up. The old Mum was gradually coming back.

She moved out of Hesketh Place into a bedsitter in St Peter's Place. I didn't realise it at first, but half the girls who lived there were on the game. It got on well with all of them. Mum started having her regular visitors around, so I had to be careful whenever I went back. There was always a secret sign that let me know whether or not she was entertaining. Once, she went into hospital for a week after taking an overdose; I had a key and stayed at the flat every evening. Several times her clients turned up. When I opened the door most of them made excuses and disappeared, but if I fancied one of them I used to invite him in and make a play for him. Sometimes I was successful and at other times I nearly got a good hiding.

At one stage I was meeting a large percentage of my mother's ex-lovers, and even had an affair with her regular boyfriend. I'm sure that if she had ever found out she wouldn't have minded. I was heavily involved in the gay scene, and used to visit the toilets in Fleetwood. I occasionally went to Blackpool to visit its only gay bar and club, where I had a super time. Lucy's Bar was outrageous. It was a brand-new bar, and holidaymakers from all over the country used to visit it. One could be ultra-camp down there and get away with it.

One night I was standing in Lucy's and the organist was bashing out his camp songs (he'd sung the same songs very night since the place had opened – and, believe it or not, when I revisited the place nearly ten years later the people were different but the organist and songs were the same). Two queens from Manchester walked in; their hair was permed and they wore heavy make-up. Their outfits were very camp, with jeans tucked into knee-boots. They received a lot of attention that evening. I thought I'd like to try the same thing – but, being an exhibitionist, I took it one step further. I told my Mum that I was going to a fancy-dress party; she set my hair in rollers and made me up in full slap. I wore a white shirt with a big collar and a pair of blue-and-white striped jeans I'd bought in Fleetwood market. I borrowed Mum's old fur coat and topped the outfit off by wearing her tortoise-shell boots and carrying a matching bag. I looked in the mirror and couldn't believe the difference. I looked like a real woman without tits. My Mum treated it all as a big joke.

When I walked into Lucy's that evening, Lucy behind the bar burst out laughing and everyone had hysterics. I ordered half a pint of lager and blackcurrant, and stood there and sent everyone up. I was really enjoying myself. I had such a fun evening and everyone kept telling me that I looked great.

I decided to keep the image, and I started to buy very camp and flamboyant clothes. It became a regular thing, borrowing my mother's coat and boots and make-up. She had told me that my father had been bisexual and was worried in case I had caught it. I denied it and told her it was just hippy fashion that I was involved in. She accepted that.

About three months later I met a guy from London in Lucy's and things began to change. This guy was called Nick; he was Irish and had dark curly hair and a thick 'tache. I thought he was lovely. He used to wear a red velvet jacket with gold braid and was really nice. I didn't realise at first that he was down with his lover. We met most evenings when I had finished work and sat under the balcony by the Metropole Hotel. As his holiday was coming to an end he asked me if I would go back to London with him. I jumped at the chance. We agreed that I'd tell my mother that weekend and travel up the following week. I went home feeling elated. At last I had met someone whom I could live with. The following morning I had planned to tell my mother that I was gay; but just couldn't get up the courage. She was meeting a guy who owned an off-licence and she was quite friendly with his wife, Myra (she wouldn't have been if Myra had known what was going on). I thought that if I told Myra she would be able to break it to my mother better than I could. I explained to Myra that I was in love with another man and I intended to go and live with him in London. He'd left me his number and I was to ring him every night at eight o'clock and travel down the following week. Myra accepted my declaration and passed the information on to my mother that evening while I was at work.

My mother met me from work that evening and told me not to worry. She had fully understood, and as long as I was happy she didn't care what I did. I was so glad that she had accepted it, and started making plans to leave for London the following Sunday evening. I handed my notice in at the hotel and phoned Nick as promised. He worked as a chef at a club in the West End.

Mum gave me fifty pounds the day I was travelling, and there was what I had managed to save. She took me to the coach station that evening with my luggage in a taxi and waved me off. I promised to write.

When the coach arrived in Victoria I looked around for Nick, who had said he would meet me. I sat down on a bench with my luggage to wait. There weren't many people around at that time; I thought maybe he had had trouble getting up so early in the morning, or perhaps he'd slept in. But by nine o'clock I was getting very worried. I put my luggage in the left-luggage office and hung around the main entrance. I was feeling very down. By lunchtime I had convinced myself he'd got the wrong time and would turn up at 6.30 that evening. I felt a lot better and went and had something to eat. I went into the West End, and with the money my Mum had given me I bought a long black cloak with a red lining and gold fastening. In Carnaby Street I bought a pair of purple velvet trousers and a purple silk shirt that was very baggy. The outfit looked great on and was very camp. I was sure Nick would like it.

At about five I returned to Victoria and stood around the area where the Blackpool coach arrived. By seven p.m. I was feeling as bad as I had at lunchtime. I rang the club and couldn't get a reply, so I decided to walk round. Eventually I got to the club. It looked very posh with its marble entrance and antique furniture. I asked the porter if Nick was in, realising that I didn't even know his surname. The porter disappeared and came back to tell me that the only Nick that had worked there was a chef, and he'd been sacked the day before.

My heart sank. I returned to Victoria station not knowing what to do. I thought about my conversations with Nick. He'd been so genuine – perhaps he'd got the day wrong. I was so naive that I convinced myself he would turn up at six o'clock the following morning. By this time it was nine-thirty. I didn't know any clubs around Victoria at that time, so I settled down with a book.

At about eleven-thirty, when I went for a walk, I noticed that a lot of gay men were cruising around the station. I wasn't in any kind of a mood for cottaging so I drifted back to the coach station. I was sitting reading my book feeling terribly cold, when I was certain I could hear Nick's voice. I stood by the main entrance and, sure enough, Nick was walking up the road. Rolling about with him was his lover. (He'd told me on the phone earlier in the week that it was all over with him.) I just couldn't believe my eyes.

As they came level with me I called out Nick's name. He looked and came staggering over and asked me what the hell I was doing here. I told him that he was supposed to have met me the previous day at six-thirty a.m. He looked slightly awkward, and apologised. He said he had a few problems to sort out with his friend that evening, but that if I rang him at eight in the morning he'd come and pick me up. He gave me his home number and staggered off after his friend, who was shouting all kinds of obscenities from further up the street.

I felt slightly better as I settled back into my book. It was nearly two, so I didn't have all that long to wait until everything would be O.K. Nevertheless, the night seemed to drag on for ever. At last eight o'clock came round and I telephoned the number Nick had given me. He answered. I said hello and asked him how we was, and if everything had gone O.K. There was silence on the other end; then I could hear someone giggling in the background. I called Nick's name two or three times, and he then spoke. He told me he hadn't thought that I would come up to London and had only been joking anyway. He'd since decided to stay with his friend. He was sorry if I'd been put to any trouble. Before I had any chance to reply, the receiver was replaced at the other end. I was stunned, but soon came out of that. I redialled his number and when the phone was answered I let out a whole line of abuse; but it wasn't Nick. It was his friend. He just said, 'Piss off, dear,' and put the phone down.

I went straight to the left-luggage office when it opened, then bought a single ticket back to Blackpool. I caught the lunch-time bus and was back at my mother's flat by eight-thirty p.m. She was surprised, of course, but I told her exactly what had happened. She replied that I'd soon learn my lesson. All men thought about was their bellies and their pockets. If both were full, the rest of the world could get screwed. How right she was!

She had arranged to go out that night, and I decided to go with her. She like my new purple shirt and trousers and she thought the cloak was great. We went to a big night club. I looked so camp and the club was so straight; all the younger fishermen drank there with all the working girls of the night.

A few heads were turned when I made my entrance; my mother loved it – until someone called me a poof. Then she just let fly and knocked the guy over a table. I thought all hell was going to be let loose, but Mum just stood back and the guy nearly begged for forgiveness. During the course of the evening several guys who had lost their girls tried to pick me up, such was the ambiguity of the men in that small seaside town.

I spent the next few nights sleeping on the floor in my mum's bed-sit. I tried to find another job, but it seemed impossible. One night we were in a terrible position, as one of Mum's punters turned up;

he paid quite a bit and she didn't want to lose the cash. She went to see one of the girls who had a bedsit further down the hall. She too was on the game, but was having a quiet night in. She came and had a drink with my mum and the punter, then we both went back to her room. It had been decided that the punter was going to stay the night. She had a big double bed, so we settled down for the night, as I was only sixteen, and a virgin where women were concerned. She was thirty-six, a divorcée and a nymphomaniac. Once the light went out she made a play for me. She knew that I was gay, but that didn't seem to make much difference. I didn't know what to do. I had a vague idea, but all the foreplay was beyond me, and I told her so. She just laughed and pulled me to her. She led the way and told me what to do. It took all my concentration just to keep an erection, and when I was inside her it felt like one great big sloppy mess.

Thank God I was gay – I couldn't have done that every night. I performed all the actions and groaned as she groaned. I eventually completed my duties, but it had taken a long time. She laughed. I wasn't a virgin any more, and wasn't it better than being with a man? I agreed, but if she had seen the look on my face she'd have died. I moved to the end of the bed and prayed that she wouldn't have another go. Luckily she didn't. I don't think I could have stood it.

Next morning I was out of bed and dressed in a flash. I couldn't bear to think that I might have to share a bed with her ever again. I looked at her as she lay in bed; her false teeth had been stuck under the pillow and her breasts hung halfway down her over-sized stomach. She looked a mess. I was glad to get into the open air, and I walked along the sea-front.

As I passed a small hotel I noticed a sign advertising the post of general assistant. I rang the bell and a Spanish-looking man answered the door. He was the manager, about thirty-five years old and very good-looking. When I told him that I was interested in the job, he looked me up and down and invited me into the lounge. The wages were terrible, but there was a converted bedsit in the back that went with the job. The only staff were the manager, his girl-friend and one other boy, so one had to do a bit of everything. The job seemed quite attractive, and the manager even more so. I thought I'd have to make a start somewhere, so when he offered it to me I took it.

I moved in that lunchtime. The bedsits in the back were no more than parts of a converted garage. The other guy who worked there was a dopey sod. On my first night he showed me some photos that Manuel, the manager, had given him to look at. They were porno-pictures – some of heterosexual sex and others of two men and two women. That set off a little interest in me; what was Manuel doing with gay pictures?

The following day I let him know that I'd seen them, and he gave me loads more to look through. Some of them made me feel quite horny. I dropped a few hints that I was into gay sex, but Manuel didn't seem to take much interest. It took about three weeks to eventually catch him alone in one of the bedrooms at the hotel. I jokingly pushed him on to the bed and we groped about a bit. I grabbed him where it mattered and he didn't seem to mind, so I eventually undid his trousers and began to have oral sex with him. I wanted him to screw me, but he refused. He said he only screwed women. I jokingly said that he'd have to meet my mother.

He jumped on that straight away, and told me he'd screw me if I introduced them. I explained that she was on the game and he'd have to pay. He said he didn't mind as long as it wasn't too much, and I agreed to take him that evening. He was really excited by this time, and I felt hard done by, because he screwed me and it was over before he had even begun.

My mother didn't mind at all. I waited in Manuel's car for him. He was only in the flat ten minutes, but on his return he said that he had enjoyed it and it had only cost him three pounds. He started to visit my mum regularly, and wasn't interested in me any more.

I started going round the toilets and picking men up again; but that only lasted about six weeks. I used to feel so ashamed of myself, standing in a toilet, playing with another guy. There was no love in it at all. I started to look at my situation and realised that I was no better than my mother. I was a whore, and no one was doing a thing to discourage me. In fact, I was encouraged into some of my more weird encounters.

If I was going to be saved, I had to save myself, and the sooner the better. I visited an agency in London and was offered a job in Folkestone as a trainee manager in a hotel. The money wasn't too bad and the future prospects looked good. I agreed to go on a month's trial.

I didn't even give in my notice at the job – I just left. I called at my mother's and the sign was outside that she was entertaining. I thought to myself. What the hell, I can write later. I decided to leave a short note just saying I'd left town and would be in touch. I took all my clothes to the station and travelled to Folkestone.

By the time I'd been at the hotel about six weeks, I had worked hard and proved that I was capable of doing the jobs that were expected of me. But one morning the receptionist came into the linen room and asked me to go to the manager's office.

The manager was sitting with two strange men, whom he introduced as CID men from the local police station. While she had been drunk one day, my mother had reported me for stealing her fur coat, boots and bag. One of the officers asked me if I had them. I said yes, I'd had them nearly six months. They were up in my room. The manager looked at me in disgust as one of the officers stood and said: 'George William Roberts, we are hereby arresting you for theft of your mother's property. If you have anything to say, you may do so, but anything you do say may be taken down and used in evidence against you.'

Then I was taken to the police station.

Chapter 8

Porridge

After spending a sleepless night in a cell at Folkestone, I was transferred back to Fleetwood in the custody of two policemen. I cursed my mother. I know the coat did not belong to me, but I had had it for many months. She never wore it, anyway – that annoyed me more than anything. I vowed never to speak to her again.

We travelled down on the train during the afternoon. I had been very embarrassed. After settling myself down, thinking that it was going to be an easy journey, I received the shock of my life. I was handcuffed to the luggage-rack with both hands, which meant that I could no longer sit. People were continually passing the window, and once they spotted the handcuffs they skated off, giving me filthy looks.

When I arrived I was harassed by all the station cops. One of them asked me if I had nicked the coat because I was a poof. I ignored him, and he lashed out at me and smashed me in the stomach. I buckled over, and as the cop walked away he repeated he didn't like poofs.

The new cell I found myself in was very cold; all I had to lie on was a wooden board that was fixed to the wall and a single blanket. The walls were a bright green and looked sickly; the bare brickwork was only just visible. I was lying there, ignoring all the slander that was being shouted through the door by cops as they passed, facing the wall and pretending to be asleep. I was frightened in case the big cop that had hit me would start on me again. I could hardly believe my ears when I heard my mother's voice asking one of the officers if I was alright. I heard the key go into the door, and I froze. I did not want to see her. I held my breath. I wished that I could just disappear.

She entered the cell and asked me how I was as if she hadn't a care in the world. I just ignored her. She called my name three or four times. I told her to go away. I refused to turn round. She soon became impatient. She pleaded for me to forgive her, but I retorted that the pubs must have closed already – or was she on her way to the club?

She tried to reason with me. She had brought me some chicken sandwiches and a bottle of coke, but I still refused to turn round. She laid the food and drink behind me and turned to leave, re-marking that I could please my bloody self from now on. I was also a little thief. I was furious at that, and swung round. The packet of sandwiches followed her through the door and the bottle of coke smashed against the far wall outside the cell. A cop grabbed the door and swung it shut. I could hear my mother walking down the corridor calling me such an ungrateful bastard, but I felt better after she had left. Just then I hated both my parents. I began to wonder why they had ever brought me into the world.

I was awoken the next morning by the sound of someone kicking the cell door. I jumped with fright. I had had a sleepless night. The wooden board had been very hard and sleep had only come as day started to break. The cell door flew open and I was told to move my arse and quick. I had to wash before breakfast. There was only a cold tap. I splashed my face, dried it on a small musty towel and re-turned to my cell. Breakfast was pushed through the small hole in the door – a cold egg that felt like rubber and a slice of burnt toast made up my first meal since the previous morning. I had to eat it, I was so hungry, and I can remember cursing the fact that I had thrown away the chicken sandwiches.

Later I was transferred to another cell, just below the courtroom. The statements that I had already made were checked and signed. Then I was conned by a police officer. I had been pleading not guilty and had intended to fight my case. The cop that came in, suggested I should plead guilty, was very friendly and said he was only offering me advice. He left, and another cop came in, who threatened me. Of course, anyone in that situation is going to turn to the helpful one. Clever tactics on the part of the police, as I changed my plea with only minutes to go before the case came up. As soon as I had signed the new statement, the decent cop turned out to be as bad as his mate. They laughed and told me that they had me by the short-and-curlies now. I realised that I had been set up.

I walked into the courtroom and sat in the box allocated to the criminal. Mine was the first case to be heard. I was a little dis-appointed to see that my mother wasn't there. I was pushed to my feet and the magistrates entered. One was a man, and he looked in one hell of a mood. He was joined by two women; one of them was an old girl who had used to live quite close to us; we used to nick flowers out of her garden and she used to chase us with a stick. I prayed that she wouldn't recognise me, because after a chase I always used to stand and shout back at her that she was an old bag.

A hush descended over the courtroom as my name and the charge were read out. Then came my plea of guilty. I had been told by the police that because it was my first offence I would get a warning. Social reports were read out, and my family history. The fact that we had come from a broken home seemed to have no effect on the bench, and before the hearing was over I could see that they had already reached a decision. When they left the courtroom to confer, my stomach was turning over and I felt weak at the knees. The policeman at my side told me to sit down, but no sooner had I done so than I was on my feet again. He said that that had been a quickie; it did not look at all good for me now.

The male magistrate told me that they had taken into consideration the fact that it was my first offence – but I had stolen from my mother, the mother that had loved and cared for me for many years. I felt sick. What was he babbling about? They had decided to give me a chance: three months in a detention centre would stop me from ever committing another offence. I thanked him weakly, left the box and was returned to my cell. I held back the tears until the police officer had left. It was my mother's fault. Why couldn't she have been like everybody else's mum?

Later that afternoon I was taken by police escort to the detention centre, Buckley Hall. Through the van windows I could see the high fences and the black brick building that looked so much like the Harris children's home. As the van drove round the grounds I spotted some of the other guys. They all had cropped hair and wore the same uniform. They weren't walking – they were being run at the double.

I was taken to reception, all my valuables were taken off me and I was told to strip. There were two prison officers in the room and three detainees, and I felt very embarrassed; as I slowly undressed I was told to pull my finger out. Christian names were gone – I was Roberts. One of the officers called out my name, and even though I was naked I was searched from head to foot. I was given a pair of blue trousers that barely fitted and a blue-and-white striped shirt that hung on me like a sack. The uniform was finished off with a pair of huge black boots that were two sizes too big, but they were the smallest they had. When one of the boys that had my size left, I would be able to swop.

I then had to sign several forms; I wasn't allowed to read any of them, and I could have been signing my life away for all I knew. Next was a trip to the medic. The hospital area stank to high heaven of antiseptic. I saw an orderly who read out a never-ending list of diseases. As I had never had any of them, I was allowed to eat. Everyone in the dining-room wanted to know who I was, where I was from, and what I was in for. I met a few of the boys I had known at school. At least I wasn't the only one in Fleetwood that got into trouble.

After I had finished eating I was taken down a maze of corridors and put into a single cell. The windows were all barred and the door was made of two-inch steel. It was painted light blue. The officer who took me down was a right bastard. As we got into the cell he told me to stand in the far corner until he came back. I stood there for hours, not daring to move; I had heard many stories about detention centres, and I didn't want to upset anyone. A bell rang, and over the loudspeaker a voice commanded that everyone had to bed down because the night lights out would be in fifteen minutes. I started to make up the bed, and once finished I undressed, climbed in and lay waiting for the lights to go out.

I heard footsteps coming closer to the cell. The little spy-hole in the door swung to the side and an eye appeared. I heard a key in the hole and the bolt drawing back. In walked the officer that had brought me down to the cell earlier. He screamed at me to get out of bed. I dived out and stood there; he lashed out with his fist and sent me flying across the cell. I collapsed against the far wall. He told me to stand up. When I did, he asked if anyone had given me permission to get into bed. I started to explain that I had heard the loudspeaker giving out instructions, but before I could finish I received another swipe in the stomach. All the blows that followed were precisely aimed so as not to cause any bruising. I cried out in pain but still the brute carried on. I thought I was going to black out. As I lay in a heap on the floor, the officer pulled my bed to pieces and told me to remake it. I bent to pick up the bed-clothes and did as he said. The officer stood in the doorway, watching me and calling me names that I couldn't even start to repeat. The minute I had finished, he stripped it and told me to make it yet again. This happened several times. Then, after a while, he pushed me on to the bed. He grabbed me by the throat and pulled me towards him. He warned me that I would be under him all the time I was at Buckley Hall, so I would have to watch myself. I was gasping for breath. He threw me back on to the bed, went out and relocked the door. I didn't know what to do next. I lay on my bed, but all through the night, each time I heard footsteps approaching the cell, I got up and stood by the side of my bed. I dreaded the key going into the lock again. It was out of sheer exhaustion that I fell asleep.

Next morning a different officer unlocked my door and told me to make my bed and have a wash in the bathroom opposite. I did so and was then locked in my cell again. Breakfast was brought along by one of the other cons on a metal tray, with a real knife and fork, not like the plastic ones I had been using for the last couple of days. Later that morning I was collected by another officer and told that I would be having my medical.

I was taken back to reception again, and into a room where a formidable-looking man in a white coat sat at a large desk. He barked at me in a deep voice to strip off. I did so. He had a file with my name and number printed on the front, which he quickly looked through before asking me a few questions. He already had the answers in front of him, so it all seemed a waste of time. Then he asked me what I was in for. Stealing a woman's coat: was I bent, then? The answer took him aback a little. He stood up and towered over the desk. I felt an inch tall when he laughed and said, 'So you take it up the bum then, Roberts. God they get younger.'

As I was dressing he picked up the phone and asked to speak to the governor. 'Jim, we have a little poofter in our midst – yes, this new one, Roberts. Yes, I think it's advisable that we move him, before he corrupts any of our straight little boys.'

At those words I was taken back to my single cell, and within an hour I was back in my civilian clothing and in a minicab with two officers. I asked where I was being taken, and one of the officers told me that I was going to the place where they beat up poofs all the time. After the beating I had received the night before, I felt my stomach turn. I spent the rest of the journey in silence.

After a while we pulled into the imposing entrance of Walton prison in Liverpool. Within two minutes about six officers were standing all around the car, and I was taken down to the prison hospital with an escort of the size usually reserved for murderers.

I was taken through the hospital at quite a swift pace, stripped off and placed in a room that had no furniture or windows; the walls were padded. I was desperately confused. Why the hell was I put into a padded cell just for admitting that I was gay? I felt lost. I had been in there about three hours when the door opened and a guy in a white coat walked in. He asked me if I was O.K., and I told him I felt fine. He smiled and told me not to worry. It was the first time that anyone had showed me any form of courtesy. My clothes were passed into the cell and the guy stood there while I dressed. He then took me down to the orderly room and asked them to put me in a single cell.

I was taken to a cell on the ground floor that was quite comfortable. It even had a radio fixed to the wall and a shelf full of books; it was like a little bedsit, really. I had been in there about an hour when the door opened. I flew to my feet and stood by the side of my bed. The officer who entered told me not to be so jumpy. He laughed and said I was in prison now; they didn't treat you like they did in borstals and detention centres. I began to relax.

I learnt that I had been transferred to Walton to see a psychiatrist and would most probably be staying for a few weeks. After a while I was told to clean the cell up, and a pair of clean sheets was brought down by one of the prisoners who worked in the hospital. He was shocked when he saw me, and asked me how old I was. When I told him, he looked disgusted: 'Fancy sending a young kid to mix with this bloody lot.' He started to tell me about some of the other prisoners. There were about thirty men in the hospital – one or two of them were murderers, and there was the odd rapist.

Mick was a nice guy and he took me under his wing. He was coming to the end of a five-year sentence for armed robbery. He wasn't how I had imagined an armed robber would look like. Instead of a rough, scarred face he had a soft, gentle complexion, with deep brown eyes. No big muscular body, either; he was quite small – yet still tough. There was an aura around him that let you know you didn't mix with Mick Patterson unless Mick Patterson wanted to mix with you.

He glanced up at my card hung outside the door and raised his eyebrows. 'So you like men – hey, baby.'

I looked up at him and asked, 'How do you know?'

He said that it was on my card.

I went outside the cell to have a look. I expected to see 'THIS MAN IS A POOF' written all over it, but I couldn't see a thing – only a green star drawn in the left-hand corner. I was later to find out that different things in the left-hand corner had different meanings. It let the officers know just what they were handling – whether they were gay, suicidal or whatever.

Mick walked into the cell and told me to let him know if anyone threatened me or tried it on. With that he stuck a Mars bar in my hand and disappeared again. Later he put his head round the door and asked me to go down to the servery and give him a hand. I asked him about the officers, '"OFFICERS"! they're not "officers" – they're screws.' The one in charge of our wing was O.K., and told me it was all right to give Mick a hand. It was better than being shut up all day behind the door. I helped dish out the food to all the other prisoners; it was certainly a change from the beating I had taken the night before. I ached terribly, and several bruises had appeared on my side. I told Mick about the beating, and he told me that I should complain to one of the screws and they would have an enquiry. But I didn't want to bother, so I let it ride.

I settled down to read a book and listened on and off to music on the radio. At nine-thirty the lights went out and the night officer did his rounds. I was just drifting off to sleep when I heard something tapping at my window. I climbed up and had a look, attached to a piece of wool that had been unpicked from the edge of a prison blanket was a tobacco-tin. I pulled it in and opened it. Inside was a little note from Mick. He was in the cell above. Also in the tin were two roll-up cigarettes and a couple of matches. The note just said that he thanked me for the help he had had that day, and that he would try to get me out again to give him a hand the following day – but that it depended who was on duty. I didn't have a pencil so I couldn't reply to him; all I could do was shout, 'Thank you.' At least I had someone who was friendly. The sight of all the other guys had worried me a little – they all looked so rough.

The prison clothes were just the same as those at the detention centre, but at least this time I had a better fit. I snuggled down into the bedclothes and soon drifted off to sleep. I don't remember the radio going off, but the sound of it blaring out at seven in the morning certainly woke me up. I dressed and made my bed, then got stuck into Agatha Christie. At seven-thirty all the cells were unlocked and everyone had to slop out. I hadn't used my bucket but judging by the smell that wafted down the corridor, everyone else had. It was terrible, and most men considered the chore the most degrading part of their sentences.

I gave a hand in serving the breakfast. Once that was done Mick dished up our breakfasts, which we had to take back to our cells. We had nearly double what everyone else had. It was one of the advantages of working while in prison.

I wasn't allowed out after breakfast, because I was to have my first meeting with the psychiatrist at ten o'clock. I tidied myself up to create a good impression, but I hadn't asked to see a shrink and I had no intention at all of co-operating.

When the time came I was taken into a private office at the far end of the hospital. The doctor introduced himself and asked me all kinds of questions – some very personal. I refused to answer many of them. Our session went on for nearly an hour; we talked mostly about my family and family life. The conclusion was that I had had a hell of a time and had a head on my shoulders that should have been on the body of a much older man. I wasn't really complaining; there was only night in my life that I really wanted to forget. Even to that day I couldn't bear to see my father again.

My interviews with the doctor were every other day. We seemed to talk about the same thing all the time. At about the sixth interview, his whole approach changed and he caught me off guard. That was many years ago, but there was one question and answer that, in a way, sorted out all my problems then and there. He asked me, if he could grant me one wish, what it would be.

My answer was, 'To have been born a girl.'

Once I had said that, I sat and thought about it and couldn't understand just why I had done so. I thought it over for many hours that day, and then it just disappeared to the back of my mind. But it was to recur in a similar interview later in my life.

I had been in Walton prison nearly three weeks, and I had only another five weeks to do before my discharge. I was beginning to think what a cushy life I had. I was very rarely banged up behind my door, and I spent a lot of time with Mick. He used to be really kind to me. I found in him something that I had never found before: he was straight and a friend. He did not want me for my body – he wanted to know me just because I was me. For someone who had been used and abused by so many people it was a really nice feeling. We used to write each other letters, and when Mick sent me one down at night in the now familiar tobacco-tin. I would have my reply all ready to go. When I think of all my silly poems, and the things I used to say to him in those letters, it seems hard to believe that he was straight. He always called me 'lover-boy' and I called him 'marvellous Micky with the twelve-inch dickie'. It was a standing joke for he was a very big boy; I knew that because we often shared a shower together. We had become very close. We had exchanged contact addresses and swore to keep in touch with each other – so, one morning, when they told me that I would be leaving the next day, I was very upset and decided to take drastic action.

That evening I barricaded myself in my cell and refused to leave the following day. As soon as the night officer had done his rounds, I jammed my bed and bedside cabinet against the door so that it was impossible for anyone to get in. It wasn't until I sent my nightly note up to Mick that I realised he had done what I had done. About midnight my barricade was discovered and about six officers tried to get into the cell. They were worried in case I tried to top myself. The duty governor also came down. I was threatened and coaxed for hours, but I just would not give in.

Once they realised that, they tried an attack from the outside. First of all a water-cannon was put through the window and I was soaked, along with everything else in the cell. The cannon was aimed at me while an officer tried to hook the bed and pull it free, but he found it impossible because I had used the books from the shelf to jam it tight. I heard a lot of activity outside the cell door. They intended to jack the door off its hinges, and I knew that it would soon be all over and they would get me out. Outside, all the other prisoners were shouting abuse at the officers and telling me not to give in. I just sat in the corner, watching the door pushing against the bed.

When it eventually gave, there was a mad scramble for me as the bed was pulled out of the way. They took me down to the padded cell for about ten minutes until the doctor arrived. I was given an injection, and I don't remember much more about that evening. I woke the following morning feeling terrible, still in the padded cell. I thought my action of the previous evening would stop me being moved that day, but it didn't. I was terrified in case they took me back to Buckley Hall. However, they told me I was going to Strangeways prison, in Manchester. I managed to say goodbye to Mick, and gave him a quick kiss the first and the last. He is still in prison, serving another life sentence for the murder in 1987 of a guy who had made sexual advances towards him. The judge recommended that 'life' should mean just that.

When I arrived at Strangeways I again went through the all-too-familiar routine of signing forms and receiving new uniforms. Again I was taken to the hospital, but this time I was put on a ward. There were other boys of my age who were in for operations. There were also about twenty adults on the ward. Life was a bit more promiscuous in Strangeways, and I could get away with far more. I had to play it cool, though, as there was always an officer around and most of them had read my file. I was a screaming queen. I knew it, they knew it, the prisoners knew it – yet no one gave a damn.

I spent the next five weeks at Strangeways, and they were most enjoyable. In there it wasn't hard or tough. The only thing I resented was having to go to bed at nine p.m. – but then again, sometimes it wasn't too bad if I had company. There's something adventurous about having sex with a guy in the middle of a ward with prisoners all around, some pretending to be asleep, and the night officer sitting at the far end of the room reading his books.

Unhappily those days came to an end. Roberts G31246 was discharged on a Tuesday morning with a six-pound discharge grant and a travel warrant back to Folkestone, the area where I had been arrested. I didn't know whether my job was waiting for me, but I was soon to find out.

Chapter 9
Fairies in Folkestone

I arrived in Folkestone at about two-thirty on the day of my discharge. My first job was to report to my probation officer. She had been in touch with the hotel and they had refused to take me back. Luckily her brother worked at a four-star hotel and she knew that they were desperately short of waiters. She had already spoken to the manager, who was willing to see me and would be able to offer me a living-in post.

I went for the interview. I was quite truthful about my past and because I had been so honest he took me on and I moved in. But it sickened me that everyone knew I had been in prison. Rumours were rife, because no one except the manager really knew what I had been inside for. In the first day or two it became obvious that people were talking behind my back. It depressed me to think that even though I had done wrong these people saw fit to persecute me just that little bit more. Working at the hotel turned out to be worse than serving my sentence.

When I had finished work I didn't hang around like everyone else. I tried to keep myself to myself. I needed to cut my way out of the atmosphere that was built up every day – and the only escape I knew was into the gay scene. Gay people can be bitchy, but at least they stand by their own kind. I knew that there had to be a gay scene somewhere, I just had to find it. They only place to turn was back to the toilets to see if the writing on the walls gave any clues. It did not take too long to find out which public toilets were in constant use by gays.

Once I had found a good toilet, I frequented it most evenings after work and occasionally in the afternoon if I had the chance. One night after finishing work quite late I decided to take a walk down to the park toilet. It was below ground, and as I descended the steps I had a feeling that something was wrong.

At the bottom of the stairs I found a young man of about twenty-four lying on the floor. He was bleeding quite badly from a cut on his hand and a gash above the eye. He was crying and defenceless, just like a little baby. I knelt beside him and tried to find out what had happened. It turned out that he had been beaten up by four queer-bashers. I said that I would get the police, but he grabbed hold of my leg and begged me not to. I told him he must go to the police, because next time it happened the guy might not be so lucky. He explained to me that he couldn't; his parents would find out that he was gay, and he just could not let that happen in case it hurt them.

I helped the young man to his feet and cleaned up his face and hand as best I could. His hand had stopped the knife from going into his guts. I decided to walk him part of the way home, as he was terrified in case he was attacked again. The men who had attacked him had stolen about two pounds.

I ended up walking John to his front door. On the way I learned quite a lot about him. He had been gay since he was fifteen. He had never been to London. He had a regular boyfriend, who was away on holiday, and he had only popped into the toilet to use the urinal. But he told me that there was a small club in this backwater. It wasn't completely gay, and it was not even legal. It was in the basement of a little bed-and-breakfast hotel not far from where I was working. It was supposed to be for the use of residents, but if you were introduced to the owner you would always be welcome.

We arranged to meet the following weekend in one of the local pubs, and that night we ended up in the club. I was introduced to the owner, a seventeen-stone mass of blubber and laughter. I remember thinking, Yeah, I bet you laugh all the way to the bank, the prices you're charging. I was given a Yale pass key that would let me into the side door of the club if the front door was ever closed. There must have been about sixty people there on my first visit. Only about twenty-five per cent of them were gay – the rest were all straight; but one large crowd of women that were sitting in a far corner by the piano interested me. There was something not quite right about that gang of ladies. I was to find out later that evening that they were transvestites. I should explain that a transvestite is a person who adopts the clothes, appearance and to some extent, the stereotypical behaviour normally associated with the opposite sex. Only a small percentage of transvestites dress for sexual pleasure and neither is it common for a transvestite to be homosexual or even bisexual. A transexual, however, is someone like myself, who believes he or she has been born in the wrong sex, and should really be of the opposite sex. They suffer from a profound form of gender dysphoria.

Although I was always uptight at work, I could relax in the friendly atmosphere of the club. No one knew of my past – I was just another gay guy who visited for a drink. But one evening I actually got up the nerve to speak to one of the transvestites when he was at the bar, ordering several pints of bitter and a Babycham. I was by myself and there wasn't anyone of interest in, so when he invited me over to join the crowd I accepted. It surprised me to find that two of the group were women. Tom, who had been at the bar, introduced me around the table; the names varied from Anastasia to Petal. Pam, one of the girls, was Tom's wife. I could hardly believe it. She turned out to be the life and soul of the party. As the evening drew to a close she invited me back to their house for a drink. The babysitter left as soon as we arrived – she seemed oblivious of the fact that Tom was dressed as a woman. The kids were all sound asleep, so Pam went off to make a few sandwiches.

Tom asked me if I had ever cross-dressed. I said that I had occasionally worn make-up, along with camp clothes, but had never tried to impersonate a woman completely. He told me I should try it. I agreed that one day I would. Tom was about thirty, quite well-built, with a ragged-looking face; the little make-up he had on somehow suited it. The blonde wig hid his own hair, but it was immaculately groomed. The only flaw was the very old-fashioned black blouse and skirt he wore. He did not look too bad, though; there had been others around the table in the club that had looked better, but others had looked far worse. None of them seemed to give a damn, anyway. They were all happy enough.

The drink flowed and the sandwiches filled an ache in my stomach. Suddenly Tom stood up and asked me if I would like to dress up. I looked over to Pam for some kind of support; she just nodded and said I could if I wanted to. I was pissed and didn't really care. Pam took me upstairs. We were both giggling like a couple of schoolgirls. She sorted through the wardrobe and pulled out a short blue dress. I took off my jumper and trousers and tried it on. It was quite tight: the top fitted so tightly that there was no room for any titties. I lay on the bed while Pam did my make-up. When she had finished my eyes I looked in the mirror – it looked great. My hair was long, so Pam quickly back-combed it, sprayed on plenty of lacquer and lifted it as high as it would go. A pair of tights soon disguised my hairy legs.

When I walked into the living room behind Pam, Tom's mouth just dropped open. He told me that he had met hundreds of transvestites, but I was the nicest he had seen. He turned to Pam and said that I should have been born a woman – I suited the role. I laughed, not realising just how right his words were.

We sat and talked for what seemed hours. I was very puzzled about the situation between Pam and Tom. They were happily married, yet Tom always dressed as a woman at night. Was he bisexual? I could have understood him dragging up if he was gay. But he explained that he was a ladies' man. Other men did not excite him at all – he screwed only women.

His answers only puzzled me more. I put the same questions to

Pam. How did she cope with her husband wearing women's clothes? Pam just laughed and said that she encouraged him to do it. She enjoyed his making love to her when he was dressed as a woman. This was beyond me, and I couldn't cope. It was late, so I made my excuses and slipped upstairs to change back to my 'masculine self'.

As I climbed up the stairs I felt really good inside, and confident. I stood in the bathroom and looked at myself in the full-length mirror. I looked like a woman; I felt like a woman, too, and that's harder to explain. I felt different from any way I had ever felt before. I was relaxed; the struggles in my life had buried themselves. I was shocked to find that I was turned on by my own reflection. I had an erection. I pulled my dress up and looked at my reflection again. I stood boldly erect behind my tights – not very feminine. I touched my legs, and the feel of the nylon made things even worse. I relieved myself standing in front of the mirror watching myself, and I was still shaking as I entered the bedroom. I took off my make-up and dressed in my male clothing. I went back downstairs, said goodnight to Tom and Pam left promising to see them the following evening. Later, as I lay in bed, my mind churned over the events of the past few hours. The rest of the night was spent tossing and turning. I had looked good as a woman. I knew that I would have to try it again.

The following morning I went down to work as usual, but my mind was still on the events of the previous evening. I decided to spend the afternoon shopping for some new clothes and make-up. I didn't even stop for lunch. I walked up and down the high street, trying to pluck up enough courage to go in and buy a dress. I was terrified in case anyone should guess that I was buying it for myself. In one of the large stores I saw exactly the same dress that I had worn the previous evening. I went into the shop and up to the ladies' department. An assistant came over and asked me if she could help. I explained the design of the dress and she took me to the appropriate rack. I had thought up a story, so I babbled on to the assistant about how I was buying my sister a present. She just smiled and gave me a knowing look. I felt very uncomfortable. She asked me what size my sister was. I wasn't quite ready for that one. I just said, 'Oh, she's about my size.' The assistant's eyebrows arched. About a size sixteen. The dress was wrapped and I paid the bill. I felt terribly embarrassed, and the assistant was to have the last dig. 'I do hope it fits your sister, sir.'

My next stop was Boots. I explained to the assistant that I wanted some make-up to give to my sister for her birthday. The assistant was very helpful, and I tried to describe exactly the colours

I had been wearing the previous evening. The next stop was the shoe shop; I tried several before I found one that stocked size eights. I had quite a choice, and I picked a pretty white pair; they had very high heels, but I was sure that they would be all right. A couple of pairs of tights from Woolworths finished off my little expedition.

It was nearly four o'clock when I got back to the hotel, and I was not on duty until seven-thirty. I locked my door and laid out my new clothes on the bed. I tried to put on my makeup as I had worn it the night before, but I made quite a mess the first time round, and the second and third attempts were not all that much better. I still wasn't discouraged. After several more attempts it was looking slightly better. It took over two hours to get it perfect and I had used most of my make-up just practising.

When I was eventually satisfied with the make-up, I slipped on my new tights and dress and returned to the mirror. This time the dress had room for boobs, so I stuck a pair of rolled-up socks in the appropriate places. The shoes were all that was needed to finish the picture. I slipped them on and half-hobbled, half-stumbled back to the mirror. I felt so tall that I was terrified in case I should fall off and break my neck. It didn't take long to learn to walk in them, though, and they added that little extra to my legs.

I lifted the dress up and my legs looked a treat. I stood there for ages admiring myself, I was so vain. I felt different, but the fact that I was cross-dressing didn't worry me even though my homosexuality did. If anything, I was only worried about what other people would say. It's easy enough to explain to a friend that you're gay but a lot harder to explain why you're wearing dresses when society says you should be wearing trousers. I dreaded to think what the consequences would be if anyone in the hotel found out what I was doing.

I felt so happy. I was only wearing women's clothes, yet it made all the difference. I dressed as a woman every available moment. When I had been doing it for three weeks, I felt confident enough to go out on the street. I was a new person. I had brought several dresses, but I always had to sneak out of the hotel very carefully.

I felt a little apprehensive as I approached the club as a woman, but I walked into the place as though I owned it. The owner looked at me, puzzled. He had not recognised me, so he was probably wondering how the hell I got in. He made a move towards me, but, before he got any further, Pam shouted from across the club, 'Georgie, darling, you look divine.' The owner's mouth nearly hit the floor. He said he didn't believe it – it couldn't be true, it wasn't possible. I winked at him and said, 'All right, mate?' He was really taken aback. Pam threw her arms around me. She and Tom were sitting with the usual old crowd. I was taken over and introduced as Sandy. Over a period of three weeks I had been lightening my hair; it was now a nice sandy colour, hence the name. Most of the guys did not believe that I had got myself ready. I just laughed and said I had been practising a lot and had a good teacher in Pam. Tom and Pam both laughed and explained about my first night at their place. It did not embarrass me at all. I felt good.

What did embarrass me was that some of the men did look like men with dresses on. I was in a class of my own and I knew it. I would be able to get away with a lot more than any of them. Tom asked me how I had travelled from the hotel. I said, 'On the bus.' Everyone gasped: on the bus! They all arrived concealed in their cars. They had neither the looks nor the guts. I broke away from the group as the evening wore on and became bored. I drifted around the club, talking to many of the new friends I had made. Most of them were very surprised, but just accepted it. My ego was boosted several times and by the end of the evening I never wanted to be a man again. I preferred dancing with a man when I had women's clothes on and I was later to find out that sex with a man while wearing women's clothes was a big turn-on.

One or two people asked me why I was in drag. I couldn't explain to them, and I didn't even want to. I told them I was doing it for a laugh. So I thought; but deep down inside me I could not explain the change either. I should have been worried about my situation. It was abnormal. Why did I enjoy being abnormal? If I could only have lived as a woman all the time my life would have been a lot easier.

I visited the club most evenings after work, and managed to cut my preparation time down to about twenty minutes. I very rarely went out as a man now, and I always had the same problem of leaving the hotel. God knows what any of the neighbours thought if they saw a blond running out of the doorway and flying up the road at fifty miles an hour. My secret life was kept in a suitcase. Chambermaids used to clean our rooms twice a week and they were all nosey bitches. I wasn't prepared to let anyone at the hotel know. It was easier to just let them think I was a bore and a pain in the arse. I used to double-check my room all the time; the slightest hint of anything feminine might have given me away. It became a constant worry.

One evening when I arrived at the club Tom was more excited than I had ever seen him before. He had seen his doctor and had asked him if it was possible to change his sex. Pam didn't mind and was encouraging him. It shocked me because I had thought Tom really was a ladies' man. I asked how it was possible for someone to change sex. What happened? Did they cut it off? No one at the table seemed to know, but Tom would have all the answers next week, as he was travelling to London to see a specialist.

The next time I met Tom he was even more elated. He told me that he was taking hormone tablets that would help him grow a bust. Pam shouted over that she was going to borrow them, as her tits were small. We all fell about laughing. The more I thought about Tom's situation the more jealous I became. I wished I were a woman, but I was terrified of needles and dentists, and I wasn't prepared to have an operation to change my body.

One evening while I was standing at the bar in the club I nearly had heart failure – the door opened and in walked one of the lads from work. He came over and stood about a yard away from me, and just smiled as I moved away and sat at a table. Bob just stood at the bar watching me. I felt very uncomfortable; I was sure that he had recognised me. I would not meet his stare, but every time I did look up and catch his eye, he smiled. After about an hour of playing cat and mouse, I smiled back. He left the bar and started to walk towards my table. My heart shot up into my mouth.

He sat down, introduced himself and asked me my name. He hadn't recognised me. I relaxed a little, but raised the pitch of my voice slightly. I told him that I was Sandy. 'Oh, you don't look like a Sandy,' he replied, 'Anyway, aren't all Sandys randy?' I felt myself going red, but I sat and listened to him. He told me that he was one of the managers at the hotel and an eligible bachelor. The lying sod was a porter and he had a wife and two kids with another one due in about a month's time. The lies went on and on, and after a while it all became very boring. I excused myself and went to the ladies toilet. As I passed him he tweaked my bum. While in the toilet I thought it would be better to leave the club quietly.

Before I reached the entrance Bob caught me and asked me why I was leaving. I told him who I was, and he froze. I turned to go and he grabbed me by the arm. I swung round, ready to hit him, but he just pulled me towards him and said that I looked great. Such was the ambiguity of this married man. He wasn't getting his nooky at home, and he was determined to get it elsewhere – at whatever cost.

That evening Bob returned to the hotel with me and my first sexual experience as a transvestite took place. I had to leave my pants and bra on as it was a sexual turn-on for him. Apart from anal intercourse, all things we did are usually relished by heterosexuals. Bob became a regular visitor to my room. If he caught me dressed as a woman he would stay. If I hadn't changed, he always cut his visit short. Our little affair lasted until his wife had given birth to the baby; then he drifted back to her.

One other guy that I met at the club knew from the start that I was a man. He owned his own building business, just outside town. He had about a hundred men working for him. He was young and single and all the gay guys who used the club always tried to get off with him. I didn't even have to try. Every time I went in the club, there was a drink waiting for me from him and we used to go and sit in a little corner and talk and giggle the nights away. One evening he asked me to go home with him. It was impossible, as I would have had problems getting back home later and I needed my other clothes. Alan was very disappointed, so I invited him back to the hotel. He accepted and wanted to leave straight away. We crept back. Once we were in my room, he told me that he had never been to bed with a man – or a woman, come to that. I giggled. I would tell him what to do. What I didn't know wasn't worth knowing.

We had a lovely little relationship, neither of us asking too much of each other. It was obvious from the off that it was a hit-and-run affair. Alan was meeting a girl about once a week. They were engaged to be married, but she lived a long way away. As Christmas approached, Alan invited me along to his staff Christmas party. I was to go as a woman, and I would be the only one there.

The party was in a restaurant. The meal was eaten upstairs, then everyone went down into the cellar for the fun and games. Blue films and strippers were continually on the stage, and the booze flowed freely. All the guys knew that I was in drag and they were all supposed to be straight. Well, they say that one in four is bisexual, and once I was drunk I set out to prove it. I remember having about five guys in the loo while they were waiting to use the toilet. Then, as I came out, a guy grabbed me and dragged me into a corner with a mate of his; they wanted me to have them both at the same time. I told them where I lived and that they could pop round later, never thinking that they would show up. I also gave a couple of other guys my address, I was so drunk.

Alan was pretty sober and could see that I was the worse for wear. He grabbed my arm, dragged me out of the party, threw me in his car and took me back to the hotel. We were in bed within minutes of arriving back. We had been there about ten minutes when there was a knock at the door. I swaggered over and pulled open the door. One of the guys from the party had turned up.

I went rigid. What the hell was I going to do? I had his boss in my bed already. Alan would be furious if he found out. I ushered the guy over to the bathroom and told him to wait for me. I had sobered up no end. I knew that I wouldn't see much more of Alan, as he was getting married in a few months' time; but I didn't want to upset him just yet. I climbed back into bed and prayed that the other guy would get bored and go away. I fell asleep cuddled up to Alan and was only awakened by a loud knocking on the door. I called out to see who it was. The call came back, 'The police'.

We both shot out of bed. Alan climbed into the wardrobe with all his clothes – he was shaking like a leaf. I glanced in the mirror and noticed that I still had make-up on, and it wasn't a pretty sight. I tried to rub as much as I could off with a towel, but the knocking on the door was becoming more impatient.

The policeman was standing with the two guys from the party who had wanted the threesome. He asked me if I knew them, and I told him that I had met them at a party earlier that evening. They had been spotted hanging around outside the hotel and the night porter had called the police. A very embarrassing ten minutes followed. As we were talking another policeman and the night porter turned up. They had just reached my room when the bathroom door opened and the guy I had put in there earlier came out to see what all the commotion was. I had just got over the shock of that when someone opened the top door and came walking down the stairs. A hush descended over the passage as yet another guy from the party appeared at the foot of the stairs. One of the cops stepped past me and went into my room. I prayed that I would wake up. Surely this couldn't be happening?

The policeman came out of the room and just winked at me, then went to speak to his mate. He walked back and addressed the assembled party. 'I think you crowd of perverts and sex-maniacs should get back home to your wives before I run you all in.' He turned to me and asked me what I was up to. I just shrugged my shoulders. He asked me if I was trying to have enough cock to make a hand-rail for the M1, because the way I was going about it I was halfway there. I wanted to crawl under a stone. They must have thought I was a real whore.

The guys all disappeared and left the night porter standing at the bottom of the stairs. It had all been too much for him. When Alan came walking out of my room I thought the porter was going to have a heart attack. The coppers disappeared back into my room with Alan, and I had to think quickly. I grabbed my bag, stuck ten pounds in the porter's hand and told him to forget it. He just shrugged his shoulders and walked away.

The policemen were leaving my room as I got back. Alan shut the door and said that it had been close. I could just imagine the damage the scandal would have caused the company. Then he made his excuses and left; after all, it was nearly four a.m. We said goodnight, and before he left the room I knew that I had ruined a good relationship. I felt sick; but Alan felt even sicker, for it had cost him a fortune to buy off the cops.

After that little episode I didn't go out so often. Every time I bumped into the night porter he just used to raise his eyebrows, which brought an instant giggle as I pictured the scene in the corridor that lustful night.

Tom's bust was growing ever so fast now with the tablets, and Pam tried to convince me that I needed treatment more than Tom. I knew she was right, but I was terrified of doctors. After much persuasion from Tom and Pam I wrote to the Gender Identification Unit at Charing Cross Hospital. I received a letter from a senior consultant's secretary telling me to go and get a letter of recommendation from my GP. I felt very small as I tried to explain the situation to my GP, but the letter seemed to do it, and an appointment was arranged for the following month.

It was only a few days before my appointment that I realised I would be going on to the street as a woman for the first time in daylight. I was also going to be travelling quite a long way. It was easy getting out of the hotel staff quarters at night, but during the day there were a lot of people about. I decided that I would have to leave early, as a man, and change on the way down to the hospital.

I left Folkestone by train with the aim of changing before I got to London. Once the train pulled out of the station I went to the toilet and started to put on my make-up. It took ages to get it right, with the train jogging all over the place. I left the important parts until we stopped at stations. I was terrified in case I stuck the mascara brush in my eye and the tears caused all my make-up to run. Then I slowly got dressed, replacing my male clothing neatly in the bag. I would need it to get back home.

My confidence had completely disappeared by the time we pulled into London. I felt as if everyone was watching me and pointing fingers. I desperately wanted to go to the toilet. I hung about outside the ladies for ages, and when I felt as though I was going to burst I shot in. I felt as if my knees were going to buckle under me before I got into the cubicle. I sat down, and relief flowed through me as I passed water. When I stopped for a moment I was very conscious that a woman in a cubicle made a very different sound, so instead of aiming directly at the water I aimed at the side of the pan.

I checked the time. My appointment was closing in fast. I was shaking uncontrollably – my nerves were all on edge. I knew I had to go, so I opened the cubicle and fled. A woman at the basin gave me a funny look as I rushed past her. At the hospital I had to push myself to go through the door and up to reception. I was about five minutes late. Damn my nerves. I felt as though my teeth were going to shake themselves out of my head.

The receptionist looked up and said in quite a loud voice, 'You're late, Mr Roberts. Take a seat over there.' It was obvious that people had heard her. Some of the looks I got were of pity – others were of disgust. In the crowd I could see one other guy who was in drag, although everyone else seemed oblivious of the fact. He ignored me completely, and I later found out that all transexuals like to be anonymous.

I waited nearly two hours before my name came over the loud speaker and I was called to the reception desk again. As I rose I could feel everyone turn to follow me, and as I approached the desk I heard one woman say, 'Oh, poor thing, look at him.'

I just turned and glared at her. I was given my directions, and as I passed the old girl again I said, 'Don't worry about me, girl. You're nearly dead – I'm just starting to live.' It was a cruel thing to say, but I did not want people to feel sorry for me. I was happy.

When I entered the doctor's outer office his secretary was very kind to me. She gave me a cup of tea and told me that she had some bad news. She asked me why I had been late. I told her that I had been very nervous; staying in the toilet too long had not helped, either. She replied that because I was late the doctor would not see me anyway.

'But it was only five minutes!'

'The doctor likes people to be on time.'

I felt like crying. She came over and patted me on the shoulder and told me the interview wouldn't have done me any good anyway. I was far too young for the doctor to help.

I asked why, but she only said, 'The best thing you can do is go away and come back in a year or two's time.'

My heart sank. No one was willing to help me – and I did need help, if only to sort my own mind out. Everyone had made fun of my situation; the only people who took me seriously were Tom and Pam. I left the doctor's secretary's office feeling very dejected. I wandered down into Trafalgar Square and sat there for ages. Occasionally men would come over to me and chat me up, but when that happened I just moved away.

Gradually my depression turned into anger. No one was going to hold me down or tell me what to do! I wanted to live as a woman, and I was going to. I returned to Folkestone in a vicious mood. I had to change my clothes again, but I couldn't bear to take my make-up off. Sod everyone at the hotel; if they didn't like it – tough. I was in such a state that when I got back into my room I just went berserk. I banged my way around, smashing anything that would smash. Even my new stereo unit went in the holocaust. I threw myself on the bed and tried to cry it all out of me; but it did no good whatsoever.

I spotted my evening suit hanging on the back of the door, and I flew at it and started to rip it to pieces. I was going wild. By the time I came to my senses it was too late. Every article of male clothing was ripped to shreds.

I felt slightly better as I collapsed on to my bed and fell asleep amidst the flow of tears. George Roberts was dead, and I never wanted him to exist again – ever.

Chapter 10
Becoming a Chambermaid

When I awoke the following morning I lay on my bed trying to re-arrange my life.

I had convinced myself that I was a woman trapped in a man's body. No one, at that time at least, could have persuaded me differently. I looked around the room at all the ripped clothes that had belonged to George. I jumped out of bed and viciously ripped up a shirt that still bore some resemblance to its original form. The hatred that was welling up in my heart frightened me. I had never really been vindictive or vicious, so I could not understand why I rebelled against my masculinity so much.

I should have been at work hours before, but I was not unduly worried. I intended to leave; I was going to go to London. I was going to live in my true form, that of a woman. I telephoned the hotel manager and told him of my decision. He tried to remonstrate, but I wasn't in any mood to listen. I cut him short and told him that I would collect my money at three p.m., then slammed down the phone. I was not normally so rude, and I could not really understand my own aggressive attitude.

I quickly dressed as a woman and went into town. Gone was the obsession about creeping about without anyone seeing me. If they did, it was just too bad. It wasn't until I entered my bank that I realised I would have a lot of explaining to do. It cannot be very often that a woman walks into a bank and tries to withdraw money from a man's account.

I walked over to the enquiry desk and rang the bell. A teller appeared and greeted me with the usual 'Good morning, madam, how can I help you?' I retorted that I was not a female but would be soon. The poor girl looked as though she was going to pass out. I gave her my pass-book and told her that I wanted the account clearing. She carried the book away at arm's length as though she might catch some terrible infection from it. I watched her talk to several tellers, who tried to look at me without being too obvious. She then disappeared into the manager's office. She reappeared two minutes later with a formidable-looking gentleman in his early forties, who joined her at the window. His attitude was rather flippant, and he started to ask me questions that were not relevant.

I shouted out that I had fuck-all to explain to him and I wanted my money. Suddenly the bank door flew open and four policemen came rushing up to me. I was thrown against a wall and a policeman gave me a complete body search. If it had not been in front of so many people I might have enjoyed it. I was dragged into the manager's office. It took me about twenty minutes to get the police to understand me, and it was only after they had rung Tom and Pam that they believed my story. Then one of the policemen took me back to the counter to draw my cash. The manager was still grumbling under his breath that it was most irregular.

I composed myself again as I entered the high street. I had some shopping to do and time was getting on. I entered several stores and bought all the garments I needed to complete my wardrobe. My ego was boosted beyond all belief. I hadn't been stared at or looked upon with curiosity since leaving the bank. When I returned to the staff accommodation, I bumped into one of the porters. He stared at me blankly at first; then a quizzical look spread across his face. When I was sure that he still had not recognised me, I asked him what he thought he was looking at. The shock of hearing my voice sent him reeling back in disbelief. Then he followed me down the passage to my room and asked me what I was doing. I told him that it was none of his business really, but, if he must know, I was going to London to have a sex change. He said that he did not believe me, but once he had all the facts he was off. No doubt everyone in the hotel would know before lunchtime.

I quickly packed my cases with all my feminine clothes, and cleaned up the room. At three on the dot I walked over to collect my money. As I neared the hotel entrance I could see several of the staff looking from different windows. As I climbed the hotel steps it felt as if hundreds of pairs of eyes were watching me. I just held my head high and walked over to the reception area.

It seemed as though they were, expecting me. The head receptionist asked me to sit and wait. During the five minutes that followed, nearly every member of the hotel staff found some excuse to pass me in reception. Their attitude annoyed me. I could hear snatches of conversation as they drifted away. One old chambermaid told her companion that she had always thought there was something rather strange about me. But the general attitude though was one of amazement. I had been such a nice boy.

The head receptionist called me over and asked me to go into the general manager's office. When I entered, his expression did not change. He, too, must have been warned. His first words were, 'Well, I can't call you "George" any more.' After he had handed me my wage-packet, I stood up to leave, but was cut short when he asked me to be reseated. I had always found him a hard man, but as I looked at him his face was full of compassion. He told me that he had heard rumours that I was going to have a sex-change and I admitted that it was true. He said that he wished he had known of my problem. I told him that it wasn't a problem and that I was now far happier. He then told me that I looked much better as a woman and he only hoped that I was doing the right thing. After wishing me luck he escorted me to the hotel entrance and shook my hand. The head porter's face was a picture. I smiled and thanked the manager for his concern. In those last few moments I had changed my opinion of him.

Just then I had more money on me than I had ever had before, plus a new identity. George had been corrupt, but I was determined to lead an honest and decent life. I picked up my cases and made my way to the railway station. The sooner I got away from Folkestone the better – away from all the people who knew of my former identity, the identity I wanted to forget about for ever. London was a big place, big enough for me to hide. As I bought my ticket I began to work out a history for Sandy.

I was Sandy St Claire: the name had a nice ring to it. I was a bubbly little blonde number, slightly overweight but with personality and a charming face. My mother and father were both dead and I had been an only child. I did not even have any relatives alive; I was alone in the world. George had been sixteen. Sandy was twenty-one years old and looked it. The easiest job for me to find would be that of a chambermaid. After all, it was only making beds and hoovering – anyone could do that. I should be able to pull it off without attracting any undue attention.

The train journey was soon over, and when I arrived in London I asked a cabbie to take me to a bed-and-breakfast hotel in Earls Court. He dropped me at the first hotel on the Cromwell Road that had a 'Vacancies' sign. The old woman who shuffled up to me in the hallway took my money and booked me for three days into the only room available.

The following morning I awoke with sunlight streaming in through the window. I looked like Dracula's daughter, so I washed my hair and repaired my make-up. It was only nine a.m. when I was ready for off.

As I entered the Frith Street branch of the Alfred Marks Agency I was amazed at the amount of people waiting and at how fast they were being dealt with. I was given a form to fill in before I got to the interviewer, so I was able to set out all the lies about my new identity without too many problems. Once I reached the desk the task became even easier. I never once spoke a word, and nodded my head only twice. Within five minutes three interviews had been arranged for me.

The first interview was at midday. I had nearly an hour to kill, so I travelled down by tube to my destination in Kensington and viewed the area. The hotel was very impressive and was handy for the gay scene in Earls Court. My interview with the head house-keeper was short and sweet. She was a frumpy old Spanish woman dressed in black from head to foot. She told me that she needed staff desperately, and as long as I could make a bed I could start straight away. I was on a months' trial – if I kept my area clean then there would be no problems. If I didn't, I would get my arse kicked out of the door. Again I had hardly spoken a word. She escorted me round the hotel at breakneck speed. I was to be responsible for the eighteen rooms on the fourth floor. Four of them had bathrooms, and there were four public bathrooms.

Suddenly she stopped in her tracks and looked me up and down. Surely she had not seen through my act? She shook her hair out of her eyes and said that English girls were usually very lazy, but as I looked like a strong girl the job was mine. With that she slapped me on the back, and I agreed to start the following morning at seven. The job was living-in, and the room was ready to move into straight way. When I returned to the guest-house to collect my suitcases, the old girl was adamant that I could not have a refund. So while packing my belongings I slipped in four towels from the bathroom and two china ornaments off a table in the hall.

Back at the hotel, I decided I would have to get rid of all the bad habits that George had had. He had basically been an untidy person and most undesirable character; thank God he had gone. I had to start as I meant to go on if I was going to pull my new life-style off. I unpacked my clothes slowly, taking great care to ensure that they were hung and folded properly. Then I started to prepare myself for the following day.

My hair was long, so I washed it and started to put it into curlers. It was nearly dry by the time I got the last roller fixed. I removed the final traces of make-up that hadn't been obliterated when I washed my hair. Then I mixed up a face pack and spread it all over my face and neck. I looked a right sight in the full-length mirror. There I was, stark naked, my three-piece suite all on show, with rollers in and a pure white face. I stopped and looked again. For some reason the fact that I could see my testicles bothered me. I slipped on a pair of pants and never allowed myself to view those monstrosities again. After washing the cement-like face pack away, I looked in the mirror. I hadn't changed a little bit. I had expected the treatment to make me look beautiful; it had said that it would on the packet. Feeling less glamorous than I had expected, and slightly disappointed, I decided to retreat to my bed. It was gone ten p.m. and I would have to be up by six.

I put on the nightie I had bought the previous day. I had always slept in the nude before, but now I wanted to complete the feminine effect. I jumped into bed feeling quite relaxed, but sleep was not going to come that easily. The rollers were digging into my head. But I knew I would have to get used to them, so I persevered, thinking that all women must be masochists to want to endure this discomfort every night. I tossed and turned for what seemed like hours.

I woke up shortly after three with the sensation that someone had his hands around my throat and was trying to squeeze the last breath out of my body. I tensed up and opened my eyes, but I couldn't see much in the dark. I slowly raised my hand to my throat, only to find that my nightie had worked its way up and twisted around my neck. I did the most unladylike thing – I jumped out of bed and ripped it off in disgust. It wasn't until I had stood up that I realised just how badly my head was throbbing where the rollers had embedded themselves. I pulled them out as fast as I could and threw them into the washbasin. Jesus, it was going to take me ages to get properly used to living as a woman. Surely all women didn't suffer in the name of beauty as I suffered that night.

I was awake at five-thirty. I knew that I could no longer just throw on my trousers and shirt and go to work, as George had done. I had to consider my every action, and I had to take time getting ready. I was a woman. I shaved, made up my face and combed up my hair. It all seemed to take so long, although the fact that I was half-asleep helped. I had not expected it to be like this; I had always had the impression that life as a woman would be easy.

I was ready to go by seven and went down to my landing. I knew the usual procedure, so I got on with the job as best I could. I made a few mistakes with the early-morning teas, but it was my first day. By nine o'clock I felt as if I had been working a week. I was completely shattered, and I had yet to change sheets, dust and hoover in rooms that had been badly neglected for weeks. The prospect wasn't very exciting. The dirty cow who had been working the landing before me must have sat in her servery all day. I spent nearly an hour on my first room. It looked much better when I had finished, although it did mean that I had to rush all the others.

The housekeeper occasionally looked around my rooms, always nodding with approval and never complaining. I occasionally over-heard her telling the other girls that if they all worked as hard as the English girl the hotel would be a much cleaner place. She had no idea at all about my true identity.

One day I was called into the office. I thought I was for the high jump, as I had been late that morning; but all she wanted was to warn me that she had been in the kitchen shortly after me that morning and had heard the chefs talking about what a good lay I would make. She reckoned that several of them fancied me and warned me to keep my door locked. Little did she know that my door-locking procedure each night was to protect the living-in male staff. They would have died of heart failure if they had opened my door by mistake and caught me in a compromising position. I had changed my lock the day after moving in, and had also added a bolt. Not satisfied with my own security arrangements, I also wedged a chair under the handle, especially when I was in bed or changing my clothes.

The other girls were all foreign, mostly Spanish. Their English was not all that good, so we had very little to say to each other. Occasionally in the afternoon I would go out with them on their shopping trips. They all liked my style of dress and tried to imitate it. I went along to give advice about colours and styles. They even asked for advice on make-up and hair-styles. I always took great pride in my appearance and great care over my hair and make-up. I knew the styles and colours that suited me and chose my accessories meticulously. Most of the girls were dark-haired and dark-skinned, so the brighter colours suited them. They seemed very grateful for the advice, especially Sally.

Sally was a Filipino girl who was very sensitive. She had joined the staff shortly after me and always clung to me for advice. She was trying to learn English, so everywhere I went she followed. I was most embarrassed one day when we were out shopping. Sally was trying on a dress in a cubicle and called for me to help fasten her up. I entered without thinking; imagine my shock when I found myself standing in the middle of a communal changing-room with about ten women. I couldn't get out quickly enough. I tried to keep calm, but being at close quarters with so many women in various states of undress brought me out in a hot sweat. I just stood outside the cubicle, my mind in a turmoil. I so much wanted to be a real woman like them. It really hurt me.

That evening Sally asked me to go along to a club with her. I had been at the hotel nearly four months without going out, so I accepted.

Sally met me in the hotel lobby at nine-thirty p.m. and we went to a local pub for a drink. At closing time we set off for the club that Sally was a member of. The entrance to the Gateways was very inconspicuous. I sat with Sally in a dark corner for about an hour while she continually plied me with vodka-and-orange and refused to accept a drink from me. In the end I just couldn't take any more. I like to pay my way, so I got up and went over to the bar to order a round. It was only then that I realised something was drastically wrong. The barman was a woman. Her hair was cut short and greased back and she was wearing trousers with a shirt and tie, and it was only when she repeated my order that I knew. She had really fooled me, and I am not one to fool easily. I looked around the club. It was quite dark, but I could see that all the men down there had busts under their shirts. I was completely taken back. There was not one man in sight. They were all lesbians. Surely Sally wasn't a lesbian?

I returned to the table with the drinks and told Sally that the man behind the bar was a woman. She said she already knew that. I sat down, and Sally placed her hand on my leg and told me she had only brought me down because she had thought I might like it. I told her in no uncertain terms that I liked men and men only. I was a straight woman. Sally argued that she had never heard me talking about men or ever seen me go out with one, and with that she slipped her hand further up my leg. I could have died. She asked me why I didn't at least try it just once. 'You shouldn't knock it till you've tried it' was her line – a line I have used on several occasions since; but it had gone far enough for me. I told her to take her hand away or I would break her fucking arm.

That really shook her. Her hand moved as though it had been stung. My aggression came flooding back. I downed my drink and stood to leave. As I got to the door Sally pulled at my arm and begged me to reconsider. I turned on her and said, 'Look, baby, you want a woman, go and find one. I'm still a man.'

It would have had the same effect if I had hit her with a sledge-hammer. I walked out into the street, but Sally followed me, screaming that she didn't believe me. I stormed back and told her that if she wanted to prove it she could. She realised I was serious, and burst into tears. I stopped a cab and fled back to the hotel. Sally was such a nice girl. Why did she have to be a lesbian?

The following morning, during the tea-break, one of the girls asked me if I had seen Sally, as she had not turned up for work. She was never seen at the hotel again.

Believe it or not there are estimated to be over 100,000 people adopting the role of their opposite sex all the time. My voice, although quite masculine, was never a problem when I was living as a woman. After all, many women have deep voices including some very famous actresses such as Lauren Bacall and Bea Arthur. What gave my real gender away was silly mistakes like opening doors for women and letting them through first, rather than the sound of my voice.

On the whole, life at the hotel was great. I had been there nearly six months and my secret was still safe. I was the head housekeeper's favourite. The other girls just came and went; I hung on. I enjoyed the work. A couple of the male staff had taken me out on the odd occasion, but I always ended the night by telling them that I was an honest girl and I was saving myself for my wedding-night. So after a passionate embrace and a kiss, and on the odd occasion a quick grope on my part, I managed to keep face. All the rest of the staff thought I was such a nice girl.

Looking back, there is one moment in my early months as a woman that always makes me smile. It was one bright Sunday morning in room 409. The room was at the end of my corridor, and a young man of about twenty-five had been in there for about a week. He had taken early-morning coffee every morning at seven, and even on the morning of his departure it was ordered. Each morning during the week he had been in various states of undress. I just used to laugh to myself, realising that he was trying to shock me, but the joke was really on him. That last Sunday, I tapped on the door and received my usual 'Enter' call from within. So, with my pass-key, I entered. That morning had not seemed special, but as I pushed open the door the young man wasn't to be seen. I walked over to the dressing-table, and in the mirror I could see the man's naked reflection behind the door. He didn't have a bad body, either. He pushed the door to. I wasn't perturbed in the slightest. I just opened the curtains to their fullest and wished him good morning.

He just smiled and looked down upon his form with pride. Life stirred where life should not have been stirring that time on a Sunday morning. I walked across the room towards him with an evil smile spreading across my face, my mind working overtime and summing up the situation. I picked his penis up in my hand; he got an erection straight away as I started to rub him.

Then I squeezed with all my might; he let out a cry of pain and I sent my right fist straight into his jaw. He reeled across the bedroom and landed on the bed. As I walked towards the door he asked me what the hell I had done that for, especially after getting him erect. I retorted that I wanted to see if it would grow as big as my own.

A look of horror spread over that sickly face. I pulled the door to and went down the corridor giggling like a little school-girl. I bumped into the head housekeeper as I approached my servery and she asked me what was wrong. Tears were streaming down my face and I just burst into fits of laughter.

The thought of that guy's face sent me into hysterics for weeks afterwards. I never saw him again, but I hope that if he has read this he has felt a twinge between his legs. I would do the same thing again.

Chapter II

A Fair Cop

I was happy at the hotel. I had a lovely room which I had been able to decorate to my own taste. My new ambition was to fill a third wardrobe with clothes – I had already succeeded filling two with all the latest fashions. My former identity very rarely raised its head.

But, deep down inside, even though I was living in my perfect dream, something was missing. George's attitude to life had been 'screw 'em all'. I was different; we were opposites. I had everything I needed to live my new life except love. Not sex, as George had craved. I was basically very lonely and wanted someone to want me. The sexual act no longer interested me. Wearing women's clothes had turned me on at first, and I had got my sexual kicks by masturbating. Now, for some unknown reason, I could not even obtain an erection. Out of sheer frustration I used to try all types of weird things to turn myself on, but it was pointless. Something was causing a blockage, and I could not – or did not want to – understand it.

The only way for me to find a lover was to return to the gay scene. But then I would no longer be a woman – I would be a drag queen. It was a risk that I was not really willing to take. At length I thought of advertising in the gay press and some of the more dubious of the underground papers. So I wrote out an appropriate message: 'Young man living in London as a woman longs to meet suitable companion for life-long relationship. Someone please answer. A.L.A. Sandy.'

Within three weeks I had received about sixty replies. Some of them seemed quite genuine, so I replied to them, using a post-office box number. Other letters were disgusting. Only perverts could have written them, and some of the things that they suggested doing to my body made even me blush. These perverted letters, along with nude photos that had been sent, ended up in the hotel boiler.

Following from the dozen or so letters I had replied to, I eventually met three people. None of them were men I would normally have chosen but go with them I did. All three were married, and they all insisted on wearing frilly underwear when in bed with me. That put me off straight away. I understood why I wanted to change sex, but could not begin to comprehend why a married man with children insisted on wearing feminine underwear, especially when his sexuality was basically heterosexual.

After my disappointment with the advertising campaign, I decided to visit a few gay pubs. That was the worst step I could have taken at that time. As I walked through the door of a pub in Earls Court, I could have thrown up. My whole being rebelled against the homosexuality that was being so openly paraded. I stood at the bar, and after ordering a drink I viewed my surroundings with displeasure. Young boys were openly prostituting themselves with old men, and older boys were wearing outrageous clothing with their peroxided hair and traces of make-up. They were trying to send up the female image and the sight angered me. It should not have done, as, a few years before, I had done exactly what they were doing. I felt like taking them all in my arms and mothering them, yet beating them at the same time. I could not even finish my drink.

Back at the hotel, I lay on my bed. What on earth was I do to? I wanted love, yet society was not prepared to accept me; it had not even bothered to make plans for my arrival. I burst into tears. Why couldn't I be real? Why did I have a cock when I did not really want it? Why did I have to have it cut off? Why couldn't I make my own choice and rip it off if I didn't want to keep it? I just wanted to throw it away and be the real me. Why was life so difficult? I made a vow that evening that I was going to become a woman even if I had to cut it off myself.

It took me several days to get up enough courage to go out again. I decided that I might as well throw myself in at the deep end and go up into the West End. There were so many foreigners there that I could always plead lack of communication if I got into a sticky situation.

My first visit was not all that successful. I sat in a pub drinking all night without speaking to a soul except the barman. Men always looked in my direction, but I tried to avoid their glances. Those I did fancy never made an advance. This happened several times, and it puzzled me. One night I found out why.

Four men entered the pub I had chosen for the night. As they ordered their drinks one of them winked at me. I just smiled back. One of the guy's mates had seen it and jeered at him, but I could not hear what was said. The one who had winked came over to the empty table beside me. I just smiled even more. His mates joined him and started to rib him. He kept smiling at me and telling them that he was on to a good thing. The general response was that he stood no chance. I was too classy a bird, especially for a yobbo like him. I admit that I spent more money on clothes than a normal woman; I also had my make-up and hair done to perfection.

The guy eventually got up enough courage to ask me if I would like a drink. I accepted his offer, and he joined me at my table. His mates went deathly quiet, and after about ten minutes he asked me if I would like to go somewhere a bit livelier. I said yes, and to the amazement of his mates we stood up to leave. He helped me on with my coat and, as he had his back to his friends, I winked and gave them the thumbs-up sign. A loud roar broke out from their table and my companion could not understand what they were laughing at.

We wandered around a few pubs, and I accepted his invitation to a disco, where we danced the rest of the night away. He confessed to me that he had honestly thought he didn't stand a chance. I just laughed. During the later part of the evening, after the drink had been flowing quite freely, things started to get slightly out of hand. As we danced to a slow, smoochy number our legs and bodies seemed to become intertwined, and where our bodies rubbed together there was a definite stirring. I tried to discourage the guy by standing back slightly. I must have appeared terribly frigid. He was convinced that I was a woman. I only wished that I could lie on my back and open my legs and prove that I was. He was getting hornier all the time, and kept pulling me towards him. The more he pulled, the more I strained, and as the dance finished I grabbed my bag and dashed into the toilet. But there was no escape – I had to go out of the door by which I had entered; so I returned to the table. I told him it would be impossible to do anything that evening because I was in the middle of my bad time of the month. He told me that in that case I could at least relieve him. This I did in the back of his car in the hotel car park. Promising faithfully to meet him the following week, I was able to slip into the hotel without a big scene.

I had to take a serious attitude towards sex. If I went out with a guy I could only go so far without being discovered; so it became a routine exit line to blame my frigidity on my period. But I started to wear low-cut dresses, and to make the effect look good I used to Sellotape up all the loose skin on my chest. This was a long and painful process. I had to run tape across, pulling my skin closer together with each piece – making a cleavage that was well worth looking at but bloody murder to get off. It was on a night when I had pulled out all the stops and looked great that I met Chris.

I had been out to the West End and missed the last tube, so I decided to walk back to the hotel. It was a warm night and I only had a shawl over my arms. I had been walking for nearly an hour and was reaching my destination when a car pulled up and asked me if I was all right. I nodded and said that everything was fine. The man did not push it any further, but told me to be careful and then drove off. But no sooner had he disappeared than the heavens opened.

I dived into the nearest doorway for cover. I had been there about five minutes when the car pulled up again, the driver ran towards me. He asked me how much further I had to go. Home was only about five minutes' walk away, but I would get drowned, so he offered to run me to the door. I declined at first, and it was only because he said he was offended after trying to help that I agreed to accept.

Chris introduced himself, and we chattered quite freely, as though we had known each other for years. I felt at ease in his company. We discussed my job and my past; he had a knack of extracting information from me. I didn't falter from the story I had made up when first embarking on my new identity. He seemed genuinely surprised that a nice girl like myself was only a chambermaid. He too was an only child; he had been brought up in Dorset, where his parents lived. The rain had stopped and we had been parked outside the hotel for ages, so I made my excuses and bade him goodnight.

At about eleven o'clock next morning one of the Spanish chambermaids came flying into my room, telling me that I must go at once to the head housekeeper's office because a telegram had arrived for me. I felt my stomach turn. No one knew of my new identity. No one would send me a telegram anyway.

I ran to the office. The telegram just said: 'PHONE ME URGENT. CHRIS.' along with a phone number. I had to think for a minute who the hell Chris was.

When I rang him, he asked me out for dinner that night. The rest of the day was like a nightmare. I just could not concentrate. Chris was a nice guy, but he was straight. I would have to watch myself, and I decided that this would be the first and last time. It had upset my usual pattern. I was normally the hunter and my men the hunted; now the roles had been reversed. But I was terribly excited as I prepared to go out. I chose my nicest dress and took great care over my hair and make-up. I wanted to look my best and not like a cheap tart. That evening I think I looked far better than I had ever done before.

Dinner was at the Wheatsheaf Hotel in Virginia Water, and we had a wonderful time. When we got home, we arranged to meet again the following evening. I shot up the stairs three at a time, I was so happy. It was two o'clock when I fell into bed. I tried counting sheep, but sleep would not come, so I started to count down the time to our next meeting: only seventeen hours. The next morning I was singing and dancing my way around the hotel. As I delivered the early-morning teas and coffees I greeted everyone with a grin. My mind was definitely on Chris as I sprayed furniture-polish about the rooms and air-freshener on the furniture.

We met every night for a month, but he did not even kiss me. I couldn't understand why not. After the first week we were telling each other that we loved each other. What a situation! There was I, a faggot, a homosexual, telling a man I loved him – and he had never even laid a hand on me. I wanted him to kiss me, to touch me, but if he did he would find out the truth. I made myself believe that if I dated him long enough he would accept my situation – or, if I thought it wouldn't work, I could have a sex change and he would never know. What a fairy-tale I was living in. If I had been a real woman it would have been the perfect romance. Cards and letters and surprise bouquets of flowers. I would have married in white and been a virgin on my wedding-night. That is how Chris would have wanted it.

Things had been going so well that they just had to start going wrong soon. My life wasn't usually as uncomplicated as this, Something drastic was due to happen, and I started looking for faults. I looked for faults in Chris, in me, in work. I couldn't find any within myself. I had made myself the perfect woman. The only disadvantage was that I was still a man.

One of the biggest shocks I have ever had came when I was walking down Edgware Road one day about three months after meeting Chris. A police car pulled up in front of me and Chris jumped out in full uniform. He grabbed my arm and dragged me into the back. To anyone watching it would have looked as though I were being arrested. I could have died – the number of times I had called the police pigs and perverts in front of Chris! He just started laughing and told me I had seemed so dead against the police he thought he had better not mention it until I knew him better. I would never have dreamed that he was in the force – it just did not seem to go with his nature.

I spent the rest of the afternoon being chauffeured about in a police car while I did my shopping. Once I had got used to the idea that Chris was a policeman, I enjoyed flying down the full length of Oxford Street in about two minutes with the old blue light flashing and the siren screaming.

I had come to love Chris dearly, yet he still hadn't made a play for me. I thought that it might be easier to quit while the going was good. If my situation ever got out, it could ruin Chris's career. I toyed with the idea for weeks and one night decided to tell him the truth. We had been to the local for a drink, and I had had far more than was normal for me. I needed Dutch courage. Once or twice I started to tell him. I would say, 'Chris, I have something to tell you,' but when I had his full attention and he was looking into my eyes I would lose my nerve and say, 'Oh, it doesn't matter.'

As we walked back, Chris tried to prise my problem out of me. He thought it might be something he had done, and he begged me to tell him about it. I was choking back tears; I couldn't get out the truth. We stepped into a shop doorway. As he raised my chin to look in my eyes I could not stop the flow of tears. He pulled me towards him and held me tight. I clung to him for dear life. Chris tried to dry my eyes with his hankie.

Once I had calmed down, he told me that he loved me and would do anything for me. I only had to ask. All my determination disappeared. I looked up into his eyes and tried to smile, but I never made it. He kissed me – slowly at first; only as I hungered for more did he comply. We ran our tongues inside each other's mouths, touching, probing and holding each other tight. He broke away, gasping for breath, but I only wanted more. Deep inside me something stirred that had never stirred before. I felt as if my head had been blown open.

I don't remember walking back to the hotel, saying goodnight or even getting into bed. But I do remember clinging on to my pillow, squeezing it with delight as I relived that first kiss.

We spent more time together than ever before. I even attended the annual police ball with him. I bought a special dress and fur wrap for the occasion, and spent the whole day of the event having my hair done and my nails manicured and polished. I looked and felt like a million dollars as I entered the ballroom that evening, and I knew that Chris felt proud of me. I was introduced to many of the hierarchy from Scotland Yard and all Chris's workmates and wives.

While powdering my nose in the ladies' toilet with the other women (this now came quite naturally to me) several of them asked me how long I had been dating Chris. They had always thought him the most eligible bachelor the force had to offer. It had only been five months, but it felt like a lifetime. When one of them asked me if wedding bells were in the air I went crimson. One of the girls noticed and told her friend off. Then she gave me a little bit of advice. 'Never marry a copper, love. You'll never know whether or not he's going to come in on time, or whether he'll come home at all. Me and my old man haven't had a bit for weeks. He's always working, and if he isn't working he's too bloody tired.'

That night Chris was very excited. After the raffle had been drawn (we won second prize – a statuette that I still have) he whispered in my ear that he had found out that very day that he was no longer a sergeant. He was to be promoted. He was determined to make it to the top. I congratulated him and kissed him tenderly.

He had not yet told his parents about his promotion, and as their wedding anniversary was coming he intended to tell them then. He wanted me to go down for a long weekend. I agreed without giving it a second thought. I had not had a holiday, and I had been at the hotel nearly a year.

I was very worried about meeting his parents. I knew that I wasn't in the same class as them. I had only spoken to his mother once, on the day I got the telegram, and she had sounded very grand indeed – too grand for me. Chris had an air of elegance and money about him when we visited the posher of the restaurants together. He knew how to conduct himself, although it was obvious the force had knocked a lot of that out of him.

I chose very sedate clothing for the weekend – nothing too flashy. Chris tried to put me at my ease all the way down to Dorset, but any girl in my situation – even a real one – would have been as nervous as hell. I felt even worse as we pulled into the estate and motored up the never-ending drive towards the manor house. I was so nervous that I was visibly shaking, and as the house came into view I let out a shriek. Chris stopped the car about a hundred yards from the front door and leant over to kiss me reassuringly. We did not notice his mother and father coming out of the house and heading towards the car until it was too late. But it was nice to have a large glass of brandy thrust into my hand the minute we entered the library, and to sit in front of a large log fire. The family had already eaten, but Cook had left some sandwiches in the kitchen. After a light snack I was ready for bed.

When I awoke the following morning, the immense size of the bedroom startled me. It hadn't looked that big the night before. The house had been built in Regency times, and still had the original furnishings. Chris's mother brought me breakfast in bed. I always look terrible first thing in the morning, so I kept my head under the bedclothes. She told me that they were off riding for an hour, and would see me later.

My bathroom led off the bedroom. It was that sort of house. I could never have lived in that life-style; but I did come very close.

That evening about thirty special guests were attending the great anniversary party. I had willingly given Cook a hand with the preparation, and Chris's mother was impressed by my versatility. I heard her telling Chris that I was a fine girl. I only wished I could have felt a little more at ease.

During the toasts Chris grabbed my arm and led me into the library, away from the madness in the drawing-room. I had already wanted several times to throw my hands around his neck and kiss him, but had had to remember my place. Once we were alone we kissed and held each other tight.

Then he sat me down on the chaise-longue and took hold of my hand; I was giggling but he was deadly serious. I wondered what was coming next. He stumbled over his words, and what he did say did not make all that much sense. The gist of it was that he had bought me an engagement ring.

I fell into his arms. As he pushed me back, he asked me if I would marry him. I said yes.

Chris bounded out of the room, leaving me holding the most beautiful ring. It had three small diamonds and two sapphires set in it, and I didn't dare touch it. Chris shepherded his mother and father into the room and announced that I had accepted him. With that he took the ring out of its box and slipped it on my finger. Their reaction was not what I would have expected from such a grand couple. His mother came over and threw her arms around us both, and the major shook both our hands. I was completely overwhelmed.

I was being ushered from the library into the drawing-room. The major called the gathering to order and announced the good news. Everyone started clapping and cheering, and I was being kissed and having my hand shaken by the whole assembly. I was on a new high. It had all happened so fast.

Yet, amazingly enough, I still had not considered the implications. It was after we had all departed to bed that it suddenly hit me. I couldn't marry Chris. I was a man! But if I told him now, it would kill him.

I hardly slept that night and, when I did, I woke up sweating after having a repeated dream. I walked down the aisle of a church for a wedding service conducted by the devil. The minute we had taken our vows the devil ripped up my dress and pulled off my testicles.

The following morning I was reprieved, as everyone went riding again. I dressed and went down to the library; but when I sat down and thought over the past twenty-four hours I felt sick. Surely I was dreaming it all? The ring on my finger told me it was no dream. It was for real – yet I wasn't real. I burst into tears.

I tried to get back to my room before anyone saw me, but I had to bump into someone and that just had to be Chris's mother. She asked me if I was all right. I blamed a bad toothache and said another hour in bed would cure it. The hour spread into a day, with Chris and his parents popping in very ten minutes to make sure I didn't need anything.

The more I thought about my situation the worse it became. I had to tell Chris the truth – there was no other way. I decided that it would have to be done the following day, as soon as we got back to London. But I wanted to be a woman; I wanted to be able to marry Chris. I wanted to make him happy. That bastard of a doctor – this was his fault. If only Tom had never given me his name.

The thought of Tom and Pam sent me off on a different track. I wondered if Tom's operation had been a success. If it had . . . Could I possibly get away with it? If only I could have got the operation without Chris finding out.

I put on a brave face as we left Dorset telling my would-be in-laws that I looked forward to meeting them again the following week when they came to London. God knows how I got through the journey. My mind was toying with all kinds of ideas; yet I still managed to talk over wedding plans with Chris as if nothing were wrong. He dropped me at the hotel that afternoon and we arranged to meet the following day.

The first thing I did was to call Tom and Pam. I had to talk to someone. I had not contacted them since I had left Folkestone, so I had a lot to tell them. It took a long time for the phone to be answered, and when Pam eventually picked it up her voice seemed dull and lifeless.

'Hi Pam! It's me, George,' That statement shocked me. Who was George? He had been dead for over a year. Yet I had brought him back to life in one short sentence. It was terrifying but somehow comforting to know that he was still around.

'Hi, George. How are you?'

'Oh, I'm fine love. How's things with you?'

'I'm fine.' She didn't sound it.

'How's Tom?'

'Tom? You haven't heard, then?'

'Heard what?' This was becoming a mystery – she sounded so strange.

'He's dead.'

Tom dead? He couldn't be.

'How, Pam?'

'He committed suicide three months ago. He was very unhappy.'

Apparently Tom had been seeing the doctor and taking the tablets to develop the bust. These had made him very depressed, and he always thought that the psychiatrist was giving him a bad time. He just couldn't handle it all. He had stopped having treatment because he thought he was being treated like an animal. Such a waste; he had been such a nice man.

I felt empty as I put the phone down. If Tom were not strong enough to take the treatment and pressure, surely I wasn't?

I went for a walk to try and clarify my mind. I was deeply in love with Chris and I didn't want to lose him; but I didn't want to hurt him either. I walked for hours, my state of mind becoming even shakier. I was nearing breaking-point when I spotted an advertisement for the Samaritans. I wrote down the number and dashed into the nearest phone box. I had no sooner got the money in the box and started to explain my situation than I broke down. The young woman on the other end of the wire called me back and listened to my problems for over an hour. Then, when I had finished, she put it all back into perspective.

I was a man living as a woman. I had met a man and fallen in love with him. He thought I was a woman and had asked me to marry him. That was it in a nutshell. It was so simple when someone else was analysing the situation. But what was her advice? How did I solve my problem?

Her answer was short and straightforward: 'You must become George again to save yourself and your lover.'

I couldn't face Chris to explain the truth to him. I did not have the strength or the guts to do it. I slipped his ring into an envelope and sent it back to him with a brief note: I explained that he deserved better. He had to trust me, it would be better this way, better for us both. I honestly thought that he would come looking for me, so I covered my tracks very carefully but in 1980 I was in a programme on Radio Four at Broadcasting House and when I walked out through the front entrance, he was waiting for me. I prayed for the ground to open up as he walked towards me in his uniform. He had been listening to the programme and had come to find me. He was shocked by the truth, but he just wanted to tell me that he understood. I had fooled him but he was not bitter. Now, he is happily married and we do occasionally talk and meet. He is like the big brother that I never had or like the father I always wanted.

Chapter 12

Marriage

All through the night, I felt panic-stricken. How could I live as George again? I had been so happy as Sandy. Tears flowed, and my heart yearned all night for peace. I tried to find a good excuse for not becoming George, but each one was wiped out by the urgency of my situation. During the early hours of the morning, I made my plans.

I collected a few personal mementos of Sandy's, and dressed in women's clothes for the last time. At nine o'clock I left my bedroom. The wardrobe was full of clothes. The dressing-table was decorated with an array of cosmetics and perfume-bottles, each carefully replaced as I completed my make-up. As I closed the door, I was wiping out the happiest memories I had ever had.

I visited my building society and withdrew the balance of my account. Then I went into Marks and Spencers to buy some male clothing. I chose a casual jacket, shirt and trousers with ease. I was dressed as a woman, but buying clothes in Marks was far less conspicuous than going into a male boutique. After buying shoes, socks and other garments, I made my way to Victoria station. I entered the ladies' toilets and changed into my new clothes. It felt very strange. As I left I dropped a plastic bag of female clothing into the rubbish-bin.

I had removed my make-up, but my hair seemed exceptionally long. I went straight into a hairdresser's and had it cut short. As the barber clipped off my bleached locks, I looked at my reflection. My face remained impassive, but my brain was working overtime. I was George.

I booked into a small bed-and-breakfast hotel for the night to give me a chance to sort myself out. All I had with me was a small bag of personal effects, a spare pair of socks and a clean shirt. My confidence was soon wiped out that evening when I visited one of London's more notorious gay pubs. It sickened me. Men were holding each other and rubbing up to each other, openly picking each other up. I had done it myself for years, but now it seemed disgusting. I was rebelling against my homosexuality. I needed fresh air, and fought my way out of the place. Why did I suddenly think homosexuality was wrong? I had always believed that men and women should be allowed to do what they liked with each other.

Surely living as Sandy hadn't changed my whole attitude to life? I thought of the Black Cap in Camden Town. It was such a friendly pub; surely I would feel better there. I got the underground over to Camden and entered the pub. The drag show was in full swing, and everyone seemed so friendly. Yet I still felt it was wrong – that I shouldn't have been there. But I was gay. I always had been. I accepted that. I was a homosexual. I had been out of my closet for years. I couldn't reject the scene – it would mean rejecting myself; all I stood for.

I drank myself into a stupor, ignoring the advances that were made towards me. While I was still in control, I headed back to the hotel. I convinced myself that that night I had been saved from committing further sins with other men: I must become a heterosexual – a decent, honest and respectable young man. I'd never had the chance to be one before; now it had come. I was determined to become real.

I thought that everyone in Fleetwood knew of my past, so I decided to return to Fleetwood again. I hadn't seen Mum for ages, and she was good to have around when I was in trouble. But things weren't too good when I arrived. Mum was pissed and living in the usual filthy state. All she needed was a good man to look after her, then she would have led a decent life. But her men friends were all the same – the type who would find, fuck and forget her. After spending one night in the same room as her, I knew I must get away. She had a kind heart really, but I would only end up in the same rut.

I found a living-in-job easily enough, and started work in the Savoy Hotel, Blackpool, as a waiter. The hours were long and the hotel was busy, which gave me an excuse not to visit Fleetwood too often. I bought myself a new stereo unit and listened to records every night. But I missed socialising. As Sandy, I had had a good time meeting men. Perhaps if I visited a straight club I'd have fun meeting girls.

On my night off, I dressed casually and made for the bright lights. I had very little bother getting into the Blue Flamingo club, so I must have looked straight enough. But I spent the night sitting at a table by myself, drinking. I asked a couple of girls to dance, but after receiving rejections I didn't bother any more. I watched all the other guys dancing and approaching women in the club. Perhaps they had something that I didn't. I seemed to be the only man sitting alone, even though the women did outnumber us two-to-one. I tried to imagine what the men were whispering into the girls' ears to make them giggle so. What would they do in bed? Would I have the strength and guts when my time came? Three hours at that table didn't deter me, and I repeated my vigil night after night, always leaving as pissed as a newt and thinking that I must be as ugly as sin. Why didn't anybody ever talk to me?

One night as I made my way back to the hotel a woman in a doorway called me over to her. I went and asked what she wanted. We talked for a short while, and she made several advances towards me. I thought my luck was in. She rubbed slowly, but to no avail. I couldn't get an erection. She even undid my trousers and went down on me. Nothing. Perhaps I had drunk to much. As she stood up, I began to fumble her breasts. She pushed my hand away and demanded a five-pound note for wasting her time. It was only then that I realised she was a prostitute. I started walking away telling her to piss off. Then she started shouting that she'd scream rape if I didn't pay her. One scream broke out, and I ran back and pushed a fiver into her hand before she had regained enough breath to scream again. I felt sickened.

Over the next few weeks I became lonelier and lonelier. I tried the gay scene again, but it didn't work. I rejected men and women; what a predicament to be in! I was so mixed-up. Sex had played such an important part in my previous lifestyle. The lonelier I got, the more frightened I became. Would I be alone forever? Was there no one who could stir the dying spirit in my body?

As I had always done when in trouble, I moved. I dreaded moving again, but I had to. I felt everyone knew of my past. I had to go where I wasn't known. So, like a rabbit, I ran. I travelled round the north-east of England, feeling more and more rejected. I'd sunk so low that I felt like copping out of life. Hull was my last stop in England; from there I travelled by ferry to Rotterdam, in Holland, then by train down to Amsterdam.

I'd never been abroad, and the adventure added a new sparkle to my life. Every day was worth waking up for. I couldn't speak Dutch, but I managed to survive for a few weeks, just visiting museums and art galleries, walking around the old city and admiring the sights. The red-light district had been an eye-opener, with all the prostitutes showing themselves in the windows. But although it was all done blatantly, there was still an air of respectability about it. At least the girls weren't on the streets. Nevertheless, the sex shops and pornographic books on display were far pornier than anything I'd ever seen in England. And homosexuality was openly accepted. Everyone just carried on with their own lives and didn't give a damn whether the Joneses next door were gay or even perverts, as long as they kept it to themselves.

Even drugs were openly used. During an excursion on the canals, the boatman pointed out an open market with a brightly coloured building on its right. A big sign declared that it was 'The Head Shop'. I asked him what that meant and the old sea-dog explained in broken English that people in there were mad. I didn't understand what he meant, but before I visited the Head Shop the following day, I never thought that it would change my life.

I spent the night sleeping in the railway station, as money was getting short and I was saving it for food. I slept next to a young American guy who said he'd slept in the same spot for nearly six months. We struck up a close friendship that night, and the following morning he invited me to join him for a cup of coffee. We ended up in a little café a few doors away from the Head Shop. I enjoyed his company and enjoyed talking about America. But I noticed he was becoming more and more restless. I asked if everything was O.K., and he told me he would be fine. I eventually found out that he fixed heroin in his arm and was waiting to see a pusher. The Head Shop was the 'in' place to meet and push or buy drugs. Within two hours the boy had become a nervous wreck. Eventually his pusher turned up and he dragged me into the nearest toilet to fix himself. I felt sick as he rolled up his sleeve and jammed in the needle. His veins stood out prominently where he'd injected himself time and time again. But within twenty minutes, he was fine. I was amazed at the change. During the day we hung around together, meeting all kinds of strange and 'beautiful' people – mostly addicts and pushers.

Everyone was in a world of their own; if you had stabbed one of them in the back he'd just have turned round and shaken your hand. The buzz was that that evening some girls were having a party on a barge. My American friend insisted that I join him until it was time to go to the station to kip down for the night. I agreed, and we spent most of the day just hanging around until it was time to set off.

When we were approaching the barge, I couldn't believe it. People were lying on the barge and all over the canal bank. I was dragged down into the smoke-filled depths, where bodies were crushed together in a small room. I couldn't understand why everyone had one drag on a cigarette and passed it on to the person next door. It was a very strange party. There was no food or booze – just cigarettes. It took a while to sink in that they were smoking dope.

I accepted a cigarette several times, but only pretended to inhale the smoke. This game lasted a couple of hours; then I realised that all those around me were really enjoying themselves. So, the next time I received a cigarette, I inhaled as if there were no tomorrow.

I felt as though I'd left my body and was looking down on it from above. My arm- and leg-movements, though slow, were precise and calculated, and I began to feel as though I didn't have a worry in the world. All my problems were solved as soon as I posed the questions to myself. I thought I was answering them all rationally, even when I asked myself about my sexuality. I was right – I was a man, and all I needed was the right woman.

Through the cloudy haze of the cabin, I saw a girl sitting in the corner by herself. I slowly moved over to her, trying to keep upright and avoid standing on too many bodies. I casually introduced myself as I sat beside her. She told me her name was Helena. We laughed and giggled for hours, talking about nothing. It was all rubbish. That night we slept arm-in-arm. The following morning, as soon as we woke, another joint was passed around, and then another, and then another. I remember someone having a collection to buy some more dope. I threw in a few guilders, and stuck the rest of my money deep inside my shoe. Helena and I laughed, talked and slept, holding each other closer and closer. God knows how long it took us before we actually kissed each other, but people came and went, and I hungrily pulled on any joint that was going round the cabin.

I can't remember how we ended up in bed together, but next door to the main room on the barge was a small bedroom with a bed that nearly filled it. We were only two out of about ten people in the bed. I remember kissing Helena and feeling her silky body rubbing against me. She was lying beneath me and I was aware of enjoyment. I was making love to her. I had an erection and I was actually screwing a woman. I could do it! Those thoughts soared through my brain as I screwed faster and faster, until I felt my whole body shudder and convulse. I'd ejaculated into her. She threw her arms around me and screamed for me to do it again. Others in the bed were making love, some were sleep. I just carried on and made love to her again and again. She hungrily sapped all the strength out of me until I collapsed exhausted upon her and slept.

When I eventually came around, people were dressing and preparing to leave. Helena and I slowly found our clothes, and as we dressed we broke off occasionally and hugged each other. She whispered in my ear that she wanted me to make love to her again. I wanted to, too, if only to prove that I could do it again. She was Dutch, but spoke perfect English. She asked me if I'd like to stay with her for a few days before moving on, and I agreed. As we got into the open air I felt hungry. I couldn't believe it: we'd been on the barge for nearly four days. God knows where the American had got to. It had been quite a party, and I hadn't even had a drink. My head felt heavy and I badly needed a shave, so we went straight back to Helena's flat – two rooms in the basement of her family's house. It had its own entrance, and she came and went at her leisure.

It was only when we arrived that I could study her properly. She was very dark-haired, slim-faced and tall, a very straggly pretty girl. She had manicured nails, and her flat was elegant and had all the furnishings. It was quite obvious that her parents had money. I couldn't fathom out why she bothered to go to such parties.

During the next three weeks we spent most of our time in bed. I was performing four or five times daily, and Helena taught me all kinds of tricks. My money soon ran out, though, and I hated having to depend on her. I felt deeply for her, but didn't want to become too involved. She even hinted at marriage. I had a vision of a ball and chain tying me down for ever, and felt it was time I ducked out of her clutches. I had proved to myself that I was a man, so I shouldn't have to bother with girls any more. After making an imaginary phone-call, I said that I had to go home. I promised to write every day.

Money was a problem. I'd run out. How the hell was I to get back to England? Helena advised me to go and see the British consul. We visited the consulate and explained my situation. The people there were very good, and they gave me tickets for my ferry back to England. I was told that as soon as I arrived in Hull my passport would be taken off me, and when I paid the money that was owing to the British consulate I would get my passport back and be able to leave the country once again. I agreed and signed the necessary forms.

It was a tearful goodbye in Rotterdam, but I felt good once the ship set sail for Hull again. I spent the whole passage at the bar, chatting up a girl. If I'd had enough money for a berth, no doubt I'd have tried to pull her and use her for immoral purposes.

Once in Hull, I hitch-hiked to Blackpool. It was a cold night and my journey was made in seven different cars. The guy in the last car, who took me from Preston to Blackpool, was gay and made a pass at me. As he rubbed his hand up and down my leg I got an erection. We pulled up in a lay-by and I ended up screwing him. Only four weeks previously, I hadn't been able to face a man or a woman. Now I'd had both within twenty-four hours, and enjoyed it. I wasn't a homosexual. I wasn't a heterosexual. I was a bit of both. I was bisexual. What could be better? I had the best of both worlds.

After telephoning around the bigger hotels I soon got a job. I started working at the Cliffs. It was only two blocks away from the Savoy and, when I told them during my interview that I'd just left the Savoy, they took me on straight away. There was a bit of rivalry between the two managements.

I kept my promise to Helena and wrote to her every day at first. Then it dwindled to twice a week. I pledged my love for her in every letter, but went on the rampage every night, and screwed anything that was willing. In a six-week period I made love to women between the ages of eighteen and forty-five, and men between sixteen and sixty. No holds barred. The more I made love, the more I wanted it. I learned sexual tricks from the older women that I used on the younger girl, and I experimented more and more with younger gay guys.

Then the shock of my life arrived in an airmail letter from Amsterdam. Helena was pregnant. She was expecting my baby. I was elated at first and ran around the hotel showing everyone the letter. Then after a short while the seriousness of it all struck me. I was to become a father. Financial commitments. What of Helena – would I have to marry her? I didn't really love her as much as I'd told her. I had just enjoyed abusing her body. I'd got myself into a mess – again.

Her letter was a tear-jerker. She pledged her love for me again and asked me if she could come to live with me. She was only two months gone, but if her father suspected that she was pregnant he would kill her. She as good as asked me to marry her.

The sooner I talked to her, the better. I telephoned her that evening with all the answers I thought I'd need in my head; but as soon as she realised it was me, she broke down in tears. I tried desperately to pacify her. She eventually told me that her father knew. The doctor she had seen was a friend of the family – and, as she took drugs, the doctor had thought that her father had the right to know about the situation. When her father had questioned her, she had told him that I had already agreed to marry her.

I wasn't really prepared for that, so I agreed to go to Amsterdam the following weekend to meet her parents and discuss her future. I was too naïve to take on the responsibility of a wife and child. Helena's father had seemed so demanding when I had seen him during my visit, and I was sure that he'd only want the best for his daughter.

I dressed very conservatively. When I arrived I was taken to his study by the housemaid, and was confronted by Helena's father, mother and two elder brothers. I was questioned rather firmly by her father. Her mother kept bursting into tears and babbling in Dutch to her husband. He explained to me that his wife had wanted much better for her daughter; now she was being degraded into marrying me.

Once we had reached agreement, I was allowed to meet Helena, with her mother as chaperone. We were to talk about the agreement to see if it was acceptable to both parties. I'd agreed to let Helena stay in Amsterdam with her parents until she was six months pregnant. I was to move from Blackpool to Nottingham, where she had an uncle who would be responsible for keeping an eye on us. I was to marry her before she left Amsterdam, and her parents would then escort her over to check the home I was to have prepared for us both. They would leave after they were sure she was settled. Helena was in full agreement and we bade each other farewell once again, under the watchful eye of her mother.

All the way back to England, the agreement played on my mind. Why couldn't I just move and forget Helena? Surely it was possible. The only thing that put these preposterous ideas out of my mind was the fact that I wanted a child. I wanted to be a daddy. I wanted to be able to look on a young child and say, 'I created that.' I wanted a child that I could love and cherish. I adored children – but I had never ever dreamt that I would be in a position to feed and bathe one of my own.

Back at the hotel I worked ever so hard. Every hour I could, I worked overtime to earn extra money. All I earned went straight into the bank in preparation for starting my new normal life-style. I wasn't as randy as I'd been; but then again I had a new purpose in life. I advertised in the Nottingham papers, and with the help of Helena's uncle was able to get a nice little furnished terraced house at a reasonable rent. I spent a few hundred pounds on bedding and special things that we would need, and as the wedding-day approached I became more and more excited.

Helena's letters arrived daily, and she continually told me that she loved me dearly. Perhaps in time I could learn to love her? I moved to Nottingham and got a job in a night-club. The money was good, and the job held its own excitement for me. Cabaret was staged every night and the shows became part of my life. I loved to watch the very big stars and the way they acted, and I dreamed of a day when I would stand in front of a big audience, receiving the same applause.

I travelled back to Amsterdam with just an overnight bag and a return ticket in my pocket. All the arrangements had been made by Helena's parents; we hadn't had much say. We didn't even meet until we stood side by side in the registry office. The registrar raised his eyebrows as he entered the room; Helena was so big. It was obvious that she was with child, and he flashed me an accusing look. The rigmarole of the service took ages, and I was glad to say 'I do', if only to stop Helena's mother from sobbing.

The dress that Helena wore was revolting. It looked very uncomfortable, and I had the impression that she wouldn't be able to get it
off quick enough. Once the service was over, it was back to the
house with all the family for celebrations. Everyone was congratulating Helena. I stood like a prat for nearly an hour until Helena
grabbed my hand and dragged me up the stairs. She told me how
much she'd missed me and how glad she was I was back. All her
clothes were packed ready for travelling, and a large box of wed-
ding-presents stood unopened.

Over the next few weeks I grew to hate the sobs of her mother
and groans of her father. The day they left Nottingham to go back
home I breathed a sigh of relief. The only time I'd had alone with
my wife was when we were in bed – and we were different somehow. Marriage wasn't what I'd expected it to be. I was trapped;
there was no way out at all. Helena sat around all day and expected
me to be at her beck and call. I cleaned and cooked for us both; she
hardly ever lifted a finger, and when we argued about it she blamed
her pregnancy. The child was becoming a pest even before it was
born.

Helena's pregnancy was normal, according to the clinic, and as
her time approached arrangements were made for her to go into the
local maternity hospital. I was working seven nights a week, and
had bought a new pram and cot in preparation. Helena's mother
regularly sent parcels of clothing she'd knitted. However, Helena's
attitude towards our child changed as she approached the day. She
complained of the eighteen-year burden we would have to carry,
and she said she wished she'd never ever told me or her family; she
wished she'd just had an abortion. I convinced myself that she
would change once the birth was over and the baby was put into
her arms, and that she was only frightened of the childbirth pains.

The day came, and she eventually went into labour. I was a bag
of nerves. I paced up and down the corridors like any normal father
– but it was special for me. I was a reformed homosexual who had
never thought that he would enjoy fatherhood. For nine hours I
paced, read and fidgeted, until the double doors opened and a black
nurse called out my name. I half-ran over to her and nearly tripped
myself up in my excitement. She congratulated me on being the
father of a bouncing 8 lb 4 oz baby boy. I let out a whoop of joy
and threw my arms around her, I was so excited. I was told that I'd
be able to see Helena in about an hour. I talked to anyone who
would listen. I was a father, a daddy; I'd be able to take him out
and play football, and one day we'd even be able to stand and drink
in a pub together. Oh, what a future we all had – or so I thought.

I was eventually allowed to see Helena. I wasn't unduly worried;

she'd been through a lot. And the baby, the baby looked so lovely – a shock of black hair, just like his mother's. But he had my nose, I was definite about that. The nurse stood by the cot and smiled and agreed with me. She lifted the baby out and brought him closer. He looked so cuddly, but she wouldn't let me hold him. She walked over to Helena and offered her the baby.

But Helena just turned away and faced the wall. Only then did I realise I was going to have problems.

Chapter 13

Peter

Helena's rejection of Wayne, our first son, shook me. How a mother could just ignore a child as he lay in his cot crying was beyond me. I had spent the first two weeks after the child's birth at home, trying to make them both comfortable, but I had to keep the money coming in. Every hour I spent at work was nerve-racking. I had visions of the baby crying in his cot while she just sat and watched television. I tried to treat her with the respect a wife deserved, but she was playing the role neither of a wife nor of a mother, and it annoyed me beyond all belief.

I came in from work one night feeling exhausted. The baby lay screaming in his cot in the front room. I opened the lounge door. The room was stiflingly hot. I lifted him out of the cot and calmed him down. It was obvious from the smell that he had messed himself, so I got a clean nappy and talcum-powder and changed him. I was sickened by what I saw. His bottom was raw where he'd been left in wet and dirty nappies. My temper just snapped, but I calmly fed him from his bottle. The way the poor little mite drained it, it was obvious that he hadn't been fed all day. I placed him back in his cot and stayed with him until he went to sleep.

Then I sent up into our bedroom. Helena was asleep. At the side of the bed was an empty bottle of wine and a half-eaten box of chocolates. The little puppy that I had bought for her the week previously was curled up asleep on the pillow. I was so annoyed that I made a dive for her and struck her. I'd never struck a woman before, but she was ignoring my son. She turned on me and started lashing out, and my temper got the worse of me. I tried to throttle her. The fight seemed to go on for ever, but I eventually got the better of her and left her crying on the bed. I returned to the baby's cot, carried him upstairs to the spare bedroom and kept him by my side all night. It was a restless night, and as soon as dawn broke I changed him again and took him out of the house.

I spent the day just pushing him around in his pram. I'd prepared two bottles for him and had a few spare nappies, so I was able to feed and change him without going home. I had no choice but to go home that evening, though. I couldn't take the baby to work with me. When I walked through the front door Helena was quiet, but she took him out of his pram and started to nurse him. I bathed and changed, and as I left for work she apologised to me for neglecting Wayne.

Her attitude had changed; but that wasn't to last for long. She no longer neglected Wayne, but she still neglected the house. Every day I cleaned the house and cooked our meals. I didn't like complaining, because I enjoyed playing mother. Helena was basically lazy – I had known that before we even married. But I was still sure that she would change.

My sexual appetite had dwindled since she had had Wayne. I was lucky if I could make it once a fortnight, and I only did so to stop her complaining. I found it a labour to make love, and it took nearly an hour to complete the task. I was glad to turn over and go to sleep. Sex had become boring.

Wayne was eight months old when Helena told me she was pregnant again. I had serious doubts as to whether it was my child or not. But when I accused her of having an affair with someone else, she denied it; and when she hinted one night that she was going to have an abortion, I let her know in no uncertain terms that I would cut her throat. She was carrying my child, and it should be given a chance to live. If it didn't, neither would she.

Helena had succeeded in changing me. She had changed me into a vicious, disgruntled man. We had rows daily. She started to neglect and mistreat Wayne again. If I hadn't kept cleaning the house, it would have looked like a pigsty in a matter of weeks. I was very unhappy. I wanted so much for my child, but every time I bought him a new toy I was accused of spoiling him and neglecting her. The fact was that she no longer mattered to me. Wayne and the child she was carrying were my only worries.

Soon Carl was born. He brought a little more happiness into London Road. Helena doted on him; she even seemed more interested in Wayne, and started taking them out for walks. For the first time she looked proud of her offspring. Perhaps Carl was all she'd needed to get her back on the straight and narrow. The only problem now was that I was no longer interested in Helena. She only needed me to supply the money to keep the house running. Sex was out, and I was told to go and find it elsewhere. I didn't argue with her; but, again, I thought she would change with time.

On my regular night off, I now used to go out for a game of darts with the boys in the local pub. I had become celibate. Sex didn't interest me; I just worked and slept. There was nothing else to distract me. Helena kept the boys occupied all the time. The change in her was remarkable – she was a mother at last; but she didn't consider her duties as a wife mattered any more.

One night, after a visit to the pub, I called in at the local fish-and-chip shop to get something to eat. There would be no chance of food being ready for me at home. When I entered the shop, the person in front of me struck me as familiar. He looked so much like Simon, the love of my life. At first I was sure it was him; but once he ordered his food the idea was dispelled. He had a Midlands accent, he was dressed in a black leather jacket and he carried a crash helmet. There was some delay as the assistant was waiting for fresh chips to be cooked, so we started talking to each other. It turned out that Peter only lived in the street next door to London Road. He offered me a lift home and I accepted it; he had a spare helmet in his bag. Peter worked as an engineer and was bike-crazy. He had three bikes and kept them all ready for the road. As he started the bike I climbed up behind him. I had to put my arms around his waist, and as we pulled away from the kerb and sped off down the road I held on tight. Peter's body was warm, and down in my groin I stirred. I rested my head on his back. He was so much like Simon.

The journey was soon over, and when Peter brought me back to the gate I invited him in for a drink. He said he had to get back to his wife, as she'd be worried. It hadn't crossed my mind that he'd be married, but we agreed to meet the following day at about six o'clock to go for a run on the bike. I went into the house. Helena was in bed, and I didn't fancy sleeping with her, so I crept into the spare room.

The following day we ended up in a little country pub where we were the only customers. Peter talked about his wife and two children. He had two girls, slightly older than my two boys. Judging by the way he spoke, he seemed dead straight. I let him believe that I was the same.

We had a very pleasant evening, and I was sorry it had to end. Peter hadn't been in Nottingham long, and had only moved there because of his job. I asked him to bring his wife and kids round the following Sunday for tea. It would be good for Helena to make a new friend. I knew that I must keep my feelings to myself. Peter would never accept my old way of life, and I'd rather just have him as a friend than never see him again. But all evening I'd thought of his likeness to Simon, and twice nearly called him by my former lover's name.

By the Sunday, Helena was looking forward to meeting Mary as much as I was looking forward to seeing Peter again. When they arrived, Mary's beauty astounded me – I had never seen such a good-looking woman, and Peter seemed so proud of her. Yet, underneath, something was wrong.

The kids got on well together, and Helena had made me such a nice spread. She had really put herself out. She and Mary struck up an instant friendship; I had never seen Helena be so cordial with anyone. The girls were arranging to go out shopping one afternoon, so once tea was over Peter and I slipped out to the pub. He seemed a little subdued, and I asked him what was wrong. He didn't want to talk about it at first, but after a few drinks he became more amiable. It turned out that Mary was money-mad, and spent Peter's money as quickly as it came into the house. He also thought she was having an affair with an antique dealer. I tried to cheer him up but he was very depressed. I wanted to take him into my arms and comfort him; but that was impossible. I told him that he'd made a friend in me, and that I would stand by him if I was needed. He sounded grateful, and that evening we became even closer.

Mary and Helena took to going out together nearly every day. Mary was definitely a bad influence; no wonder Peter was upset. Helena was always asking me for more money. She wanted new clothes. The boys were happier, though, and enjoyed playing with Beverley and Joanne, Peter's little girls.

I met Peter two or three times a week for nearly three months, and became very fond of him. It was very difficult to control my emotions, but I did. We spent hours riding about in the country and visiting country pubs, and stripping down and rebuilding one of Pete's bikes. I even took one of the bikes on the road one night, with Peter riding another bike behind me in case anything went wrong. It was an amazing experience being in control of a Norton Commando, speeding down the road with 750cc throbbing between my legs.

We drove back into Nottingham that evening before we went for a drink, as I hadn't wanted to drink while driving. The bike had really turned me on, and I was feeling as randy as hell. I was washing my face in the bathroom when Peter walked in and started having a pee. I couldn't help but watch him, and he didn't seem to think it was odd. When we sent down to the pub I drank far more than I'd ever done in Pete's company before. He was aware that something was disturbing me, and tried to coax it out of me, but at first I would not give in. Inside I felt as though I was being ripped apart. I hated my wife, but I loved my children and I loved Pete. Yet, while the children were mine, Pete belonged to Mary.

Peter wasn't put off very easily; and I eventually told him that I was gay. He told me that he found it difficult to understand but was sure that I would be cured in time. That wasn't enough. I had to tell him that I loved him.

He was shocked, and the expression on his face showed it. He seemed to step back from me a few feet, and tried to keep me at arm's length. I knew straight away that I'd done the wrong thing. I felt sick. I wanted to throw up. I wanted to turn the clock back just two minutes; then I would have kept my big mouth shut. I ran away from Peter. I couldn't stand to look back at the distaste on his face. I went home, into the spare bedroom where I'd slept for the last three months, and cried myself to sleep. I prayed that Peter would come round at the weekend as usual, and that he wouldn't treat me any differently.

When the time came for Peter to visit, only Mary and the kids came round. Peter had made excuses that he was very busy. It was obvious that he hadn't mentioned anything to Mary, but I was hurt by his actions. I went out and got so drunk that by nine o'clock I was falling about; when I got home, Mary was still there. She helped Helena put me to bed. Helena started screaming that I shouldn't come home in such a condition – especially in front of the children. I was too pissed to answer and I went on behaving in the same way most nights. My relationship with my wife, never good, got decidedly worse. Every minute was spent rowing and fighting. I craved to see Peter again and wrote him several letters, but it was nearly three weeks before he came round.

Helena opened the front door and called that Peter was there. I half-rose from my chair, my heart beating at an extraordinary rate. Peter smiled at me as he entered the lounge, and sat down on the settee by the fire. I offered him a drink but he declined. He seemed rather edgy as Helena came in, and at the first opportunity hinted that we should go out for a drink, as he wanted to talk to me alone. I, too, wanted no more than to be alone with him. I wanted to apologise to him. I wanted to tell him to forget all that I had said. I just wanted to secure his friendship; I had missed him so much over the last few weeks.

We sat in a small pub and talked for ages. Peter no longer considered my homosexuality a problem. He said that he'd missed my company, and my being gay shouldn't affect our friendship. Once we'd sorted that out, we talked quite freely. Peter wanted to know how on earth I could possibly be in love with him. I explained that was how I felt inside my heart. He smiled and held my hand and told me that it was nice to know someone thought so much of him. I told him that I couldn't cope with life at home any more. How could I live as a father and a husband when I was in love with another man? I had decided I would leave Helena, and told Peter that I was going to live in London again. I should never have got married in the first place, Peter promised to write, and to visit me as often as possible. He seemed very understanding, and in those four hours together we had re-established our good friendship. When I left, though, I felt more in love with him than I had done before.

I didn't tell Helena that I was leaving, and waited until she was out with Mary one day before packing and going. It was a heartbreaking decision to make. I loved my children so much and so deeply that it hurt. But I wasn't fit to be their father. I was gay; what good would I ever do them? They needed a good father and a better chance in life.

As I closed the front door in London Road I realised that I was closing yet another door in my life. I felt like a gypsy, always moving on. I remember faltering at the gate with the image of our children playing on my mind. But I had to be strong, I was doing the right thing for us all. The further away from the house I walked the bigger the lump in my throat got. I felt totally gutted and it took a long time for the burden of guilt in my heart to lift. On reflection this was one of the hardest decisions I've ever made in my life but I certainly would not have become who I am today, if I had stayed there. I would have tried to be a good husband and a good father – I would have done my duty and waited until the children had flown the nest to start their own lives. Only then would I have contemplated changing my own life. Indeed, many transexuals are in this very position today, hiding their time and perhaps, even waiting for their partner to die.

I managed to get accommodation in Battersea, in south London. I was one of five guys, all gay, who shared a house together. The house was clean, and as I was alone, missing Peter and my children, it was nice to have other people around me. I got on so well with the other boys and often spoke to them of Peter. There were several photographs of us together, and they were my pride and joy. I always showed them to anybody I met for the first time.

I got a job in a factory as a chef. I was responsible for cooking for about five hundred people, so I always took plenty of food home for the gang. I kept their stomachs full, and I was known as Billy Bunter – the cook of 'em all.

The highlight of each night was when I settled down to write to

Peter. He replied to every letter, and phoned every other day. After I'd been in London about four weeks, he rang me and said that Helena had suddenly packed her bags, left Nottingham and taken the children back to Amsterdam. I was relieved. At least her mother would ensure that the children were well looked after. He also said that he was coming down for a few days the following Friday. I contained my excitement until I put the phone down, then ran around the house telling all the boys that he was coming down to see me. One of them asked me where he was going to sleep. I hadn't really thought about it. I only had a single bed in my room, but we would just have to manage. I could always sleep on the floor.

I prepared a special meal for Peter's arrival. I was very excited, and when he eventually came I gave him a big hug. He held me back and smiled at me and called me a silly prat. We ate, and then I took him down to one of the gays clubs I'd started frequenting in Earls Court. I thought it better to warn him beforehand; he didn't seem to mind, so we took him down to the Masquerade club.

We had a fabulous night. Peter was amazed as he stood and watched all the gays dancing together. We drank at the bar until about two a.m. As the dances slowed down, Peter asked me if I wanted to dance. He knew it was what I really wanted. We danced, holding each other really close. Two of the guys I lived with gave us a lift home in their car. We hadn't talked about sleeping arrangements, and we didn't until we were behind my bedroom door.

Peter started to undress and got into bed. I undressed, pulled two blankets around me and lay on the floor. I turned off the bedside lamp. I dearly wanted to climb in bed beside Peter and just hold him. I didn't want sex; I just wanted to feel the warmth of his body. I lay in the dark on the hard floor for what seemed an age. I just couldn't sleep.

Peter asked me several times if I was all right. I said I was, but after a short while he insisted that I share the bed with him. He couldn't see why I was sleeping on the floor. He said he trusted me and knew that I wouldn't upset him in any way. I knew what he meant, but wasn't so confident of my actions. I eventually got into bed and lay with my back against Peter. He put his arms around me and held me tight. I had a prominent erection and found it impossible to sleep, but Peter snored on contentedly behind me.

We spent all Saturday visiting the sights and shopping in the West End. Saturday night went as well as Friday had, but we also took in a drag show. That had Peter in hysterics. He didn't believe that the hideous sight on stage was really a man. That night we slept together again.

The weekend flew past. The following morning we were invited by one of the boys in the house down to the Pig and Whistle pub in Belgravia. It was a fabulous gay haunt, very famous – although like many other gay pubs, it was only gay on Sunday mornings. We both had a little too much to drink, and I suggested that an hour in bed would do us both good. I was first in. It was good to feel Peter's body pressing up against me. He had his hand on my stomach, and slowly started to stroke me. His hand slid down to caress my private parts. At first I thought I was dreaming; the sensations were gushing through my body and I could hardly contain myself. I turned to face Peter and he just lowered his eyes. He too had an erection, and I touched him slowly, caressing him. Then I started to kiss him from head to foot. His body reacted to every caress and every kiss. The more excited he got, the more I touched him. Without our even realising how we'd got into such a state, Peter was screwing me, holding and clinging on to me. I was so happy as I felt him thrusting deep inside me that I started to cry. He was lying on the bed on his back and I was straddling him. He reached up, brushed the tears away from my eyes and pulled my head down towards him. He kissed me in a way that I'd never been kissed before. It sent a tingling sensation running through my whole body. My tongue sought deeper into his mouth, and his tongue flicked about mine.

Peter eventually climaxed, and I collapsed sobbing into his arms. He comforted me and we slept. I woke with a start; my legs were entwined with Peter's, and I was lying half across his naked body. I too was naked, and the memories started to flood my brain. I wondered if Peter would feel the same way when the drink had worn off. It took ages before he opened his eyes.

Then he started to stroke my hair and just held me tight. We kissed for ages and ages, then eventually got out of bed and had a shower together.

Peter had to leave at six the following morning, so we didn't go out that Sunday night. We went up to bed and experimented with all kinds of things. They were all new to Peter and he enjoyed them all. The only thing he couldn't stand was when I squeezed his bum. It must have been a threat to his masculinity, as he always pulled away.

We didn't sleep all night, but what fun we had. Peter got into the bath at about four a.m. I went to clean his back and ended up in the bath with him. We giggled, but once back in the bedroom we both knew that it would be ending. He had to go back to his wife. As he dressed I lay in bed watching him. We didn't talk about the next time; I wasn't even sure whether there would be a next time or not. I just smiled and encouraged him as he dressed. After a quick good-bye kiss, Peter left the bedroom and went downstairs. I went to the

131

window and watched. Peter mounted his bike. I couldn't contain myself. I opened the window and waved as he disappeared down the street. I felt a heavy load had been laid upon my heart. I prayed to God that I would see him again, and see him soon.

Nearly a week passed before I heard from Peter. It was a nine-page letter. He apologised for his actions over the weekend, and hoped I wasn't annoyed with him. He finished with a little foot-note: 'Thanks for the good time.' After rereading the letter, I was sure that I would never see him or hear from him again. I wrote him a short note, just saying that he'd made me very happy at the week-end, and that I would miss him dearly and there would always be a place for him in my life and in my heart.

I didn't hear any more for about two weeks. Then, one night, I was sitting watching television when I heard a bike draw up outside the house. Every time I heard a bike, I thought it was Peter; but this sound was followed by a ring on our doorbell. I was the only one in, so I went to answer it. I couldn't believe my eyes. There was Peter with a case in his hand. I threw my arms around his neck and started gabbling out questions. He just pushed me aside, closed the door, pulled me towards him and held me tight.

He had been very upset about our activities the weekend he'd been down, and he'd promised himself that he'd never see me again. Then, all of a sudden, Mary had left him, taking the kids, and gone to live with her antique dealer. Peter hadn't known which way to turn. He'd tried desperately to get her back and when he had realised it was no good he had vowed he would never get involved with a woman again. Therefore he'd packed in his job, and he wanted to know if I was able to help him. He wanted me to show him how to appreciate gay love, and the gay scene. He asked me to be patient and said he would try to be a good pupil. He only wanted to learn how to love me as much as I loved him.

Chapter 14
Girls for Sale

Having Peter around me was very refreshing. A new wind had swept into my life and blown all the fears and cobwebs away. It was touching to feel wanted.

Peter soon got a job in engineering, and I used to love rushing home to prepare dinner for him. The minute he took off a shirt or a dirty pair of socks, I was there, and had them washed and ironed before he even realised it. Peter loved it; even his wife had never treated him like this. I couldn't do enough for him. I became so possessive that I was terrified of losing him. For the first two weeks of Peter's time in London we never ventured out, but used up curl up in front of the fire and just talk ourselves to death. I felt very self-satisfied. Peter was all I really needed, and all the false, plastic people I knew were swept aside. But I made the big mistake of sweeping away some loyal friends as well.

From the day Peter returned he refused to have sex. When, in desperation, I questioned him about it, he told me that he was very mixed up, especially now Mary had left him. Although we'd had sex before he left Nottingham, he felt he had pushed himself too early. He assured me that he would eventually be able to make love to me with true feelings; but what, he asked, was the use of just pretending? He would only be hurting us both. His words touched me, and at least he had been honest with me.

After two weeks, sex still hadn't happened between us, and my frustrations had reached their peak and started to ebb away. I felt content enough just holding and cuddling him. He did the cutest things for me. It may sound silly, but I really enjoyed it when he knelt by my side in bed and massaged my back, and whispered silly things in my ear at the most unusual times. We used to send each other telegrams and cards for no reason, each trying desperately to prove he loved the other.

At the weekends we used to go shopping in the West End. The big stores such as Harrods and Selfridges terrified him – not because of their size, but because of the fact that once inside I didn't know when to stop spending! When we walked in the street together we used to clown about, and always seemed to be laughing together. We never had a cross word, and even when I made the most obvious blunder, Peter would just smile and say, 'Don't worry.' Once I was sure he didn't mind, I felt a lot better. People on the street must have thought we were nuts – we walked hand-in-hand, and it was obvious that we were both males; in those days homosexuality wasn't really openly displayed. But I was damned if anyone's criticism was going to stop my happiness. Occasionally people catcalled, but, the minute we stopped and faced the challenge, the challengers disappeared. One could be gay, but people didn't like you to be able to stand up for yourself and prove it.

After a month or so we started visiting the many gay pubs and clubs that had suddenly started opening up. After having had a limited social scene, the gay world seemed to be growing every day. No sooner would we visit a new club than an invite to another was given to us as we were leaving. Pubs became popular, and the established gay bars began competing with each other. At last a part of society had realised there was money to be had from poofs. I'm not sure whether that was a good thing or not. Gays came out more and more, but queer-bashing increased drastically, and some of us had to pay. Luckily Peter and I never got involved in any scuffles, and at night we mingled and tried to act as normally as possible on the street. Most of the time we travelled on the bike to gay pubs, but we avoided the heavy bike scene.

It was surprising how quickly the gay scene split into different categories. If you were gay, there was a place for you. The leather boys and bikers congregated in the Coleherne in Earls Court, the camp in the Green Man in Euston Road and the Boltons in Earls Court. The drag scene revolved around the Vauxhall Tavern, the Elephant and Castle and the Black Cap in Camden Town. The rent boys all used the Golden Lion in Dean Street, whilst the piss-elegant were at the King William IV in Hampstead or the Pig and Whistle in Belgravia. The cruisers all drank in the Queen's Head, the Champions, or the theatricals in the Salisbury on St Martin's Lane, mingling with the tourists. The old queens visited the City of Quebec in Marble Arch, fondly known as the Elephant's Graveyard. These were just a few of the many pubs, and each section had several clubs to match their tastes. Even perverts and deprived ones had a look-in late at night. There was a little club in the King's Road where people all crammed into the cellar. There was a coffee-bar – no alcohol, but people masturbated or fucked against the walls in the midst of a crushing crowd who just looked on. Or those people just went walking up and down Holland Park for hours, or on Hampstead Heath, until they found the sex they were so desperately searching for.

Peter and myself had an open mind when we visited most of these places. It was obvious that most of the pubs and clubs were rip-offs, and only the nicer side of the scene ever employed gays. Queens always used to terrify Peter. They had only to flash their eyes or wiggle their bums and he'd come running back towards me. Many times I egged him on, telling him that someone was deliberately watching his every movement and even following him when he went to the toilet. He ended up so frightened that he wouldn't even go to the toilet without me.

I had become bored with work. I would just stand in a steamy kitchen all day, waiting to feed the hungry 500, checking that the meat was tender, the vegetables cooked and the apple pies browned enough. I was bored and under-paid. Life was more exciting at home, so going into an everyday job was no fun at all. But if my work was affected, in time my home life would take a bashing. I had to find something new. The idea of interviewing appealed to me, and I soon secured a job with Reed Employment in a small office in Edgware Road.

After a week in that office I felt trapped. I wasn't used to a desk job, and all I really knew about was catering. I ran the catering section, but the agency's rules and regulations were very tight. I was able to offer only appointments paying £3,000 and over. Many people came in desperate for work, but the hotels – even though they were crying out for staff – paid only a third of that. The girls I worked with bitterly complained about one another when the others' backs were turned, and I spent my last day telephoning round to find a good job for myself.

I ended up being interviewed for another position, through an agency that specialised in catering staff. Jane, the manager, wasn't as I'd imagined her. During our conversation on the telephone she'd sounded very efficient. In the flesh she was only four foot six, yet she ran the first branch the firm had opened. She specialised in beauty-trade and shop staff. She was immaculately groomed; her hair and make-up were done to perfection. She explained that her boss wanted to expand the agency's business by going into catering. I knew enough about catering to convince Jane, and ended up on a short-list of three. She asked me if I could meet her boss in the roof-top restaurant at the Hilton. I made sure I looked my best. Whoever her boss was, I wanted to impress him. The money was good and the commission even better.

I was surprised when I met him. He couldn't have been more than five years older than myself. His handmade suit and shoes were impressive, and he had a suave, sophisticated air. We sat and ate an impressive meal and discussed catering. It was obvious that he didn't know a *chef de rang* from a chambermaid. I was in my element, and impressed him enough to be offered the position there and then. I was to work in Oxford Street to start with, while the new offices in Earls Court were being decorated. I left the Hilton that afternoon with a new aim in life. If I played my cards right, I could earn a fortune. All I had to do was to keep him happy. For money, I could keep anyone happy.

My first few days in Oxford Street were closely scrutinised by Jane. I contacted most of the personnel management in the central London hotels, and started laying out my new track record. Business was good. The boss was very attentive too, and I must have looked keen enough to him, because the following evening he asked me to dinner. I was to be propositioned in a way that I'd never been propositioned before.

He had decided to take me into his confidence. He was sure that before very long I would find out anyway about the other business that he operated from Earls Court. The catering agency was to be a legitimate business run from the ground-floor offices. But it was a cover for a massage-and-prostitution racket run from the floors above. During the day my offices were open for the usual employment-agency business. Upstairs, two women manned a series of telephones, and occasionally a young girl would ask for Annette. That was the password to let someone up. Anyone sitting in the office would notice nothing out of the ordinary.

I had my doubts about the practices upstairs, but for the first month or two I kept very quiet. The catering business took off. Numerous hotels were opening up in the area, and we had a number of advertisements in the *Evening Standard* and the *Evening News*, and my office was continually full of chambermaids. Sometimes they were homeless. It wasn't long before I realised that some of these girls could be an asset to the business upstairs, and one evening I asked the boss if I could have a word with him. He just smiled and told me that he had expected me to come to that conclusion; and that evening I was taken up to meet the people who worked in the offices upstairs. I'd never been upstairs before. There were just two bare offices with four desks covered with telephones. Annette was the elder of the two women there. She turned out to be the boss's mother, the real brains behind the business, and for many years a prostitute herself. She was about forty-five, dark-haired and unkempt. The big bags under her eyes proved that she worked late every night. No wonder she wasn't fit to earn money as a prostitute any more. The other woman, Sophie, was the boss's girlfriend, a pretty girl with long blond hair. I could see why he was attracted to her.

I spent the next four hours talking to Annette, and was to hear all kinds of revelations besides seeing the office transferred into one of the busiest areas of full pretty women I'd ever seen. They stood about the room, and all the chairs were full. There was a steady flow of girls in and out of the offices. Annette and Sophie continually answered the telephones, and the many names they mentioned as they answered confused me.

It turned out that there were different businesses, with twelve different names and twelve different telephones. The boss knew a telephone engineer who ran in different lines when they were needed, and he often advertised a new company and just stuck on another name. Each phone had a name printed across it – Karen,

Angels, Goddess, Handy Girls, Screw Girls and Come Play With Me were just a few of them. Each service had a set price. When a customer rang on the Goddess phone and was told twenty pounds, he would invariably hang up. Then he'd ring another; his voice would be recognised and he would be told £25. Before long he would ring back to Goddess to book one of the girls at twenty pounds. Whatever he did, the firm got the business. They were un-scrupulous people.

It all looked disorganised, but it was the most organised prostitu-tion I'd ever seen. Annette told me about the type of girls she wanted. Once they were selected, Annette took them round to her small flat and trained them to use massage. Her training took only about an hour. Eventually I had the chance of going round and see-ing just what the girls were taught. All the methods led to sexual arousal, and invariably the girls ended up giving a 'relief massage'. They were told quite openly that it was expected of them for the price; if they wanted to go further, they would have to charge more and stick in their own pockets.

The boss also have several drivers driving his best girls around town. The collecting of cash and setting-up of the best girls in good apartments was well organised. One of the girls had appeared on an album cover, which she proudly showed me. She was totally naked and surrounded by tropical fruit. The album was called *Juicy Lucy*. For me it was just a chance to earn extra money. I told Peter what was happening; he advised me to be careful, but said that if I wanted to get involved he had no objection.

At first, I only enticed the girls who were homeless and appeared to have no family. It was obvious from the start that they didn't mind. They went straight into established apartments with a good income, and all they had to do was lie on their backs for an hour or two every evening. Most of the girls were grateful to have a roof over their heads, but they had to be prepared to do anything with-out asking too many questions. I'd had to do the same myself in the past. On reflection, we really took advantage of those girls. We caught them at their lowest ebb and then degraded their bodies by sending round a continual stream of sordid men, eager to pay for their services. But they did know what they were letting themselves in for. No-one forcibly held them down. They could have walked away at any time and some did. Others, believe it or not, were grateful and would tip us in the office to make sure we sent them the better clients.

Annette was pleased with the girls I sent her, and after a day downstairs sending out staff I started going up to help her with other business. Within a month or two I ended up manning the tele-phones along with Annette and the boss. Business was good upstairs, and since it was the tourist season all the advertisements in *Where to Go* and the porno magazines kept the phones ringing constantly. There were always plenty of heavy breathers and crank calls, and I always weeded those out to save the girls bother. I used to give the poor guys on the other end of the phone as good as they gave me.

It was policy to check out the phone number when a guy wanted a girl. He would ring and book, and then we would ring back, confirm his booking and arrange the details – the girl's size, colour, etc.

The boss was a shrewd guy. He also had a lot of the night porters in the top London hotels on his books. If someone made enquiries of one of them as to where to get a girl, he was given a card. The porters could earn up to a fiver a time for their services, especially in central London. For each hotel there was a special entry, and once the porter was alerted he used to meet the girls and take them up to the rooms. If no porter was established, the office had floor-plans of the hotel, showing where all the rooms were, so that a girl could check which floor she was going to and didn't have to keep the customer waiting. God knows how the boss accumulated all this information! But it was always right.

Within seconds of a call coming in, we knew exactly where the customer was going to, and we used to find out exactly what he wanted. It used to be really funny – all the kinks and cranks wanting girls to dress up as schoolgirls; but then again, the boss had girls who dressed as schoolgirls, so they were sent. For some hotels it was easy – we had chambermaids already established through the staff agency. Most of them lived in, so it took only a phone-call to get them out of their bed and tell them to go down and look after the customers. And the last word was that many of the girls even carried radio bleeps, paid for by the firm.

The boss went round telling everyone that he belonged to the SAS. He was a good-looking guy with the athletic build of an ex-marine. One day I was at my desk, just after opening time on Monday, when he asked me to give him a hand in counting some money. The cash was bundled into one-thousand-pound piles, and I checked the piles that were placed in my drawer. I had nearly eight thousand pounds. When I was sure I'd put it all by I called him out of the back office. He called it his weekend money. He had been counting too, and as he opened his briefcase I couldn't help noticing the gun that lay on top of the hundreds of pounds already stacked in the bag. He just tapped the weapon reassuringly and told me it kept him out of trouble. It wasn't the last time I saw the gun. Whenever he went out on business to the West End, he carried it.

That incident frightened me a bit, but the extra cash helped me and Peter to set up in our own flat. I could always buy him presents – he loved it. We ate the best food and drank the best wine. When I told Pete what had happened, he asked me to leave, but I felt too involved. I got on well with the boss and couldn't see any reason why he should try to harm me.

One day we were in the office when the boss brought in quite a scruffy girl. She had an attractive face, but her hair, make-up and clothes were a right mess. Annette told him to get rid of her because she couldn't use her. But he thought that after she'd been cleaned up she'd be all right. Siding with him as I always did, I told Annette that it was possible. I said that once her hair was washed and she was dressed properly she'd be as good as all the other girls. Annette was unimpressed, but I was determined to prove to her that it could be done. The young girl was close to desperation, and needed a break. That evening I took her home; once she'd been bathed and had her hair cut she looked a completely different girl.

When I took her back to the office the following evening, Annette could hardly believe it. The girl had on a bright new dress and looked a proper little treat. The boss was very impressed, and from that moment I was told that I was the Goddess mother and it was my job to tell the girls how to wear their hair and make-up. Each girl had her own assets, but some of them just didn't know how to use them. It wasn't long before I was teaching them how to massage as well. I became far more involved with the seedy side of the firm. But the money was good.

Every new girl after that was put through my hands. I began to neglect Peter, spending many nights asleep on the floor in the office after working late. It annoyed him, but there was nothing sexual for me to return home to, so money was my main concern. The more I earned, the more I wanted. When we did meet at home, we used to have rows and end up close to blows. Yet I desperately loved Peter, and tried to tell him so. I thought the best way to sort out our problem was to write to him, so I wrote and told him that I was sexually frustrated, and it was no wonder our relationship was breaking up. The letter must have played on Peter's mind, because shortly after that he started to become more sexually active and interesting.

On several occasions the customers asked for males, but Annette used to turn them down. One day I answered the phone and went out on a booking myself. It was in the Dorchester hotel. Luckily we knew a night porter there, so he showed me up to the right room. As I went in, I was amazed to see the huge block of flab that lay on the bed. He was American, and I was supposed to massage him. All I could do was to roll the fat about. It turned out that he wanted oral sex. I told them that it was thirty pounds on top of the fee, and he paid without any question. I got the job over with as soon as possible. After that little episode I carried a bleep and occasionally went out with other clients whenever the boss or Annette called me.

One night the boss phoned me up, sounding as though he was having a laughing fit. He asked me to come round to the office straight away. I dived out of bed, dressed, called a cab and was at the office within an hour. I soon found out that a regular customer wanted two men and six girls to go to his home for a one-hour booking. Once everyone was assembled and on their way, the boss explained to me what was about to happen. He had done this journey several times. We were to visit a retired general who lived in Chelsea, one of the most expensive parts of London. The booking was costing three hundred quid, so he wanted to keep the old boy happy. I thought he was joking about what was going to happen, but I soon found out it was no joke.

We were escorted into the general's lounge. In came a woman clad in only thigh-length leather boots and a black hood over her head. The boss whispered that it was the general's secretary and personal housekeeper. Some housekeeper, I thought, with a whip tucked under her arm. We all sat on chesterfield sofas and admired the luxurious surroundings, while the secretary poured drinks from a beautiful bar in the corner. Most of the girls had made the journey before and weren't too perturbed about what was to come.

The general didn't look as old or frail as he had been made out. And he had an evil glint in his eyes as he surveyed all the girls. No one else – they just finished their drinks and followed the secretary out of the room. I followed the boss, not wanting to be left out of the proceedings. We ended up in a large bedroom with a circular bed and rugs in the middle of the floor. The boss and I sat on a seat at the far end of the room; the girls slowly stripped off behind the curtain and emerged into the room stark naked. All they were holding was an ostrich feather each in their right hands. They all stood on the bed, holding the feathers out in front of them. The lights were turned down and the old man came scurrying from behind the curtain, carrying a bag in one hand and a bunch of feathers in the other. The girls all knelt down on the floor while he lay on the bed.

From somewhere faint music was being played. I could also hear the distinct sound of chickens clucking. It wasn't obvious at first, but it was the girls walking round the bed who were making the noises. They were flicking the old man with the feathers they held. Slowly he got an erection. When it looked as though he had reached his peak, all hell broke loose. The lights in the room all flashed, and it sounded as though it were raining very heavily. Once the lights had settled down again, I could see that the old man was kneeling in the bed, throwing seed out of the bag on to the floor. The girls dropped to their knees, clucking loudly like little hens. They all stuck the feathers in the clefts of their bums and ran around picking up the little bits of seed that he had thrown.

The old man was madly throwing himself about the bed, masturbating. He'd stuck the bunch of feathers between the cheek of his arse, and was crowing with all his might like an old cockerel. This seemed to go on forever, until he let out an almighty scream as he ejaculated. That was the cue for the boss and myself. We had to clap and shout congratulations as loudly as we could. The girls all joined in, until the old man took a bow and left the room through a side door. He looked completely exhausted.

Everyone was dressed and ready to leave within five minutes. The boss collected his three-hundred-pound fee and ushered us out into the waiting cars and back to the office. I listened dumb-founded as he explained the many ways the old man liked to climax. It seemed he booked sessions like this twice a week. Nobody ever knew what he was going to do next time until his secretary rang up and said what the new sexual adventure was going to be. I was to read in later years about the poor old general's downfall. The *Sunday People* was full of it one year, and the poor old guy and his secretary got a real slaying.

Peter had begun to demand more and more of my time, but I found that although I spent less time at work I could still earn enough money. One of the nights I did spend at work, however, was to change my feelings towards the boss.

He had a girl that had worked for him for six months. She'd been out the previous night and had earned about a hundred pounds, but had been so busy that she hadn't been able to bring the takings back into the office. Now she said she'd lost them. The boss swiped at her, grabbed her by the throat and pushed her up against the wall. Within seconds he turned into a vicious, clawing animal. It frightened me considerably. If I were to do anything wrong, I was sure I'd get the same treatment as the girl. The poor creature was flung to the ground, and he kicked and beat her for quite a long time. She left the office that evening unfit to go out and see any clients, and I don't think she was ever seen again.

The boss knew I was gay and having a relationship with Peter, so, when I told him Peter was complaining about me being out so late at night, he didn't mind me disappearing early. But, apart from that, I had a feeling something was wrong. There were two new girls working upstairs, and they used to ask me all kinds of questions about Annette and the boss – especially when they were out of the office. I avoided answering too many, but started to tread very carefully. There also seemed to be too many visits from the Kensington and Chelsea licensing authority. I had the feeling that the agencies were being more closely scrutinised than the firm would have wished. On several occasions I could have sworn I was being followed, and I became very suspicious of anyone coming into the office asking for a job and pleading that she was homeless. Especially if they were women and mentioned that they would love to find an easier way to earn a living.

My suspicions were confirmed one day when I saw the two new girls coming out of the back of Kensington police station. I knew then that things were getting too hot to handle, so that evening I took all my personal belongings from the office and never ventured to go back to work for the firm.

I told Peter of my doubts and fears when I got home that evening, and, when the boss telephoned the following day to ask why I hadn't turned up for work, Peter said I was ill. After a week of making excuses, he told him that I wouldn't be back – I had another job. I walked in fear of my life for three weeks after that, because I knew far more about the firm than was good for me. Therefore it was good to read in the *News of the World* one Sunday that the set-up wasn't all it claimed to be. It was well and truly smashed by the police, and the family were not heard of again. But I'm sure, since there is always prostitution and degradation in London, that they are involved in it somehow.

Looking back on that period of my life, I'm ashamed that I was involved in the corruption of decent young girls. Then again, I suppose I was also being corrupted – by the boss, the firm and all they stood for. It was rotten, and it stank. The main thing was that it was all over.

Chapter 15

Drag Queen

Over several nights Peter either did not come home at all or came in very late. I was convinced that he was seeing someone else and one night I erupted. We kicked, clawed and punched at each other. We said such cruel things to each other that night, that I still shudder when I think about it. He had been drinking and did not know his own strength, so that night I slept alone, not wanting him near me. The next morning I found a letter from him. My heart missed a beat as I tried to get the envelope open but things weren't as bad as I had thought, Peter was having the same identity problem as myself. He was sure he loved me, but had to prove to himself that he wasn't completely gay and could still screw a woman. On Monday night he had met a girl who had offered it to him on a plate, and he had screwed her at her flat. He'd stayed out every night since then because he'd felt so guilty. He asked me for forgive him, but to give him time to learn how to understand himself.

My feelings changed in an instant. I hadn't really given much thought to Peter's situation. He was, after all, a straight guy converted by me to become a citizen of a world that was despised by many. He had become an object of ridicule at work. His workmates knew about me and his wife, and all the tittle-tattle had got to him.

When the phone rang that afternoon I was surprised to hear his voice. He just said that he'd be home on time that evening in case I was cooking dinner. I tried to keep some control in my voice, but it was no use. Peter tried to calm me down, but all I could do was apologise and tell him how much I loved him.

Peter asked me a question I hadn't been expecting. He knew about my childhood, but he wanted to know about the happiest part of my life. Had I ever been really happy? I told him it was the day I had first met him; but he wanted to hear more than that. Without doubt my happiest moments were ones I hadn't disclosed to anyone. I tried to avoid answering at first, but when Peter pushed me, I began to tell him.

He occasionally nodded as I told him all about my life as Sandy. If I changed sex, he wondered, would I be a real woman. I thought I would be. Peter was sure that I'd be making a mistake; but then again, it would make him straight. That night in bed he continually teased me; as he screwed me he kept on saying that if only I had a fanny he wouldn't have to degrade himself by screwing my arse. Although I laughed with him, his jeers hurt me.

Not much was said about Sandy when Peter was about, but I constantly had the urge to dress once again. I eventually started buying new clothes and shoes. I was George first thing in the morning, and as soon as Peter went to work I dressed up before doing the household chores. They'd become boring jobs, but as Sandy I really enjoyed cleaning, dusting, washing, cooking and ironing. I worked my fingers to the bone. By five o'clock I was so worn out that I was glad to dress back as George again. But the more I dressed as Sandy, the harder it was to revert to George, and within a month I had got to a state of despair. Sandy's clothes, kept in a suitcase in the wardrobe, were sometimes only returned there just in time. I remember having to dive into the bathroom one evening as Peter came through the front door, pretending to have a bath and then wrapping all Sandy's clothes in a towel and hiding them.

I had a compulsive urge to show Peter what I looked like as Sandy. The thought of his rejecting me worried me, but one day the compulsion became too much. I dressed in my best clothes and headed over to his factory in Battersea. I stood outside the gates waiting for the hooter to sound. As five-thirty drew nearer I began to have doubts. I could have run home, and Peter would never have found out, but I stood rigid, unable to move.

Then I could see hundreds of men filing out of the gate, Peter among them. As he passed me I grabbed his arm. He turned and asked what I wanted. I just smiled, and Peter looked uncomfortable. Then he said, 'Do I know you?' I stood close to him and said, 'Well, you slept in my bed last night.' Peter seemed to step away from me into another world – it was as if time had stood still for me. Peter was talking away, but I couldn't hear him. All I knew was that he was surprised and I had fooled him. Then I became aware that we were arm in arm, walking away from the gate.

As we passed a bus-stop just by the car park where Peter had parked his bike, a man shouted out to Peter, 'Georgie wouldn't like it if he knew you were with a woman tonight.' Peter shouted to him to go fuck himself, then turned to me and smiled. I just started giggling. Getting on the bike proved difficult, though. I had a tight dress on, and had to hitch it right up to be able to ride on the back. I was showing more leg than was good for me, and several times whistles shrilled out as we passed Pete's workmates.

That evening Peter tried to explain how he had felt. He could only say that he thought I had guts to go on the street, but that it was uncanny how much I really looked like a woman. I didn't change back to George that evening, and I felt great as we sat cuddling on the couch. When it was time to go to bed, Pete helped me undress. He became excited as I removed my dress and he saw that I was wearing stockings with matching bra, suspender-belt and pants. It was obvious that he was horny, and foreplay that evening was a real turn-on as Peter rubbed the stocking and tweaked the suspender-belt.

I met Peter several times from work, and he often passed comments about what his workmates had said to him. He told them that I was a married woman, and they all thought he was a sex-maniac. A couple of them occasionally made passes as they left the factory gates while Peter was stuck in the clocking-out queue. I used to lead them on a little bit, so they jeered at Peter even more; but he loved it.

Dressing as Sandy didn't mean so much now, but I never went to bed without bra and suspenders. It had enhanced our sex life. I knew that once again I had trapped Peter, and that he wouldn't be looking around for other women again. We had something special; each caress was just passing on loving vibes. We were happier than we had ever been.

For me it had become a sexual fantasy. When Peter held me and touched me and screwed me, I was a woman, even though I had a male body. It didn't matter if I felt like a woman. I pretended I was Peter's wife, and used to think of all the good things we would do. The thought of having children aroused me and I insisted that Peter screwed me harder. If he did it hard enough, perhaps I'd become pregnant. I often complained of morning sickness. I think I was just trying too hard to have a baby, and wearing myself out. Peter just used to laugh.

One thing I was never allowed to do, however, was to go out with Peter socially as a woman. It was taboo. Even if friends were coming for dinner, I had to meet them as George. I wasn't allowed to introduce Sandy to anybody in case people thought we were perverted. Peter had really changed. It was all right to appear as homosexuals, but not as straights. This led to more rows. Peter was frightened in case I should suddenly give the game away and make him the object of more ridicule. He couldn't face going through the branding he had gone through when admitting to his homosexuality only a few months earlier.

One row led to Peter actually striking me for the first time as Sandy. I felt hurt. The blow itself hadn't worried me, but the fact that he could raise his hand at all had. He had hit me as Sandy, even though I wasn't dressed. It was Sandy we were arguing about. It was Sandy he didn't want to take out. He was rejecting the real me. He was saying no to my happiness, and for that I hated him.

Two friends of ours called round for a drink regularly twice a week, and the Porchester Hall ball became a talking point one evening. Phil and Brian were going along, as they had done for years. It was the drag ball of the year, and the Christmas follies attracted the most outrageous and glamorous of the gay world. When they invited us I jumped at the chance of going, but Peter was far more reserved. He wanted to know what we were expected to wear and do. Phil apparently hired a costume from Bermans & Nathans and went in drag every year. Brian just donned an evening suit and escorted him. Phil wasn't a transvestite, but used to like camping about at the balls.

Peter eventually agreed to go, so Phil and I arranged to go to Bermans the following Friday to hire our dresses. I had a field day there. The poor assistant didn't know which way to turn as Phil and I ravaged through the rows and rows of dresses and gowns. Phil insisted that the more outrageous we looked, the more fun we'd have. We decided to wear eighteenth-century-style ball-gowns with hoops. Phil looked a treat in his. The only one that fitted me had a six-foot train and looked big enough to present a Billy Smart's Circus spectacular underneath it; but it did look good. Phil decided on a powder wig with matching jewellery. I had the jewellery, and all I needed was a friend to comb up a couple of my wigs. Peter thought I looked a right idiot when I tried it on again that evening; but I didn't give a damn. I thought it looked great.

The following day I collected my wig from my hairdresser. It was amazing. He had attached every spare hairpiece he had in the shop, and when it stood on my head it looked like the Leaning Tower of Pisa. He had built in so many strings of beads and scarfs that it glistened. The only problem was to keep it upright on my head! Before I left the shop we tried tying it down, but nothing seemed to work. I was terribly disappointed, but Peter had a good idea when I got home – Bostik! And, believe it or not, it worked.

Once I had made up my face and fixed my hoops, Peter helped me climb into my gown. After fastening all the hooks and eyes, he helped me stick on the wig. No matter which mirror he held in front of me I could neither see the top of the wig nor the bottom of the dress. My make-up was outrageous and I was heavily perfumed.

We had agreed to meet Phil and Brian outside the hall at nine p.m. Our trouble really began when the taxi came to pick us up. I tried for five minutes to get in. I went in head first, then on my bum, but even that didn't work. I ended up getting in through the back door behind the driver and kneeling on the seat with my head hanging in the front passenger seat. Peter pushed in the rest of my gown, then struggled into the back seat with me. It was so uncomfortable. The poor driver didn't dare take his eyes off the road. It seemed to take hours to get to Queensway. Luckily, Brian and Phil were waiting for us; but it took them all nearly ten minutes to work me out of the back door.

At last, with feet planted firmly on the ground, I smoothed out my regalia and held my head high. Phil and Brian were laughing so much they were nearly doubled up. I turned to Peter as he finished dusting himself off, and he too started laughing. I turned my head from Peter to the boys, and back to Peter. Then I realised that something was drastically wrong. Part of my hairpiece had come adrift. We scurried through the doors and into the ladies' toilet to do a repair job. When I looked in the mirror I could have cried – the top half of my wig looked as though someone had sliced through it with a knife.

However, with the help of the assistant in the toilet I did a good repair job. Then it was up into the sparkle and intrigue of the upstairs hall. Old queens strutted about like stuffed chickens – most looked as though the dresses had been layered on to them. The make-up piled on top of wrinkled layers of skin looked abominable. People with their own particular fetishes loped around the room clad in leather bras and pants and rubber skirts. Those were the oddities of the ball, but the glamorous babes were present in greater numbers – young queens decked out from head to toe in sequins and beads, topped with feather head-dresses. Around the room were many familiar faces, as the male doubles of Marilyn Monroe, Marlene Dietrich, Rita Hayworth, Shirley Temple and Judy Garland strode about. Many were very convincing indeed.

I could pick out many sex-changes and transvestites among the male débutantes and drag queens. There was also the odd smattering of hetero-straights who seemed to be viewing the sights with utmost curiosity.

I had thought my dress would be a showpiece, but it was everyday wear compared to some of the glitter surrounding me. Nevertheless, the wig proved to be a highlight. Peter and Brian wouldn't dance with me, so Phil and I waltzed together – nearly taking over the floor. Every time we bumped into anyone our hooped dresses went sailing into the air, displaying our legs and panties to anyone who wanted to look.

The competition turned out to be the funniest part of the evening – for me, anyway. Phil convinced me that we should enter as the Hanover Square Sisters. We didn't stand a chance of winning, but anything for a giggle. The glamorous and the naive queued in line. Some of the sights were pitiful. Some I felt sorry for. Others made me sick with jealousy. Our turn came, and I didn't realise I was on a trip that was to change my life yet again.

As we stepped on to the stand, my hairpiece revealed a mind of its own. It separated exactly where we had repaired it; as everyone started laughing. I shook my head and the whole lot collapsed about my ears. I reached up to save it, trying to pull it off, but Phil pushed me down and I left the stage with head hidden up his dress. People all around me were in hysterics.

I ran to the toilet, and when I saw my face in the mirror I could understand why they were laughing. I looked like something out of a hair advert that had gone very wrong. It was so funny, I had to laugh myself. The wig was beyond repair, so I just left it. Peter told me I looked a bloody mess but, now the competition was over, people were telling me it was the funniest thing they had ever seen at a ball. Before we left, Roy Alvist and Danny O'Dell, two famous

London drag artists, called me over. They told me that they had a ladies' night at the Elephant and Castle pub by Vauxhall Bridge every Monday, and that if I wanted to do a bit on stage, I could go along any time. Me on stage – that was a joke! And Peter thought it even more so.

Me on stage, my name in lights. After all, I had seen some pretty bad shows by drag queens; perhaps I could do better. I might not be as glamorous as others, but at least I could try to be funny.

It took me a couple of weeks to get up the courage to go and even see the ladies'-night show at the Elephant and Castle. The pub was packed to the door. Roy and Danny attracted the crowd, and the ladies – I used the term loosely – gave them the laughs with their bad imitations of Dusty Springfield, Shirley Bassey, Susan Maugham, and so on. Just watching the show gave me the determination to give it a go. Roy and Danny asked anyone who wanted to get into next week's show to see them before leaving. Roy was the first to recognise me, and I agreed to do a number the following week. I didn't think that I'd be able to mime the first time, so I said I'd just have a dance if someone worked the lights.

When Peter found out what I was going to do, he was furious. Nevertheless, on the night of the show I put on my make-up with all the other ladies. Roy and Danny had their own dressing-room; we were stuck in a spare bedroom with an old mirror and a naked light-bulb. It was also bloody cold. Roy had told me to put on far more make-up than usual as I could be under stage lights. I was wearing a very short dress and very high shoes. My legs were my asset, and I knew it.

I didn't have a name so I was lumbered with Go-Go Girl Lil. Then the stage was mine. The number struck up and I danced with all my might in front of a packed pub. Peter was right at the front and kept pulling faces to try and put me off. But the crowd cheered as I cocked my leg in the air, and a roar broke out as I fell backwards into the drum-kit, sending cymbals flying through the air. In three minutes I had succeeded in wrecking the stage and upsetting the drummer – but the crowd were in hysterics. I was getting an ovation, and the poor cow who followed me could hardly hear her music as the crowd called out for more.

Roy was delighted. I had planned on doing only one number, but he asked me to close the second half with Lulu singing a version of the hit 'Satisfaction'. I knew most of the words, as the Rolling Stones were a favourite pop group of mine. I stayed in the audience with Pete until it was time to reappear.

The minute I got the first words out my mind went blank. I didn't know what to do. So I picked up the mike and started to rub my hand up and down it in a very suggestive way. The crowd cheered me on, so I grabbed a bottle off the bar, stood on the stage and simulated a love act. The number ended, but the crowd still screamed for more, so Roy re-ran the tape. I was holding the whole finale up. I had been suggestive the first time, so this time I went even further. I went into the crowd and returned to the stage with a good-looking guy hanging over my shoulder. I then slowly removed his top clothes, making suggestive passes. The guy was loving it, and I ended up on the floor on top of him. People all round the stage were being pushed forward as those at the back tried to see more. I was glad to get off after I had taken about six bows.

During the finale Roy introduced us all back on to the stage one at a time. I was the last to be called: Danny had changed my name again – this time to Mad Lily. The crowd loved it. I had been a hit and was on a high all the way home. Even Peter had thrown his arms around my neck and congratulated me. As I lay in bed that night I thought of the applause. They had liked me. If I had tried to be glamorous I would have died the death; but to that gay audience I was sending women up gutless, and they loved it.

I became a regular at the Elephant after that, and very soon joined Roy and Danny at the Father Red Cap in Camberwell Green on Thursdays. There the stage was attached to a bar – so what does Mad Lily do? She goes up and down the bar dancing in between drinks and kicking her leg up at the bar-support. I only kicked my legs up at the bar-support once, though, because when I did I split my tights from toe to breakfast. The crowd loved it, but I nearly castrated myself.

It was at the Father Red Cap that I met Chas. He was in his fifties – but what a lovely guy. We hit it off straight away. Not sexually – Chas wasn't like that; he was just like my father, and even to this day if I'm in trouble he's one of the first I can ring. He didn't mind my being outrageous. It was good for trade at the Red Cap. Mad Lily was a crowd-puller. Then Chas left the Red Cap and moved in to take over as manager of the Elephant and Castle. Bill Murphy, the owner, knew Chas was good for trade. He attracted many people on the gay scene because he was such a nice guy. When I was talking with Chas one night after time, he offered me a booking. I thought he was joking. I hadn't really taken my drag seriously. But I had ended up doing four or five minutes a night, and the professionals were only doing two spots of about twenty minutes each and being paid good money for it. Why not? I didn't need glamour clothes. I was far better just rolling around in beer and an old evening-dress from an Oxfam shop.

We agreed on a date a few weeks ahead, and Roy helped me to

tape my first-ever show. It was no different from all the other glamour drag-queen shows – except that I was going to send the whole thing up. I had a gold coat and dress made up for my opening number. The rest would just be tat drag.

Roy and Danny, Phil and Brian and many more new-found friends were in the audience to cheer me on. I prayed to God that I wouldn't flop. (If I did, it would be Chas's fault!) All the well-wishers were amazed as I refused a drink and went on stage with only a Babycham inside me to give me the courage I needed. The lights went up.

I was no longer Go-Go Lil or Mad Lil. I was semi-pro. I was Georgie Gold, hence the gold outfit to open. Ethel Merman's 'Riding High' opened the show, followed up by a cod Bassey with NHS specs, a wig full of rollers, and blacked-out teeth. It was the original 'Kiss Me Honey Honey Kiss Me'. No flawless hand-movements and poncing; just the flat-footed gestures and expressions of a builder's labourer in pain. It went down a bomb. A send-up of a pregnant bride and an old Mother Superior singing 'The Nun's Chorus' heralded the climax of the show. To Yvonne Fair's 'It Should Have Been Me', I was decked out as an old woman with handbag and woolly cap. The bag went flying, the hat came off, the dress was badly ripped, and then I dived out of the pub on to a wall about ten yards from the door. The wall was about four feet high, and two feet wide and twenty yards long. As I made my way along it I managed to strip off the rest of the clothes, yet retain my knickers. Half the pub followed me out, screaming and laughing hysterically. Chas and Bill Murphy were on the stage, looking out through the window. The cars at the nearby intersection stopped whether the lights were red or not! I leapt back into the pub, took a bow and disappeared into the ladies' toilets to change for my final number, 'The Show Is Over' by Petula Clark. The audience were ecstatic. I was knackered, and the owner and Chas were delighted. I had caused a riot, and I stood on stage receiving applause for about ten minutes. Then Chas came on to the stage to do a closing number and assured the audience I would now be a regular weekly performer. I was a drag artist overnight.

Within two months I was working every major drag pub in London. Two nights at the Elephant and Castle, and one night each at the Vauxhall Tavern, the Castle Hotel in Lewisham, the Black Cap in Camden Town, the Royal Oak in Hammersmith, and the Wheatsheaf in Shepherds Bush. I was a riot wherever I went. Gone was the fashionable glamour drag. I started the new era of comic female impersonators, and became a firm favourite in most of the pubs I worked. I demanded more money than other acts, and usually got it, for my name generally ensured a full house. I have very fond memories of my drag days, as do many of the audiences that saw me work. I had a good following and, although the show changed very rarely, the old crowd brought their friends along feeling sure they would have a good laugh.

Drag was my life. I was soon doing early stag and hen shows and, late at night, the odd club. For me, my drag was serious. I deliberately sent up women because I was so jealous. I wanted to be a woman, but I knew I couldn't be one, so to send them up and perform like an idiot was my only escape. All the disillusion of my life was exhausted under the bright lights on stage, and I became as mad offstage as on.

It had its advantages. Peter and I were invited to many parties, where I was often the centre of attraction – the clown, the goon, the idiot. Peter admired my work on stage. He thought I had the making of a professional, and always helped me with my quick changes. Yet, socially, when I played the fool he hated it. We argued, and he always accused me of doing it to attract men.

In fact, I was happy with Peter; there was no need to look for other men. He was all I wanted. But there was always plenty of opportunity for having casual sex. It was the way of life on the gay scene. Sex was just sex, it meant nothing to either party, it was just a release of frustration, wham, bham thank you ma'am and sometimes you did not even know their name. Now, with the threat of aids some people are more cautious, but not all. However jealousy was a stepping-stone in our relationship, and when Peter threatened me one night I had to make a decision – either cut down on my shows, where I was happy, or finish with Peter. It took me several days of conflict to make up my mind; and I was soon to find out that I had made yet another blunder in my life.

Chapter 16
A Life of Crime

So Madame Drag Queen became too big for her boots. I was fast approaching my nineteenth birthday and I had heard it, seen it, done it all, but was never satisfied with my lot. I wanted to be bigger, better and I believed I could do anything, go anywhere and control anyone. I wanted to have a higher station in life, I wanted to be secure and for that I would have sold my very soul. The truth was, I was prepared to do anything to save myself, my relationship and my future.

At first it was a quick wank or blow-job backstage, but I was always left unsatisfied. I needed to feel a rough man groping and pulling at me. I needed a good screwing, so I began to get it, whether it was in a back garden or in the back of a car. Then I went home and slept with Peter. I never felt guilty about sleeping around! It was all right for me – but, if I had thought Peter had been doing it, I would have been most upset. The trouble was that I had let my stage character run into my own. I wanted to have my cake and also to eat it.

Every show I did ended up in a row between us; every party was ruined once we erupted and the fists and glasses started flying. When a party was dead, people used to hang around just to see our exhibition. It was normally Peter who started off our rowing; he became very jealous – a man had only to look at me and he was off. If I flirted, I was the one which got all the backlash; but then again, I flirted all the time. Our frequent party smashes caused me a lot of embarrassment, and I began to lose a lot of friends. The only way to win them back was to reciprocate and invite them to our place. We tended to fight less on home ground. It wasn't long before Sunday lunch with fifteen people became a regular feature in the flat. We provided everything, and it was never a cheap meal, either. I used to buy smoked salmon and lumps of roast beef at astronomical prices. There was a regular crowd that visited – and, after a while, they started taking advantage.

Peter had begun to drink very heavily. It got so bad that he was unable to get up for work in the morning, and if he did, he usually returned home drunk at lunchtime. I blamed myself; there was no reason for Peter to turn to drink unless he was having an identity problem again. But, when I questioned him, he turned violent and didn't want to talk about it. I tried desperately to help him. I tried hiding bottles of Scotch, but once he realised they were missing he would systematically smash up a room until they were returned. Even watering-down the Scotch didn't work – he noticed in a moment.

The emotional strain, however, was too much. While Peter was asleep I used to just lie in bed watching him. He was ruining his whole life. Many was the night I cried myself to sleep, ashamed of myself for letting him ever get into such a state – unable to help, unable to pull him back to a decent, sober life-style.

Even though I was earning large sums of money doing drag, it wasn't enough to pay our expenses – booze and entertaining were a drain on my reserves. Gone were my daily wages, along with

Peter's. There was a hundred pounds a week less coming in. I tried to cut down, but Peter wouldn't have it. If I didn't continue to buy him Scotch, he said I no longer loved him. If I tried to cut down our entertaining, he accused me of upsetting our friends. My bank-balance was taking a bashing and, when I received my monthly statement and found I was a thousand pounds overdrawn, I was frantic with worry. Peter was never sober enough to cope. I knew I had to pull something out of the hat. If the money ran out, Peter would run too – to the nearest queen that would pay his way for him.

While reading the *Evening Standard* one night I noticed a little advert for an assistant manager in a large hotel willing to use his own initiative and able to take control of staff. I sat and thought about it. Hotels have safes, safes have money and managers have keys. With these thoughts in mind, I telephoned for an interview the following day. The senior manager sounded jovial enough, and when I spoke of my past employment – all bullshit though it was – he asked to see me straight away. As I entered his office in my new black suit, bought on a credit account at Hepworths, he scrutinised me from head to toe. A very inefficient interview followed, and I was able to start work as assistant manager the following Sunday. All the references I gave him were false; so was my name and address.

When I reported for duty, I was taken on a brief tour of the hotel, introduced to senior staff and then left to my own devices. The Majestic Hotel had about eighty bedrooms and was in a prominent position on the Cromwell Road, next door to the West London Air Terminal. Most of the customers were Arabs and the place was pretty busy. Ten minutes after I arrived, the manager handed me the keys and said he would return at the end of my sift. And, sure enough, the safe key was amongst them.

The first thing I did was to find out which key belonged to which door. I was most interested in the spirit-cellar and the safe. The very same day I left the hotel with a hundred pounds out of the safe and four large bottles of Scotch in a bag for Peter. It was so easy – no one had noticed, just because I wore pin-striped trousers and a black jacket and walked around the place as though I owned it. I had been surprised at the reaction of the staff. You only had to suggest something and they would be off. People respectfully called me 'sir'. I loved it.

When I returned home that evening Peter pounced on the bottles, and after nearly finishing one he went round the flat hiding the rest. The hundred pounds went into my bottom drawer. No one would miss the Scotch until a stock check, but the money would be missed the following day. Nevertheless, I walked into work the next day without a care in the world. Yesterday's haul had been easy – that was just a trial. Next time I intended to clear the lot, safe and cellar.

The manager called me to his office as soon as I arrived and told me about the missing money. His suspicions lingered on the new re-receptionist who had been on the later shift with him. I breathed a sigh of relief. I was told to keep an eye on her and to report any strange happenings. If only the poor sod had known how I had set her up.

That afternoon a police officer called to investigate. I told him what I 'knew', and assured him that when I had handed over the keys the money in the safe had balanced with the ledger. The receptionist on my shift backed me up; we had checked it together. I had retrieved the money from the back of the safe while she went to the loo. The following evening the officer called in again. It was about nine p.m. and I was just about to have dinner in the dining room, so I asked him to join me. We sat and ate a leisurely meal and drank a bottle of wine, talking about each other's careers and how disgusting it was that someone could actually condescend to stealing.

The next few days passed by without any disasters. I had been asked to do a cellar stock-take, so I marked into the stock the couple of dozen bottles I had removed over the last few days. My big day was still to come, though. The manager was going away from Sunday teatime till Tuesday. I assured him I could cope, and that I didn't mind covering his shifts. When he left that Sunday evening, he didn't realise what he would be returning to.

During Sunday I packed up several boxes of spirits and took them home in a taxi. Peter was delighted. There was too much to even bother hiding it. I told him I would be returning later, so not to wait up for me. I knew that by eight o'clock he wouldn't even notice I was missing. That evening I covered my tracks carefully. I closed the bar dead on time and took the receptionist's receipts as usual. At about midnight an Arab arrived; he was a little the worse for wear, and a casino was worse off for his visit – he had won two thousand pounds in cash. I assured him it would be more secure in the safe until the morning; then he could take it to the bank. He agreed. I sealed the cash in a brown envelope and wrote in the receipt book 'One brown envelope, contents unknown'. The Arab signed without question when I explained that it was better not to record that there was such a large sum of cash inside.

Once everyone was accounted for and all the room keys had been checked in and out, I sent the night porter off to make me a couple of rounds of sandwiches. The kitchen was far enough away to give me time to open the safe and check the contents. As the porter disappeared from view, I grabbed my holdall from the office and dashed back to the safe under the reception desk. My heart was pounding enough to bust my ribs, and I could hardly get the key in the hole for shaking. But once I had the door open I scooped the safe clean – even the silver and copper: if I was going to be done for a pound, I might as well be done for a penny. Once the safe was secured again I sat by the switchboard and waited for the night porter to return.

God knows how I got through those sandwiches. I was a bag of nerves, hoping that nothing was out of place and praying to God that the night porter wouldn't notice the shake in my voice and the uncontrollable wobbling of my hands. After sitting around casually for twenty minutes I decided to call a cab to take me home. When it arrived I went into the office to collect my holdall. It was very heavy. I laid the master keys on the manager's table, and only then realised that there were a petty-cash tin and a dozen wage packets in the top drawer. I couldn't find the key, so I levered it open. The contents came to another two hundred pounds.

I got the cab to drop me at Ealing Broadway. I had a feeling that I had been discovered, and I looked over my shoulder several times to make sure we weren't being followed. Once in Ealing I felt better. I took another cab into the West End, and from the West End I got a minicab to run me home. I had travelled for nearly two hours – but I had done it. I was now a fully fledged criminal.

Peter was blotto when I got in, so I sat in front of the gas fire and counted the money. When I got to four thousand pounds I decided to check it again. I hadn't even begun to count the mountain of silver and copper. By six o'clock in the morning I had finished. £4,862.84.

I hid the money in a cupboard and took out a couple of hundred quid every few days. I still did my drag shows, but spent money as if it was going out of fashion – several rounds in a pub at ten pounds a time. It just disappeared. One evening I showed Peter a little cutting from the *Evening News*: 'Assistant manager hunted by Kensington police after stealing £7,000 from hotel'. The lousy bastard of a manager had bumped the money up a bit – and, when you're doing the town and eating in expensive restaurants and buying new clothes and drinking champagne for breakfast, five thousand doesn't last very long. In fact it was a little over three months before we were as broke as ever.

Peter had helped me spend every penny, never asking where the money was coming from and just expecting it to be there. Then, one night, we couldn't afford to go out, and he wanted to know why. I soon told him. His only reaction was, 'Well, if you can do it once you may as well do it again.' That was true enough, but I wasn't going into nick for supporting him. In fact, his comments incensed me. I decided enough was enough. Peter would never leave my life – it was just too cushy. So I decided to leave him.

It was a heartbreaking decision and I knew full well that I would miss him terribly. But I was becoming a good con man, and was able to get myself into a shared mews flat near Marble Arch. A gay guy rented the place and wanted someone to share his expenses. I told him I was a hotel manager and worked evening shifts. That way I could still do my drag shows, leaving everything at the Elephant and Castle with Chas and Gary. The guy didn't look the type who would want an outrageous drag queen living with him. We got on well enough in the flat, but he was always going on about music – he was a musical director. Not my type of acquaintance, but he travelled the world a lot, and was leaving for a tour quite soon. He was away long enough for me to cause havoc.

My drag shows were becoming boring and I now had lots of competition. New drag acts were springing up every week. I was still a firm favourite in south London, but the pubs in the north and west started presenting the cheaper, shoddier acts. I was becoming too expensive. I needed a new start in life, away from London. When my flatmate went on tour, a golden opportunity arose.

A mews flat – everyone wanted to rent a mews flat. It became my goldmine. Adverts appeared in the *Evening News* and *Standard* and on several billboards, offering a furnished mews flat to let at forty pounds a week. The phone never stopped ringing, and I had people calling every fifteen minutes. I had it very well organised – forty pounds was a reasonable rent for Marble Arch, so people didn't really worry about being hurried round the place quickly. At one time I was showing four couples round at once. They all left their names and were told to call back the following day. This went on for eight days, and I saw ninety different applicants. When they called back they were all told they could move in on the first of the following month, but that a hundred-pounds deposit was required. I was lucky – no two people bringing deposits ever met each other. Each depositor received a tenancy agreement and a front-door key. I ended up with £1,500 in cash and a pile of cheques. People parted with their money so easily.

I left the flat planning a new life in Eastbourne. I decided that rather than waste the money, I would get a living-in job and save up so that I could go straight. But I thought about the chaos that I had left behind me and on the first of the following month I couldn't resist paying a visit to the old flat. It was a silly thing to do, but I disguised myself enough not to be recognised.

I couldn't believe the sight that met me as I turned into the street leading to the mews. It was terrible. Police cars were stopping the traffic, and about twenty furniture vans were parked in the street. Furniture was scattered all over the road. I walked on the far side, not daring to get too close. People were shouting and screaming, kids were crying and the police were trying to take statements from everybody. I felt ashamed – it had all been a big joke, but I had caused so much misery for all those people. How could I have done a thing like that? It was callous of me. I hadn't given a damn about those people, and I vowed I would never again do anything that would hurt individuals.

I returned to the Queen's hotel in a terrible mood. As I went into my bedroom in the staff annexe, I cracked. The portable television I had bought with the cash I had defrauded went smashing up against the far wall; I broke records and wrenched the arm off the stereo. Then I went out to the nearest pub and got absolutely paralytic. The drink soothed me until I no longer despised myself. The next morning, though, my guilty conscience also had a hangover to contend with. I was in a foul mood for days, and regretted ever leaving London. Eastbourne was dead. It was out of season and the hotel was quiet. I was a waiter in the main dining-room and worked the top table with the restaurant manager during banquets. I was good at my job, but my job was unsatisfying. I started fooling around, then screwing around.

It was difficult living in the hotel and trying to lead a double life, so I got a flat close by, above a night-club. The guy who owned it was nice enough, and I eventually started working for him five nights a week. The hours fitted well into my spare time; my screwing around usually began with enticing big, butch, straight guys to stay in the club for a drink after hours when I was supposed to be locking up. Once I had got one drunk but not incapable, I made a pass. Ninety-five per cent of the time it worked, and I ended up being screwed gutless by some virgin heterosexual. At other times I overdid it a bit with the booze and ended up screwing the guys. They probably blamed the arse-ache on too much booze. The odd one or two rejected my passes straight away, so I didn't waste my time – I just showed them the door.

That club took a hammering. I fiddled a fortune, and was screwed over the bar, on the dance-floor and even over a beer-barrel. But it could not last. Stocks were being continually queried, but the owners thought it couldn't possibly have been me – I was much too nice a young man – so they confided their suspicions in me. They were sure it was the new barmaid. I confirmed that I had seen her fiddling, and she was sacked, poor cow. But things were getting hotter, and I felt trapped again. I had to run. I sold my new furniture and eventually disappeared with a night's takings. Back in London, socialising took its toll and after a few weeks I was broke yet again. The police were most certainly looking for me – and the sooner they caught me the better.

Caterer & Hotel-Keeper magazine was my life-saver. An assistant food and beverage manager was wanted at the Palace Hotel, Buxton, Derbyshire. I applied for the post, using the name of an ex-manager at the Queen's hotel. He had gone abroad, so I have the Queen's as a reference. No doubt I was recommended, for I was accepted two days later.

I started with a pompous air in my approach to the staff. They all thought I was an absolute bastard for complaining about the standard of hygiene and service. I left quite suddenly after a few days. I took over from the night manager at seven a.m. By eight a.m. I was on a train to London with £3,600 in my bag. By eleven p.m. I was on a train to Brighton. No guilty conscience this time.

Brighton was very refreshing. I booked into a small guesthouse, bought myself some fashionable clothes and settled into the gay scene. I had visited Brighton from London at weekends several times when I wasn't working. It was the 'in' thing to go down from town, especially on a Sunday lunchtime. All the gay pubs came alive. I changed my name to Paul Riley – new area, new identity. I was sure I would never be discovered. I drank well and ate well; but I soon discovered that no matter how much money you have, it's got to run out some time. I casually looked around for a suitable job; I didn't fancy working too hard. There was no emergency – I had a few hundred pounds left and I had made lots of new friends.

The Squirrels hotel was a small guest-house in Montpelier Road. It had sixteen bedrooms, and the owner, a schoolteacher, wanted someone to run it for her. She thought I was ideal for the job. I had several schemes that impressed her, and I assured her that they would make money. Even if they didn't, I was sure there would be a satisfactory turnover. I started work, and for a month her trade increased. She was very pleased.

I had an obsession that, any day, a policeman was going to walk in and arrest me. However, Mrs T was very good to me and I was happy at the Squirrels. Until the day I walked into the 42 Club. Everyone greeted me by my new name, yet one face looked puzzled and stood out in the crowd. It was Peter. That was all I needed. He had met up with other alcoholics on the scene and had come to Brighton for a few days. My cover was blown. He threatened to tell everyone about me unless I gave him money. I gave him thirty pounds and left the club.

He asked the people in the club where I was living. I had given everyone the impression that I had bought the Squirrels, so it wasn't long before he turned up on the doorstep asking for more and more money. I was soon broke. I couldn't go to the police, because I was wanted. Peter tightened the screws until there was nothing else for me to do but to con Mrs T.

I drew up a letter heading for an American touring company and addressed it to the Squirrels hotel, acknowledging a letter I had supposedly sent. The letter offered a good deal if six of our bedrooms could have showers put in. It was a large package and Mrs T agreed to pay for the shower units. A cheque for a thousand ponds arrived for her in my name. I paid it into my account and then let off all the rooms as permanent bedsits, reaping the deposits and weekly takings. I had access to the hotel account and could deposit or withdraw at will. Mrs T lived in the country, so she had no idea what I was doing. I had opened an account in my real name, and had a cheque-book and banker's card in my false name. Mrs T and her daughter had stood as referees.

But it was getting too much to handle, and no matter which way I turned there was no escape. It was either the police or Peter. I was becoming desperate. Hours of thought turned up . . . Sandy. I could live as Sandy again – why not! No one would suspect me. I was a little bigger and my voice was a little deeper, but I could get away with it if I tried.

My cheque-book did the rounds. I bounced nine hundred pounds worth of cheques in two days in ladies' shops in Brighton. As soon as I had written my last cheque, I withdrew every penny from the bank and left the Squirrels. It was a bright sunny morning when I stepped into the cab as Sandy. I had passed several of the residents in the hall, but they hadn't noticed anything strange. The previous evening I had burnt all my old clothes and hotel paperwork in the backyard. I didn't want to leave any evidence behind.

From London I got a train to Nottingham. I had been writing to a transvestite there called Maureen for about a year; when I telephoned and I said I was on the move, she invited me to stay for a few weeks. Little did I know, but I had made a lot of mistakes. Once the police started investigating the Squirrels fraud, the cheques came to light – and why the hell had a young guy bounced all those cheques on female clothing unless he was going to use it?

I hadn't cross-dressed for ages, so all the way down I continually checked my make-up. But I had never met Maureen. When the train pulled into Nottingham Station she stood out like a sore thumb; all my worries disappeared. I looked glamorous compared to the sight that greeted me – mini-skirt covering her bare essentials and platinum-blonde hair in rollers with a headscarf tied round it. It looked as though she had the previous night's make-up on as well. I was to discover that she looked the same whether her make-up was fresh or not.

She had a room in a large house owned by a woman named Jenny. Jenny's old man was in the nick and she had a boyfriend living with her. There were two prostitutes in the basement, two butch lesbians on the first floor and a gay guy next door to Maureen. What a bloody household. I blended in well, though.

The first thing I did was to unpack my clothes. As soon as the suitcases were opened, Maureen rounded up every feminine female in the house to have a look. Everything was new and everyone was trying on my dresses.

I had a great time for several seeks. Jenny and her boyfriend occasionally went to a cabaret club, where I joined them with another ex-lover of Jenny's. We had a ball, and once Jenny was pissed I used to entice her boyfriend into the lounge and give him a blow-job in front of the fire. Her ex-lover was also a bit of a dish, and I occasionally met him at night. Living as Sandy was fun – I had more men than ever, even though most of them realised I was a man before they made a play for me. It was great. Living as Sandy brought new meaning into my life, I was more secure, far happier, and honest. Although I had reached that state via a holocaust of criminal activities, it proved that as a woman I had no need for money – only love, the thing I desired so much.

Maureen was jealous. I had good looks, pretty clothes and men after me by the dozen. When we went into town, guys were always sniffing around me and holding their noses at her. I could see us slowly separating. Jenny offered me the basement flat when the girls got nicked by the police. That was too much for Maureen; she knew I was well in with Jenny, so she planned to get rid of me in the nicest possible way.

I had given Maureen clothes and treated her well all the time I was in Nottingham, but that wasn't enough for her. She was no longer the queen bee, in the limelight, and she couldn't stand it. The last time I saw her, she was standing in the Le Chic club with her hair in rollers, wearing an old pinafore dress and slippers, drinking heavily and pointing an accusing finger at me as I danced with some hunk of a guardsman on leave. Her threats and accusations meant nothing to me – I'd heard them all before. She was always like that. But I didn't think she would call the police and tip them off about me.

I was in bed being screwed gutless by my guardsman when the door burst open and in pounced four coppers. The poor guy wilted under me in seconds and started diving around for his clothes. The cops let him go. I sat defiantly on the bed, clad in bra, suspender-belt and black stockings. 'George William Roberts, you are hereby being arrested and charged with theft and fraud. Anything you say may be taken down and used in evidence against you.'

I just said, 'Big deal, man,' picked up my make-up bag, put on a dress and pair of shoes and left with two officers, while the others ripped the room apart looking for money. There was none. I had spent it all. I had had a good time, and now I was going to be punished.

Chapter 17

Borstal

It was a quiet journey from the flat to the police station. I sat in the back of an unmarked car handcuffed to a burly officer. But things started to liven up once I was taken into the interrogation room.

At first two officers tried to assault me verbally. The fact that I was wearing a dress meant I had to face an onslaught of 'poof', 'queer', and 'pansy' labels. I just sat tight, refusing to make a statement. That made matters worse. I wasn't wanted for a local crime, but they sure as hell intended to pin something on me.

After an hour of verbal bashing, the strong-arm tactics began, and with the usual police practice of Mr Nice and Mr Evil. Mr Evil started a few slaps and punches, landing them in places where there would be no tell-tale marks. Then he left the room, and Mr Nice tried to talk me into confessing to some silly little robbery. I refused, and when Mr Evil returned and I was pulled about the room by my hair. He was hurting me, and I cried out in pain, unable to stop the tears flowing.

This cat-and-mouse game lasted for several hours, and when I was thrown naked into a cold empty cell I was exhausted both physically and mentally. I hadn't been in the cell long when the door swung open and a bucket of cold water was thrown over me. I was drenched from head to foot and unable to dry myself.

I sat on a wooden board for several hours, cold and hungry. Several police officers came to the cell peephole and jeered obscenities. The cold water had made my make-up run, and by six o'clock that evening I was glad of a chance to wash my face. Then I was made to sit about with only my dress on. My tights weren't returned in case I tried to hang myself. I wasn't offered food at all that day. At about nine-thirty a policeman came in and asked me to sign a statement. I tried to read it, but he snatched it away and told me just to sign. When I refused, he grabbed me by the front of my dress and pinned me against the wall, then repeatedly spat in my face. He threw me back on to the wooden bench. I only had my dress to wipe the spit off my face.

He hadn't been gone long when the door burst open and Evil and Nice started their fun and games again. I tried my best to fight back, and caught Mr Evil a good crack in the bollocks. That made it worse for me; but I managed to roll into a ball and fend off most of the kicks. I lay in tears on the cell floor while the statement I had refused to sign was left on the bench. I was told by Mr Evil to sign it within one hour or I would get the same treatment again.

When I slowly edged over to it, I could hardly believe what was written. I was supposedly admitting to two break-ins and a shop-lifting offence. No words can express how bitter I felt at that moment. I didn't mind admitting to the crimes I had committed and taking my punishment like a man, but no way was I going to take the rap because some crooked cop wanted to clear a few unsolved cases. I ripped the statement up into thousands of pieces, and when the two officers came back, I didn't give them a chance to say a word. I flew at them like a wild cat.

I was thrown against a wall and the dress was ripped off my back. Blood gushed from a cut above my eye. I was left alone in the cell in the dark until the following morning, and spent the night asleep on the bare boards. As light crept in through the barred window, I tried to sit up. I ached from head to foot and my lower lip felt as though it were six inches thick. The horror of the previous night's beating was reeling around in my head when the door opened. I was freezing cold and starving. My Nice came in with a pair of trousers and a shirt he had brought from the flat and told me to dress. I was taken down to a washroom, where I was left to clear up the dried blood. My lip looked a mess and my hair was matted with blood.

I cleaned myself up as best I could. Mr Nice collected me, took me back to a cleaner cell with a bed and blankets and gave me breakfast – my first meal in over twenty-four hours. As I ate I apologised for the previous evening. He told me that two officers were on their way from London to collect me, and that I would spend the night in Paddington Green police station before appearing in court the following morning.

The two men were very nice. They treated me like a human being. They knew that I was pleading guilty, so they had no need to pressurise me. We stopped on the motorway for a beer – my last for quite some time. Both reckoned that I would get at least two years in prison. Two years' peace. I didn't mind; perhaps I would be able to sort myself out this time.

Once at Paddington Green I made all my statements; I decided to plead guilty on six charges and asked for seventy-eight other offences to be taken into account. The paperwork took several hours, and after a good night I was locked in a small cell for the night with a couple of blankets. I still ached badly. One of the officers had asked about my split lip. When I told him, he just shook his head and said that bent cops like that should be kicked out of the police, but that the cat-and-mouse game was played throughout the force and was well-known.

The following morning I appeared in Bow Street magistrates' court and was remanded in prison for four weeks so that medical and social reports could be made. That afternoon I was moved to Wormwood Scrubs prison. The reception officer ordered strip searches and baths for all new inmates, and I joined the queue of naked men lining up for a bath. Then I had to join the queue to see the medical officer. Since I had already been inside they knew that I was homosexual. The hospital orderly beside the doctor informed him that here was another nancy boy to see him. But the doctor gave him a look of disgust and asked me if everything was O.K. He examined my lips and commented about the bruising on my back. I told him I had fallen on some stairs – I didn't want any more trouble.

The doctor asked me if I would prefer a single cell. That was the last thing I wanted. I didn't want to be alone; I needed someone to talk to.

I ended up in a cell with a young man on a manslaughter charge. He seemed very quiet. He had been one of six skinheads involved in a fight; he had kicked a guy in the head and been blamed for his death. He had been on remand for nearly ten months and was shortly to be sentenced. He expected six years at least. Bob was placid, but when one got on to a subject he disagreed with he became quite violent – never towards me, but he gave the screws a bad time.

We spent most of the day talking about our offences. As is normal with all prisoners, we bragged about our conquests, and each offence was grossly over-exaggerated.

At night I used to lie in bed and try to analyse where I had gone wrong. I blamed my mother, father, anyone. I didn't want to accept the fact that I was to blame.

To this day I feel deeply sorry about screwing up people's lives. But I committed offences and was punished for them in a court of law. I don't think I should be branded for ever.

My appearance in court was brief. The magistrate decided that I had committed too many offences; as the most he could give me was one year, I should go to the crown court for sentencing. I returned to the Scrubs feeling very unsure of myself. I had never been in a crown court before, and a date wasn't fixed for sentencing, so I had an uncertain future. My solicitor visited me the following week and assured me that I would be appearing within a month – the month turned out to be only nine days. No warning; and as I sat in the cell below the crown court waiting to go out, my heart was pounding, butterflies filled my stomach and I felt quite faint. When the officer called my name out my legs felt like jelly.

I had been forewarned about the judge. He was well known for his heavy sentencing. He was the terror of the criminal world and even the hardest of cons dreaded appearing in front of him. The courtroom was ten times the size of the magistrates' courts I had appeared in. All the solicitors and barristers wore their horsehair wigs, and piles of law books littered the tables. The public box was full of students and the jury box was full of so-called honest citizens.

The court rose as the judge entered. Once everyone had settled down, the clerk of the court started to read out my charges. I had to plead to each one individually. As process continued, the public and jury began to view me with an obvious displeasure. I felt more ashamed of myself than ever before. After my last 'Guilty' response the clerk asked me if I wanted the seventy-eight other offences to be taken into consideration. I agreed. Several of the jury members were shaking their heads in disbelief.

The judge queried the clerk's statement. 'Did you say seven or eight?'

The clerk set him right, and a look of scorn crossed the old man's face as he read through the list of offences that were to be considered void after sentencing. He consulted the clerk several times, then settled down to listen to my barrister's pleas for a light sentence because of my terrible upbringing.

During the speech, the judge sat cleaning his nails. After my counsel had finished, I was asked if I had anything to say. I had been rehearsing an apology speech for days, but when it came to it all I could say was, 'I'm sorry, I won't do it again.'

The officer beside me reassured me as we sat down. The judge then left the court with the two cronies who were sitting with him. They were out about fifteen minutes. During the whole period, the eyes of the public box and jury never left me. There was one old woman with fish-ball eyes in the jury box who gave me several dirty looks. I poked my tongue out at her and she turned away with a look of absolute disgust.

'George Roberts, I have given your case serious consideration and I have decided this time to give you the chance that you well deserve.'

My heart lifted. He had believed all the crap my solicitor had given him. Relief swept through my body and a smile spread across my face.

The chance you deserve is a quick, stiff punishment.' The smile disappeared. 'I'm sentencing you to borstal, where you will serve anything from six months to two years, depending on your attitude whilst inside.'

Horror set in my body as the relief was swept away. I went numb. I didn't hear much more of the judge's preaching. The smile on the jury's faces sticks in my mind even now, and that steep staircase back to the cell seemed miles and miles deep. I was convicted and sentenced; but it wasn't until I tried pacing around the small eight-by-four foot cell that I realised I was trapped for quite a long time.

Going back to the Scrubs had a new meaning. Going through reception was tougher, and when I went through the medical again I saw a different doctor. He insisted that I be placed in a single cell. My feet hardly touched the ground. As soon as I had my kit issued, I was taken away from the others.

I was a category-B prisoner on account of my cunning, but because of my high educational standard I was eligible to go to a new borstal in Leicester, called Glen Parva. I breathed a sigh of relief as I left the smell, squalor and overcrowding of the Scrubs.

Glen Parva had a new twenty-four-foot-high fence around it and cameras watched our van as it entered the large steel gates. All the buildings were double-storeyed; work was still in progress. The reception area was clean, and for the first time in a long while I felt like a human being and not an animal. The officers, in civilian clothing, questioned me about my family situation. Once it was decided what my employment inside the borstal would be, I was transferred to the reception wing, where I was to spend my first four weeks. Once I had settled in there the senior officer set out to establish as many facts about me as possible. My file was already quite thick – reports from psychiatrists, social workers, lawyers and police, plus statements from myself. It was agreed from the outset that I had had a bad time as a child. If I needed medical assistance to help me, a psychiatrist could be made available.

I was warned that I would probably serve ten months before release; that was my target. But if I worked well I could be out in seven and a half months – the record for good behaviour at Glen Parva. I made my mind up to break that record if I had to crawl on my hands and knees for six months. It was normal practice to spend four weeks on reception courses and looking at work programmes, but the kitchens were in a terrible state and the governor of Glen Parva agreed for me to go out to work straight away. I met the senior officer in the kitchen and got on fabulously with him. Mr D pulled a few strings and within three days I was at work.

On the wing I was the oldest inmate by about two years – most of the guys were between fifteen and eighteen. Most were from broken homes, and many had been in detention centres and remand homes before. They crowded in to watch TV when it was allowed, and played games, but I got down to serious studies. I intended to use my sentence to my advantage.

My reception in the kitchens was hostile at first. A young black boy who had been a baker in civilian life was the number one. He allotted jobs to all the boys and generally ran the cooking and distribution of funds. The kitchen was split up into several sections: the bakers' table, where all the bread and cakes were prepared, the butchers' room, where large sides of meat were cut up, and the coppers. The coppers were large vats where tea, porridge, curries, stews and all other liquid food was prepared. Tea cooked that way usually tasted stewed. There were also areas of vegetable preparation, frying, cleaning and washing-up. A total of twenty-two boys worked a seven-hour day, six days a week, which was normal duty. We were the best paid in the borstal, at £1.24 a week.

However, the number one was due to leave just a week after my arrival, and there was rivalry among the other boys over who was going to get the job, worth 50p a week extra. It was obvious I was way ahead of the nearest runners. I had experience in catering in every department – but I had to prove it to the other boys to gain their confidence. I wasn't assigned a permanent job, but I gave a hand around the kitchen. I made the copper-man's and baker's jobs easier by doing their heavier work.

I was eventually nominated for the job I got full approval from the guys. I was in! I had the top job in the borstal, and I had only been there ten days.

As number one, I had to down in the kitchen by six a.m. to start the ovens for breakfast. Once there I rang a bell and the gate officer transferred me to the kitchen. It was not until about seven-thirty, when the duty officer arrived, that the rest of the guys were escorted in. Within a month I had the kitchen running my way. Mr D was obviously pleased; I spent a lot of time in his office, and only came out to check the food before it was distributed to the wings.

I didn't socialise with the other guys or join in the sporting activities; I was too tired. But I did study. The educational officer supplied me with material, and after a bath at seven-thirty p.m. I disappeared into my cell.

My cell was comfortable – far superior to the cells at the Scrubs. At Glen Parva it was the same iron door, but with barred windows that opened and offered a view of the outside world and attached to each cell was its own toilet and washhand basin.

One lunchtime we had several uniformed officers drafted in from Leicester prison to check out the security. I was the only con not locked up and still working. A uniformed officer was looking after me in the kitchens.

After a while the officer went into the toilet. I was leaning up against the wall and had a full view of the pan as he had left the door open. That aroused my interest, and by adjusting my position slightly I was able to get a good view. He moved slightly so that my view improved. I was nearly busting out of my trousers. The officer slowly started masturbating.

The fact that the guy had a uniform on terrified me and yet excited me. I hadn't had a real man for ages. He wasn't good-looking or well-built, but at least he was a man.

I couldn't make a direct pass at him so we had a game of hide-and-seek. I walked into the vegetable store and he followed me. He immediately took out his cock and started rubbing himself; but when I went to touch him he turned away. He said he only wanted a wank. I pulled at him for ages but in the end we just stood and masturbated, each watching the other. Once we climaxed, he put himself away and went and sat in the office but my erection wouldn't go down, so I masturbated once again.

When I had completed five months of my sentence I was classed as a red band, which meant I had the privilege of going into Leicester on Saturday afternoons between two and eight p.m. It was great to be able to get back into civilian clothes, even if only for six hours. On Sundays I had an 'open day' too; I could either work in the kitchen or go out to a local old people's home and do community work.

On the Saturday visits into town all I used to do was cottage. We were given very little money to take out, and by the time we had spent our bus fare back into town and saved our bus fare back we only had about forty pence each to spend; so I hung around the cottage trying to earn a couple of quid so I'd be able to have a decent meal while outside. If that didn't happen I used to return to Glen Parva feeling very dissatisfied.

After five months and two weeks I was called to the general office and asked if I would like to participate in a new venture. The prison had tied in with a group from the Community Service Volunteers. If accepted I would be expected to go up to London for two weeks to work in a children's home or hospital or do other forms of social work. Mr M took me up to see the CSV offices in London, and after a short interview I was accepted. That was on Friday; on the following Monday I left Borstal under my own steam and made my way to the Katherine Settlement in Battersea.

The Settlement was a community centre that incorporated day-nurseries, youth clubs, a library and an advice centre. It was voluntarily run but seemed well funded. I was given a comfortable room and told of my restrictions. I had to work eight hours a day, six days a week; but after seven o'clock my nights were my own. On the first night I was out at the Elephant and Castle, getting pissed. It was good to see Chas and Bill and Gary, another old pal, again after six months. They tried their damnedest to get me pissed, though, and I returned to the Settlement a little the worse for wear; but no one seemed to notice.

On my second night out I met Alex. He was a nice guy, and we went out wining and dining every night. He thought I was a social worker, but I decided to tell him the truth before we got too involved. He was very shocked at first, but thanked me for telling him. It didn't seem to make much difference. For the first time in my life I started to visit the Festival Hall, where we listened to Mozart, Chopin, Handel and Bach.

Alex was both a lover and a friend, and he was refreshing and sincere – all I had ever wanted, really. But I had to return to Glen Parva. It was a sad parting; I could have been going back for eight weeks. However, when I arrived at the gates I was told that I would be released the following week if I agreed to go back to the Katherine Lowe Settlement until I sorted myself out. There was no time limit, but it would be part of my parole agreement that I could stay there until I found somewhere to live.

I was overjoyed. Only seven lousy days left. Alex wrote every day and seemed very pleased that I would be out early. In letters to him I pledged my love. Once again I tried to convince myself that I would be walking into an honest and decent life-style.

Chapter 18

Freedom

Once I returned to the Katherine Lowe Settlement I found my duties a lot easier. There were no longer any restrictions hanging over my head and the only things that really bugged me were the constant reminders from the warden that I was an ex-Borstal boy. If I did anything wrong I was told that ex-offenders could never go straight anyway. But I was doing my best, working a forty-hour week for only £3.60 apart from my keep. Many hours were spent slogging my guts out cleaning and scrubbing.

However, I no longer had to sit in the kitchen with Cook for meals, either. I was allowed to join the warden and other house-guests at the oval table in the dining-room. We all sat on high-back chairs and went through the whole process of a formal dinner. Conversation was stifled by the dampening influence of the warden.

The house-guests ranged from other social workers to a head-mistress. They were all old; I was considered to be a child. Comments were made about my social life. Did I have to stay out after nine o'clock? I disturbed everyone when I returned home. No consideration was given to the fact that I had been locked up for six months. It was easier to stay out all night than to stand all the aggravation. Alex was very good to me; he had come round on my first day home with a parcel of new clothes. I still cherish our full nights together. He wasn't a sexual person, but he had an aura that left me satisfied.

After only a week of freedom he insisted that I move in with him. I didn't want to make that commitment so quickly. It was finally agreed that I would stay with him until I could find a flat of my own, but under no obligation. If our relationship was to take off, it would do so over a period of time. I was glad to close the front door of the Katherine Lowe Settlement behind me for the last time.

Within a few days I approached a catering agency in Penge. All I really wanted was temporary work. The manageress was very kind to me and I thought it better to tell her the truth. She didn't hold my past against me, and within hours she had several interviews lined up. I worked for two weeks in a temporary post as catering manager at F. Francis & Sons in Blackheath. The personnel manager was so impressed when he was signing my final time-sheet that he asked me if I would consider taking on the post full-time. It was more than I could have hoped for, and I accepted straight away.

During the first few weeks I made several changes in the quality of the food, and won the full support of the chief union representative. It was very apparent that the unions ran the place and the directors were worked like puppets. With union consent I was able to turn an annual loss of fifteen thousand pounds into a break-even within six months. Instead of just a trolley service and luncheon, I introduced breakfast, lunch and evening meal to cover all the shift systems with the same amount of staff. Production was increased by two per cent at no extra cost. Bulk buying and costing held down food prices, which meant only slight increases.

Alex had approached his landlord, and shortly after moving in with him I was offered a one-bedroomed unfurnished flat in Forest Hill. Once I had bought myself a secondhand bed I moved in. The place needed redecorating, but with the steady income from Francis's I was slowly able to put up curtains and buy a cooker. I saw Alex several times a week, and lived between the two flats — until the day I found out Alex's secret.

I had left work early and gone back to his flat. As I entered the car park I noticed Alex's car. That was strange; he very rarely came home until seven. I rushed upstairs — I wanted to tell him about a letter I had received from the council that morning. I had a key, so I entered the front door. The sight that met my eyes hurt me. Alex was screwing a very young man. I stood still — unable to move, unable to turn away. Why? Alex had me, why did he want a boy? How could he — he was ruining that kid's life.

Alex had climbed off the boy and was grabbing at his clothes. As he pulled on his trousers he tried to make feeble excuses. The youth lay on the bed shivering with fright. I pulled him off the bed and told him to dress. I sat and watched in disgust. Alex went into the bathroom; he was stuttering badly. Once the young boy was dressed I gave him enough money to get home on the bus and told him that if I ever saw him again I'd tell his father about him.

I later found that Alex had picked him up in a toilet near Dulwich College. When Alex eventually returned from the bathroom, I could no longer hold back my emotions. I screamed at him. Why had he cheated and lied on me? Did he do it to everybody? No response, no apologies, just a smug expression on his face. I threw his key back at him, and after branding him a pederast I slammed out of the flat.

Letters and phone-calls from Alex could not mend the rift. When I felt low and wanted to give in to him, the picture of that youth's face came to mind and reinforced my anger. But I needed Alex's support; I was beginning to crumble. Only my work kept me going. The Elephant and Castle became my regular watering-hole again, and I started to drink quite heavily.

One day while walking through the yard at Francis's, I spotted a young man whom I thought very good-looking. His name was David. At first I thought he might be gay, but when I had a chance to talk to him the following day he told me he was married with two children. I was invited around to meet Stella and the kids one weekend, and I accepted. Stella was a right character. I couldn't see how they got on; they had completely opposite temperaments. The first time I saw their children Robert and Stephen, thoughts of my own kids came flooding back. I wondered where they were and what they were doing. I got on fabulously with the whole family, and spent quite some time with them.

But Stella and David treated me as one of the family, and in time I was allowed to take the boys out at weekends to the zoo or the pictures. Both Dave and Stella were true friends and without them I wouldn't be alive today. They talked me round when I felt down and gave me the strength I needed to face my future, which at times seemed bleak.

I had the continual torture of hiding Sandy from them. She was there inside me, causing me inner torment because I couldn't let her out to play. I didn't want to lead a double life of cross-dressing again. I had to be just George. I would have loved to have been just Sandy, but people wouldn't understand her. She would have had a deep voice – an attractive but incomplete woman, unacceptable in society.

I had coped earlier by doing drag, and in Borstal I had lost a lot of my self-confidence. I wasn't sure whether or not I would be able to face an audience again. In hiding Sandy I had built up a lot of defences. Would I be able to let her out under lights in front of hundreds of people? I wouldn't even know until I tried. Chas had always been good to me, and every time we met he asked me to do a show for him. I telephoned him and arranged to meet him the following night for a drink. When I told him I intended to do drag again, he was overjoyed and gave me the confidence I lacked.

It was decided that I should come back with a bang. Two weeks later Chas had organised a charity evening with about ten drag acts, and I was billed as special guest artist. Dave and Stella encouraged me right up to the last minute, and David even came to watch the show. He loved it.

I was to be last on, at 10.40, for a twenty-minute spot, and then I was to close the show. The audience was ecstatic when Chas introduced me; and, the minute Sandy was caught under the bright lights, that was it. The twenty minutes flew by, and before I knew it I was back on the wall outside the pub with the audience shouting encouragement. I took my final bow as though I had taken it every night since my first show. Chas threw his arms around me and I took six ovations before I introduced the others acts back on for 'Auld Lang Syne'.

I slept peacefully that night. Sandy had enjoyed herself and had worn herself out. The following morning at work I felt better for it, too. Drag was to be my life-saver. I was far more organised and capable to controlling the staff at work when I wasn't worrying about my double identity. If I could use the spotlights and sequins to earn me both money and peace of mind, both George and Sandy would be happy.

Within weeks I was back doing the full pub and club circuit seven nights a week besides working Monday to Friday at Francis's. It was tiring, but I wanted to have enough cash to be able to buy my own business instead of having to rip people off when times got bad. At Francis's I had the place running like clockwork, with food prepared well in advance so that if I turned up a couple of hours late it didn't really matter. After a while I ended up only calling in over the dinner hour and then going again. I had a good staff. Old Winnie was a diamond and worked her fingers to the bone for me. In return I treated them and occasionally gave them some meat for the weekend, or chocolates out of stock for their grandchildren.

At Francis's I became a firm favourite even with the directors, especially after making cuts in the budget that the union accepted; but there was a bad hygiene problem. All the equipment was past its useful life, and rotten woodwork and Formica tops only lengthened the cleaning processes. Even after a good scrub-down the place looked dirty. I read several reports in the local papers about other factories in our area that had had their catering facilities withdrawn until health and safety standards had been improved. Rather than face that situation, I worked on a report for several weeks, and presented the personnel and finance directors with a schedule and breakdown for completely refitting and modernising the cooking and eating areas. It would cost in the region of eighteen thousand pounds. I submitted floor-plans of how I thought it should be laid out to make preparation and serving more acceptable to both the cooks and the factory workers. I then asked them to accompany me on a tour of the canteen so that they could see the standards of hygiene for themselves. Several of the directors had never even seen the inside, and the antique equipment was enough for them. They couldn't really object to my plans, as their kitchen and dining-room had cost several thousand pounds to rebuild. I got the O.K., and contractors were called in. (The canteen moved into four disused offices for the duration, and if it hadn't been for Winnie that temporary canteen would never have survived.)

My salary at Francis's wasn't great – I was earning about seventy pounds a week; so when I was offered a job for nearly a hundred a week plus bonus I couldn't refuse it. I felt sorry leaving Francis's, and I went after an almighty row with the directors. They knew full well they wouldn't be able to get anyone to do the job I had done, as well as pacify all the different union officials.

My new job was with Fads Catering of Oxford, working on their first venture in the London area. The main restaurant was in the centre of a shopping precinct in Lewisham. It was open-plan, surrounded by large stores and shops, and there was a central serving area ringed with garden furniture, umbrellas and conifer trees. It looked really spectacular. I had complete control. The directors of the company seemed impressed enough to leave me alone after two days. I ran the operation well and soon increased the turnover.

One night while appearing at the Vauxhall Tavern I met Alan. He was six feet tall, with short dark hair and a 'tache; he looked very macho. I was having a drink during the interval when he approached me and offered to buy me another. As I turned to look at him my heart began to flutter, he was such a good-looking guy. After introducing himself and congratulating me on the first half, he began to get very familiar.

It was most unlike me – I didn't normally fall in the arms of a guy within minutes; I normally chased and caught my own prey. But Alan overwhelmed me. He came backstage, and each time I came off to change costume he grabbed me and hungrily pawed my body. I only just made it back on in time for my numbers. I couldn't concentrate on what I was supposed to be doing. I had mouthed the words of 'Tits and Arse' so many times it came out naturally, but my mind was on Alan in the dressing-room. Would he still be there at the end of the night?

I should have trodden carefully, but all the emotion was too much for me. Alan was quite smartly dressed; he asked me if I would like to go out for a meal. I told him I had a better idea. He just grinned and helped me load my drag in the car, and we went home. In the next few days I experienced love in many forms. Alan was tender and warm, caring and exciting. He didn't speak of his family or home, and when I asked him where he lived he just said north London, but I didn't really care. I just wanted to lie beside him and hold him.

On the Friday morning I had to go into work to move all the week's takings from the office, where the staff had hidden it. Alan came across with me and helped me count it out. By the time we had finished he said he was hungry, so, after locking all the money in bundles in my briefcase, I took him down to eat. It was only one o'clock and there was plenty of time for the bank. We had a leisurely meal. Then one of the guys on the till was having problems with a customer, so I went over to help. It was all getting very complicated when Alan asked me for a key to the toilets. I just passed him the bunch of keys from my belt and away he went.

Once I had pacified the customer and calmed down the guy at the till, I hung around for Alan. I checked my watch; he'd been gone for nearly fifteen minutes. I had another coffee, then started to worry. What the hell was he doing? I walked through the precinct and took the lift from the boutique hall to the preparation level. The toilet door was locked, so I walked down to my office. The door stood ajar. I called out Alan's name as I pushed the door open.

I could hardly believe my eyes. Paperwork and bank bags were scattered all over the place and the briefcase had gone. I pushed the door to and sat in my chair. Piles of copper and silver still lay on the table untouched. I slammed my fist down. Why hadn't the bastard taken that lot as well? I felt choked. What was I to do?

The obvious answer was to phone the police, but that was impossible – the police wouldn't believe me. I was lost. I had to sit and think it out. If I blundered into it, I could end up back in prison as an innocent man. I needed time. I locked the office, returned to the restaurant and calmly told the girls that I would be in the following morning at nine. I had an assistant manager who opened up and closed down for me.

I was in such a state that the only decision I could make was to run – run away, mess up my whole life again just because of some fancy man I'd wanted to bed. It distressed me terribly to leave the new flat where I had only lived a month and for the first time in my life had felt settled. I had spent a lot of money decorating it and buying furniture. But leave it I must, and soon.

I didn't have any money of my own, but I had cashed the paycheque on the way home, so I had eight hundred pounds in cash. I would leave the following day, suspected of stealing that plus the £2,500 Alan had stolen. The police would blame me for the lot. I knew that running way would brand me as guilty, but I stood a better chance on the run than in some interrogation room getting beaten up again.

I have always been a good organiser, and organising crime is no different from organising a work-schedule. I didn't have too much time. The staff would need paying at about six o'clock on Saturday, so if I cleared out just before then I would be O.K. I spent what was left of the night packing my clothes. I decided to take only the good stuff with me. The following morning I telephoned David and asked him to call round. I gave him my cassette-player and valuable statuettes, plus anything that I thought he and Stella could use. I told David I was going abroad; he knew something was wrong, and didn't question me further, but he assured me that when I was ready to talk I could phone him or Stella at any time.

After he had left I went in to work and tried to act as though it were just a normal day. My suitcases were sitting in the hall at home, waiting to be collected. I placed all Friday's takings in a bag and packed all the silver and copper off the table in bank bags. During the day I took from the till until four o'clock. By the end I had just under £1,500 – not much for someone on the run. When I left at five I cleared out the rest of the notes, made as though I was returning to the office and then slipped out on to the roof. I made my way down to a local cab office, grabbed a cab, picked up my cases and headed into the West End.

I ended up in Bournemouth early on Sunday morning. I booked into an hotel, then lay on my bed in a hot sweat. I knew I had done wrong. I should have gone to the police, but it was too late now. I had blundered. I was a coward – but at the back of my mind the incidents at Nottingham police station had played a big part in my decision.

For nearly a week I walked around in constant terror that a policeman would recognise me. I found myself looking over my shoulder every few minutes. I couldn't live in that condition. My nerves were shattered and I was very jumpy. I needed someone to talk to. I needed to confess that I had done wrong. I didn't want to go back to prison.

I didn't want to live

Not wanting to live became an obsession. I didn't have the guts to use a razor-blade – that would hurt too much; I wanted an easy way out. Sleeping-pills, if only I could get hold of some. I tried a few chemists and ended up buying several bottles of paracetamol tablets. They didn't kill me, they just made me sick. After throwing up and retching for several hours I collapsed on the floor by the toilet and slept. I awoke several hours later, feeling cold and cramped, I wanted my mum. I wanted to go home and forget.

I travelled back to Fleetwood, taking great care as I passed through London. The journey was uneventful and I felt relieved as I knocked on Mum's flat door. But the police had called. I couldn't stay there – they'd catch me; so I left my luggage and went to look for a suitable flat. I gave my mother a hundred pounds to treat herself. Within a few hours I had secured a small bedsit in Bold Street. I paid a month's deposit and told the landlady I would return that evening. I was carrying all the money in a plastic bag. I hadn't left it in a suitcase in case Mum found it – she was bound to nose through to see just what I had with me. She was like that.

As I passed the King's Arms in Lord Street I noticed a man cross the road in front of me. Then I was conscious of two more running up behind me. I was grabbed from the back and the man in front snatched the bag out of my hand. I was pushed into a car and driven round to the police station. I later found out that my mother's flat was being watched constantly, and had been since the day I left London.

Once the statements had been made and the money counted I felt a lot better. I lay in a cell awaiting collection. It was pointless being unco-operative; I was sure to end up in prison anyway. When it was all over perhaps I would have the chance to start again. I pleaded guilty to stealing £1,750 and £1,500 was intact when I was arrested. Whether the police believed me or not I will never know. I was charged with taking only £1,750. The policeman who collected me and took me back to Lewisham police station was very considerate. I spent the weekend in a warm cell, and on the Monday morning I appeared in Woolwich magistrates' court, expecting to be re-manded in custody.

The court appearance was brief. I was granted bail on my own surety of two thousand pounds. I could hardly believe it. When the police objected, the magistrate slapped them down. The police then tried to get a nightly signing tied into the bail agreement, but the magistrate wouldn't hear of it. As I stepped out into the sunlight outside the courtroom, I thought I was dreaming and had to pinch myself to make sure. Then I ran as fast as my legs could carry me.

I had been given my keys back by the police, so I returned to my flat in London. The front door was barred and all the windows locked up. I was furious. I knocked at the landlord's door; his son answered and started shouting abuse at me. The police had apparently been in to search the flat, and his father had no intention of letting me move back in. Besides holding a £150 deposit, he also had over a thousand pounds' worth of my furniture.

I had nowhere to sleep, so I called in to see Chas and Bill at the Elephant. They helped me get over the first few days. My drag was still in the pub, so I was able to do a few shows to get a little finance behind me. Sue and Peter were frequently in the Elephant, especially when I was on stage. When they heard of my plight, they offered me a bedroom in their flat. I was very grateful and moved in the following evening. They were very kind to me. I went out temp catering during the day and managed to bring home enough food to keep us all going during the week. Most nights they came out with me. Pete was a hairdresser and Sue managed an employment agency. They were great to be with – both of them had the same temperament and personality, not far from my own. They were also both soothing influences when I got worked up. Together with Chas, they encouraged me to face the future.

I made several attempts to recover my furniture, if only to sell it, but the landlord in Eliot Park was very unsympathetic and refused to release it. I went round and pleaded with him, but he just called me a queer. He was a builder by trade and owned his own company; although I threatened to sue him, I knew that it was impossible because he had the finance to fight me.

I was drinking heavily while doing drag. One night when Bill Murphy asked me what I was going to do for Jubilee Day, I retorted 'Jump off all the bridges into the Thames in full drag – what do you expect?' I was only joking, but while I was redoing my make-up for the second half I heard Chas announcing it and asking for sponsors. I nearly died. I was standing naked in front of the mirrors; I grabbed a towel and stumbled downstairs – but by the time I reached the stage it was too late. Chas had nearly £500 in sponsorship. I returned to the dressing-room and drank myself silly.

I didn't really think about it any more until Jubilee Day itself, although Chas had mentioned the sponsorship money was up to £2,750. When I tuned into Capital Radio, I couldn't believe my ears. They were advertising that I would be jumping off Lambeth, Vauxhall and Westminster Bridges in full drag between five and seven that evening. I shot down to the Elephant. The pub was full, and at four-thirty we left to jump the first bridge. I couldn't even swim properly, but for £2,750 for charity I would do anything.

Nerves didn't bother me until I was actually balancing on the side of the bridge. Chas shouted from a nearby car for me to take my teeth out, and the crowd all around me pushed closer. I just jumped. As I hit the water the current swept me under the bridge, and my wig surfaced where I had gone in. I was dragged aboard a life-raft, but I could hear people shouting 'She's drowning!' and 'He's not up yet!' Then some big butch lesbian decided to rescue me and dived in. She was furious when she saw me on the raft.

I jumped the other bridges without too many problems. The crowd on Westminster Bridge were very encouraging and I surfaced to rousing cheers. On Lambeth Bridge I did a somersault before hitting the water, as I fell in after trying to climb on to the lighting structure that sticks out all around the bridge.

Once I had jumped the three bridges I returned to the Elephant for a little drink. A little drink ended up as a drunken stupor and the following morning, when Sue came running into my bedroom, I thought an earthquake was starting all around me.

'Georgie, you're in all the papers!' I raised my head slightly off the pillow. 'All the papers' happened to be the *Sun*. It said: 'Jubilee Day went down with a splash for female impressionist G. Gold, who raised £2,750 for the Jubilee appeal fund.'

I looked at the top of the page and started laughing. Sue looked puzzled and asked what was wrong. I was on page three of the *Sun*. I was a *Sun* girl! Then I fell asleep again.

Chapter 19
Escape to Bognor

Once the thrills and excitement of Jubilee Day had left my life, I was back where I could see no escape. The trial still hung over me; the prison officer, my future guardian, stood like a hangman above my head. When I would go to prison, and for how long, I just didn't know; that only made me worse. I was sick of running. Chas, Dave, Sue and Pete couldn't talk me round. Thoughts crossed my mind of jumping a bridge for real. Even once I had returned to civilisation, I knew I would walk into another lot of trouble. Permanent sleep was the only answer, but I didn't have the guts to kill myself. It was only a fantasy I wished I had the strength to act out.

No ties, no guts, no love. I had to run – there was nothing else for me to do. I was dragging everyone down to my level.

The train to Bognor Regis was slow and stopped at every station it came to. I sat bewildered, wondering why the hell I had chosen Bognor. It didn't even have a listing in *Gay News*.

The Royal Norfolk was the town's biggest hotel. My references, false as they were, were so outstanding that the new owners couldn't refuse to take me on and I was unknown in Bognor, so I was able to lead a quiet life.

Once I had established a little peace of mind, I tried to fight my loneliness. The campaign for homosexual equality had a gay disco in a little village pub and I arranged to go along. I stood with the organiser in the garden. I was surprised when a bike came thundering up the path. A leather-clad figure sat on it for a while. My mind was flooded with memories of Peter. The young man took off his helmet and smiled, and we were introduced. Then I slipped away to the bar.

Colin didn't show much interest at first; we just occasionally smiled at each other. By the end of the evening I didn't hold out much hope. If this was supposed to be the gay scene, give me a vibrator and a box of batteries.

The road to the station was dark, when the headlight lit up my path. Colin swerved his bike to a halt a little down the lane. He asked me if I would like a lift. He offered to run me back to Bognor.

His cheeky approach attracted me, and I accepted the lift as long as no strings were attached. I laughed and hung on to him. It was good to feel his strong muscular body under his clothes. It had been three months since I had had sex. It felt like years. As we sped down the road at seventy I clung on tighter. We shook hands goodnight and arranged to phone each other the following day.

Colin had just finished a disastrous love affair; he had tried to commit suicide and had spent many weeks in hospital. I knew how he felt, yet kept my secret. Neither of us wanted to make any commitments.

Several nights a week we visited a pub in Bognor, owned by two gay women. I had never got on with lesbians, but these were different. One was a lot older than the other and they could easily have been mistaken for mother and daughter.

The couple also owned a local club and a hotel. The club was open every afternoon and was a popular drinking-hole. I visited it several times and struck up a firm friendship with the girls – so much so that they offered me a job as barman. I moved into their hotel to start in my new post.

The front bar in the pub hadn't been taking too much money that season and it was suggested that a live cabaret would attract a crowd. I tried to say no, but Sandy led the way, organising publicity and putting up posters. The first show was to be on Friday night – just one spot lasting twenty minutes. By eight-thirty the pub was packed solid, and the area that had been designated as a stage was swamped with customers. A DJ had been booked to keep the crowd in the mood, and when I was finally introduced a cheer went ringing through the pub.

Tricia and Susan stood behind the bar on beer-boxes. Susan stuck a thumb in the air every time she caught my eye, and Tricia jumped up and down. Susan's real gaze, however, was on the till as it rang happily away, cashing in on a good night.

Tricia and Susan were overjoyed – the takings were up three hundred per cent. We had only planned to do one show a week, but the place filled up every evening; the customers expected a show and I eventually went on three nights a week.

After a few weeks it was obvious that gays were travelling from

179

Portsmouth, Southampton and Brighton to see the shows. I talked to the girls and we decided to turn the club gay three evenings a week. It was possible to extend the licence if cabaret was on, so a gay DJ was booked and within four weeks the girls owned the most successful gay club on the south coast. I was promoted to manager.

It upset the girls to think that they would have to start paying for cabaret shows, and at thirty pounds a night it was going to be costly; but the profits could cope. I contacted several of my friends who worked the scene in London and booked them for guest appearances. They all went down well – but I remained a firm favourite whenever I reappeared. The gay crowd are like that: they consider home-grown stock to be the best. I had succeeded in getting them a new club with entertainment and for that I received their loyal support.

Many of the gays who visited the club were forces personnel. Wrens and naval ratings outnumbered the civilians, and once or twice military police were seen watching the club. This upset our clientele, and for that reason the wrens suddenly stopped coming. It was a shame. Gays in the services have a much worse time than gays in civilian life, since even when they attain the legal age of twenty-one the forces still consider their activities illegal and discharge offenders.

Nearly nine months had gone by without my hearing a thing from the court, and I hoped they had forgotten me. I was quite happy, but I needed the extra challenge that always kept me going. I needed a man. There had been a guy coming into the club every afternoon who was dead straight. I decided to make a play for him. It had to be calculated, and I chose the right time and place. I bought him several drinks, and one quiet evening in the club I made a pass. It worked, and within minutes we were in bed, frolicking between the sheets. Dave was unemployed and turned out to be a right good-for-nothing – another of the troublemakers that I always got involved with. All the harmless conversation and questioning led to only one thing: a robbery that was very nearly pinned on me.

Dave had spent several nights in my room and got to know the layout of the hotel bedroom areas. A bathroom connected the girls' flat with the rest of the hotel. One evening in the club he borrowed my key, saying he wanted to get a packet of cigarettes from my room; I always had a couple of hundred on the side. The club was just closing and the girls were in the pub next door. He seemed to take a long time, but he eventually came back with the key. Then he left, saying he'd be back the following day.

An hour later, I heard screaming from upstairs in the girls' room.

The filing-cabinet had been broken open and cash and jewellery had been stolen. I was just going to knock on the door when it flew open, and Tricia started lashing out and screaming at me that I was a thieving little bastard.

I stood on the stairs utterly bewildered. I would never steal anything from the girls. They had been good to me. I had been straight with them, hoping it would help me in court. But Tricia was screaming at Susan that I was to blame, and in seconds my life was ruined. The police arrived and I was taken into my room. It was thoroughly searched, then I was questioned. Luckily the investigating officer was sure I was innocent – I had an alibi until the time I had heard the screaming; but Tricia hysterically ran around the hotel shouting my guilt. It wasn't until Susan slapped her that she quietened down.

When the police had finished with me they took other statements. I remained in my room.

The following morning I was made to feel most unwelcome. Every time Tricia and Susan thought I was out of hearing distance they told people how I had stolen from them and they were only keeping me on to prove it.

That night in the club I told Dave that I was going to Worthing for the night. He had been questioned by the police, but no suspicion was on him. Colin had phoned several times to reassure me that he was there if I needed him.

I slept restlessly that evening; suddenly I was wide-awake – someone had jumped from the annexe roof on to my window-ledge. The room was dark and the curtains drawn. I could hear someone breathing heavily. I sank down into the bed, afraid to move. The shadow moved towards the door and slowly opened it. The light burst in from the landing; it was Dave. I jumped, and asked him what the hell he was up to. His excuse what that he had wanted to see me.

I reminded him that I had told him I would be out all evening. He quickly changed his excuse, saying he'd seen the window open and was dying for a pee. With that he disappeared into the hall and into the bathroom. The next morning I thought about the previous night. Had Dave stolen the money and jewels and come back at the first opportunity to collect them? I will never know. Dave was never seen again. If I had said anything to the police, I would have been an accessory, so I kept my mouth shut. I didn't know the truth, and I didn't want to.

I had made lots of gay friends, and none of them believed the girls when they relentlessly accused me. One night, after a blazing row in front of some friends, I handed in my notice. I was sick of being walked on by two people whom I had helped to make a lot of money.

On my last Saturday night I experienced a cynicism at its fullest. The two girls interrupted the last record to tell everyone I was moving on to new pastures, and popped a bottle of champagne to wish me well. Pat, Peter and others round me remained silent while Tricia and Susan gloated. My contempt must have been obvious; the following morning I didn't even say goodbye. I was glad to be going.

The trouble was that I had no work to go to; no references to take to court with me. I was doomed to failure. The only thing that cheered me up were the constant reports from Peter and Pat about the club. Trade had dropped down to nil within only six weeks of my leaving, and the gay nights were threatened.

The next weekend, the girls asked Pat to pass on a message. I was invited for lunch. They wanted to talk business. Susan was up to her eyes in debt and had to sell the pub and half the hotel rooms. They asked me to return to the club again to help restore the gay-night trade. For that I was offered twenty per cent of the profits on a quarterly basis. Susan also hinted that she would appear in my defence during the trial. Like a fool I believed the girls, not knowing that they had baited me for a trap.

I had only been back two weeks when an idiotic drag queen from London was booked. He was a pet hate of mine because he had always tried to copy my routines. Throughout all drag circles he was labelled 'the Bitch'. Eighteen months before joining the club I had bought a water-fall diamanté necklace from a guy in one of the drag pubs I often worked. Jewellery was an asset on stage and I accumulated quite a bit. 'The Bitch' noticed a photograph of me with the necklace on and asked if he could see it. I didn't think anything of his request, and showed it to him. He examined it closely. Then, when he was quite sure of himself, 'The Bitch' said it had been stolen from him. I had bought it innocently enough. He said no more, changed and went on to do his show.

The following morning I awoke with a start; it was only nine a.m. and it had been a late night. Susan was banging on the door. I opened it to find two policemen with her. She had a smirk spread from ear to ear. They questioned me about the necklace, then asked me to accompany them to the station as they intended to charge me with receiving stolen goods valued at four pounds. I could hardly believe my ears, but after telling them there was some mistake I left with them. Downstairs in the lounge sat the Drag Queen, Tricia, Peter, Pat and others. Smiles and jeers as I passed them riveted me to the floor. I turned and would have lashed out at 'The Bitch' if a policeman hadn't stopped me.

182

Once at the station I was locked in a cell while further investigation was carried out. Several hours later a detective came into the room with a bunch of keys and a gold bracelet. Susan had apparently accused me of stealing the bracelet and some keys that opened one of the vending machines! I was horrified. Why had everyone turned against me? I tried to tell the policeman I was innocent, but they wouldn't believe me, and I was put on trial for theft.

I pleaded guilty to receiving the necklace, but not guilty to the other offences. The magistrate looked at me straight in the eye and called me a liar. I was sentenced to three months' imprisonment; if my trial hadn't come up within that period I would be held in further custody until it did. Everything I had held on to vanished in seconds. In court the prosecutor had told the magistrate that Susan, my employer, had found me to be both a liar and untrustworthy. I hope the girls still have it on their conscience.

The week before my three months was up I appeared in crown court for my trial. The conviction in Bognor went badly against me, and I was found guilty and sentenced to three years in prison. Three damn years. After that, what would I have to return to?

In her summing-up to the jury, the judge blamed my upbringing, I had been raised in a corrupt atmosphere – no wonder I had led a corrupt and dishonest life. It was people like me who didn't stand a chance. But this time would be the last; I knew that. Once I could be the real me, I would be all right.

Chapter 20

Prisoner

A three-year sentence was now reality. Going to borstal had been a big joke – just mixing with silly little boys. Now I was classified as a professional criminal and had to live with old lags who had spent years behind bars. I was partly to blame for being in my present position, but my heart had ruled my head. Borstal had given me the chance to reform, but I had shunned that. My whole life was dominated by my shady past; someone, somewhere would try to destroy any future I could hope to build for myself.

I knew well, as I sat in that little room, that I would be denied my freedom for at least two years; and even after that I couldn't guarantee that I would go straight. I had a long record, and to be suspected I only had to be passing a place where a criminal offence had taken place.

From the start I decided to co-operate. The moment in the cell alone just after sentencing is the bitterest of the sentence. It is then that you decide either to fight the system or to conform. People who decide to fight come off worse. No one can beat the system. But you can con the system into believing that you are a changed person. I was a good con-man, and social workers and suchlike are easy people to fool. Moreover, from the outset a carrot was suspended in front of me. If I was a good boy and said yes and no when expected, I could get out after only one year. Everyone tries for parole but not everyone gets it. I was determined to be one of the lucky ones.

Wandsworth reception stank of stale piss. About forty of us were herded like animals into small booths. The embarrassing strip-search was followed by a cold bath. Then we huddled up together in cleaner booths to eat cold baked beans and potatoes off white plastic plates with plastic forks. The bread was stale and stuck in my throat, but I forced it down like the other frightened guys around me. Wandsworth was known for its very strict regime. Officers shouted and lashed out for no apparent reason. I blended into the crowd; I didn't want to be singled out and degraded. My homosexuality hadn't been mentioned, but one of us had his name shouted out and in front of us all was called a faggot and locked into a single cell. The poor guy was branded for the rest of his sentence.

We were marched from the reception area down to the reception wing. Anyone stepping out of line soon stepped back after a bark from an officer. The smell of urine lingered wherever we walked. The small landings in front of each row of cell doors were three feet wide. If you were standing on the ground floor, the four floors that made up the average wing block looked daunting. The occasional scream or call from behind a cell door pierced the deafening silence. It was eerie.

I could pick out the first offenders by the worried expressions on their faces. The regular visitors remained impassive. Some were impatient to get behind their cell doors and get their heads down. I joined two others when our names were called out, and we were banged up behind a door together. Total strangers – it was awkward at first. The other two were friends and had been in several times before. We introduced ourselves, then bedded down. They were in for grievous bodily harm, commonly known as GBH. They had gotten four years each. One looked like a typical gangster, with a broken nose and scarred face, and the other was a baby-face, but on his arms and back were several long knife-scars. We talked about our crimes, and the guys laughed and joked about all the guys that had smashed up and twisted glass into their faces.

I lay on the only top bunk. The cell was dark and they couldn't see the terrified expression I must have had. The tough-looking one had been on remand for several weeks and wanted sex. In the end his frightening demands became too horrible to bear and I sought help.

One morning, as soon as the cell door was open, I asked an officer to arrange protection for me. I must have looked terrified. I was taken straight down to the senior wing-officer's office. I explained what had happened the two previous nights, although I found it very embarrassing to recall to a perfect stranger. I was made to write out a statement, which I had to conclude by asking for protection under rule 43. I didn't know what rule 43 was, but if it kept me away from those thugs I wanted it.

I was taken to a separate wing fenced off from the rest of the prison – H wing. I was banged up with a guy in his fifties. He was unnaturally quiet. He asked me what I was in for; when I told him, he seemed surprised. I later found out to my disgust that he was a child-molester. Ninety per cent of the people in H wing were sexual offenders – rapists, pimps, child-abusers. Three were even child-murderers. One youth of about twenty-two used to scream the place down every night; he and his wife had smashed their baby up against a wall until it was dead. They had been given seven years each. They should have got life. Many of the Playland offenders and child-photographers were also there. It was uncanny – nearly all the cons looked like normal men. No one would have been able to point one out and say, 'That's a sex offender.'

There were also several other guys in for their own protection under rule 43. But if I had known what was in store for me I wouldn't have signed on. I would taken my chances with Kelly.

Rule 43 was basically confinement in the cells twenty-four hours a day. Everyone on the wing was classed as a 'nonce', the prison slang for a child-abuser. As other prisoners passed the wing they shouted insults. Even the cleaners who worked on the wing tried their best to get at the inmates. I was lucky; a couple of officers passed the word that I wasn't a nonce so I managed to avoid many of the traps set for my fellow inmates. Urine passed into the tea-urn, however, was undetectable unless you had been warned. Cleaners spat in trays of food, and I heard one day that shit had been stirred into a stew. I myself have pulled out drawing-pins from a piece of apple pie before swallowing it.

It was well known throughout the prison that H wing got all the rubbish from the kitchen. I knew enough about catering to confirm that everything that appeared on H wing servery was inadequate and below normal standards. If anything got burnt or ruined it was sent to H wing, as 'Nonces shouldn't have decent food'. The cons who worked in the kitchen played judge and jury on the H-wing food. I made several complaints to the assistant governor, but nothing was done. I even went so far as to refuse food for five days. Only after I had made a stand were all the cleaners removed and officers designated to serve the food.

The educational officer refused to help anyone on rule 43 and the only things available were notebooks and pencils. If anyone wanted to study they had to have the books sent in or try to get them through the library. That disgusted me; other prisoners had special educational facilities. I sent a complaint to the Home Office, and within days I was interviewed by the senior educational officer and given every book I needed to study shorthand and further account-ing. Word got round among the officers that I was a troublemaker. Some admired me for making a stand, others despised me and went out of their way to make my life awkward.

Once a day we were allowed one hour's exercise. We had to walk around an enclosed yard, rain or shine. I kept myself to myself, not wanting to listen to all the sordid stories about little boys' and girls' struggles. Occasionally, too, we were taken into a special workshop to sew mailbags. Small knives were used to cut open old bags, and, during a heated argument between two nonces, one of them got stabbed. The long silent nights were often disturbed by screams as someone slashed his wrists and was dragged off down to the cooler.

I felt degraded and wanted to get off rule 43, but the assistant governor blocked my appeals, telling me I was being kept in H wing for my own protection. I wanted to petition the Home Office, but the necessary papers were not available. I couldn't complain any higher – I was a rule 43 man. Everywhere I went in the prison I was escorted by an officer. Even in church on Sunday morning we were left sitting at the back, surrounded by officers.

It was on one of these Sunday mornings that I noticed a familiar face among the sea of others at the front of the church. We both looked at each other in disbelief. It was Peter. He had ended up as low as myself. He smiled reassuringly all through the service, and we nodded at each other. His eyes were filled with tears as he passed me. Within a couple of days I had a note pushed under my door; one of the cleaners had delivered it from Rites. Every time I sent a reply it cost me a quarter of an ounce of Old Holborn tobacco. It was that series of brief encounters and letters that kept me going in Wandsworth.

I applied time and time again to get off rule 43, until the assistant governor promised to move me to another prison. Coldingley was a new industrial prison in Bisley, Surrey. As the van approached the gate, cameras turned on us from all angles. It was one of the most secure prisons in the country. Most of the offenders were serving sentences from three years to life. Many people serving life sentences finished off at Coldingley before going into an open prison for their final years.

The fact that I had been on rule 43 was kept hidden from the other inmates. I soon found the easiest way to survive. I openly admitted I was gay. I couldn't have been more open if I had shouted, 'Hi, everybody, I'm gay.' The immediate reaction was distaste, but the heavies made a move towards my cell and I was well in.

My cell door was electronically operated, so that at night I could press a button and go to the bathroom whenever I wanted; but it was on a time-switch. After six minutes, alarms would start all over the place. The wing had three floors, each with cameras viewing each corridor; the only place where a camera couldn't see you was in the toilet.

On the ground floor were two television rooms, games rooms, a music room, a welfare office and showers, just as at Glen Parva. Gardens surrounded each wing and football-pitches and games areas separated the blocks. There was a central kitchen with individual wing dining-rooms, a gymnasium, churches and a twenty-classroom education department. If one wanted to work hard or study, Coldingley was the place to do it.

Industry was the focal point of all activities at Coldingley. After being unlocked at seven a.m. it was up to each individual inmate to get breakfast and get to his appointed place of work by eight. I was assigned to the laundry. It handled hospital laundry for about twelve hospitals. Other places of work included engineers' workshops, where road-signs were made. Shelving units were made in the metal shop, and the screen-printing unit designed and made hundreds of coats-of-arms for the forces and gentry.

My job in the laundry was on the presses. It was boring pressing old ladies' nighties all day on a foot-press. The money was good, however; for a full thirty-eight hour week we could earn up to £2.40 a week. With an extra ten hours' overtime I could earn the princely sum of £3.20. I must have shown potential, for I was moved to a stand-press and made responsible for pressing all the nurses' uniforms that came through. They then had to be folded and bagged.

Education was good for passing the time, and I joined a drama and typing class for three evenings a week. Once labour was over at five o'clock we returned to the wing to have tea. Our time was then our own until seven, when classes started. Education wasn't forced, and many of the men just sat around the wing watching telly. Once education was over at eight-thirty I used to shower and join Johnny in his cell.

Johnny was a lifer. He had already served nine years in prison, and he was a destroyed man – destroyed by the system. He didn't have the guts to face the future. When I had admitted my homosexuality he had been one of the loudest to laugh, yet we became the closest of friends. Homosexuality between long-term prisoners was an accepted form of relief. Johnny had never participated, even though several advances had been made towards him. That was until I made my approach.

Johnny was in for murder. He had killed a guy in a street-fight; he proclaimed that he was innocent, and had told that to so many people that he was even beginning to believe it himself. I felt sorry for him; his family rarely wrote to him, and the only person who visited him was an official prison visitor.

We joked about sex for quite some time; then, one lunch-time, I made a move. I thought it a challenge. Johnny could have turned on me; instead, he just went rigid. But my playful hands relaxed him and over a few weeks he learned to enjoy himself. At night he would stick love-letters under my door, and I was expected to reply straight away. He liked the idea of someone needing him. I reassured him and gave him a future to look forward to. Unfortunately, Johnny murdered another prisoner just eight weeks before his release. He then hanged himself in his cell, in 1985. We had to be sure to rip up our letters, though, as the screws nosed around the cells during the day. I always flushed mine down the toilet; Johnny used to hide his among his mail.

Cell searches were a monthly routine. We didn't know when they were going to happen, so we were always prepared. Stanley knives, razor-blades and spikes were hidden all about the wing and were very rarely found. I never risked keeping a tool. I wanted my parole. Once an inmate's bed had been stripped and his drawers and cupboards searched, that was it, unless a medic was called in for a body-search; then you were made to lie naked on a bed while he probed about. Luckily that never happened to me.

I had very few problems with other inmates. There was only one guy who tried to cause trouble; he had murdered Tommy Steele's manager on Hungerford Bridge. He was a nasty piece of work. He was only young when he got the sentence, and he fought the system and tried to avenge himself on any guy he could get hold of. He only once tried to go for me; two of the wing heavies pulled him off, took him in the bathroom and gave him a pasting.

I got on very well with the officers on the wing, and the senior officer nicknamed me 'Bubbles'. That bloody nickname stuck with me until the day I left. I encouraged advances from some of the guys as I flaunted around the wing swinging my mutton. During my stay there I was screwed by three murderers, two rapists and an aristocrat. Every one of them was gentle with me, and they made my stay in Coldingley even easier.

Johnny used to get upset when I flirted with other men. He spent most of his earnings buying me chocolates.

I only had two visits during my whole stay in prison. Chas came and kept me informed about the outside world. I enquired after Bill. He was also in prison; he had left Chas in the pub and gone to live with a young man, whom he murdered one night. Bill and I had slept together several times; I could have been his victim. I shivered inside.

Money was available to all inmates, and five- and ten-pound notes had their exchange rates inside the prison walls. The fiver could get you three pounds' worth of silver, and ten pounds equalled five pounds' worth of silver.

Every new officer on the wind wasn't fully fledged until I'd initiated him. The senior officers used to warn me in advance; when the poor unsuspecting man was sent to unlock me I used to be sitting up in bed, and the patter-line was always the same: 'Well, hello, handsome. If only you didn't have that uniform on, I'd be able to make a real man of you.' Then I'd make as if to get out of bed. The door normally slammed shut, and the poor sod went running back to the office to face the laughs and jeers of his fellows. After that, every time I appeared or went screaming through the wing, he vanished, or was too nervous to move and just tried to ignore me.

There was a nonce on the wing who had been molesting a ten-year-old girl. He had a bad time. His cell was continually smashed open and shit smeared on his sheets or bleach substituted in his shampoo bottle. Even photographs of his wife and children were slashed.

The only time I got close to being reported was one day in the laundry. Everyone was in a playful mood, and a few spanners had been thrown in the machinery to screw it all up. When the machines ground to a halt the guys were laid off for breaks until the officers could unbung them. I was always clowning about, and I disappeared into the toilet and came out with a full nurse's uniform on. The duty officers fell about in fits of laughter – but the laundry manager ticked me off.

To this day I don't know what made me do it. Perhaps Sandy had subconsciously rebelled, but usually I didn't find her too much of a problem. I had always been able to control her to some extent – until the day she came out and decided to stay out for good. Then I had another problem: how to get rid of George!

Chapter 21

Decision

Despite all the frolics, I spent many lonely sleepless nights curled up in my cell in the dark. Until I had reached an analysis of my past, I was unable to decide on my future. Without careful planning I knew I would be back behind bars within a year of my release. Somewhere in my life I had gone wrong. I had to find out where.

Was it at my birth? Should I ever have been born? I had caused many people misery, and for many my name is distasteful. Should I have been born a boy or a girl? Had someone got it wrong? And if so, who? My parents? Or was someone else using me as a guinea-pig to test whether or not the formula for masculinity and femininity was right? All I knew was that it wasn't my fault – or was it?

Had sexual corruption at an early age steered me on to the wrong path for ever? Was there no turning back? The fact was that corruption had brought me the security and happiness I hadn't known before. Had my 'uncle' damned my life – or was my first criminal offence to blame?

I had known full well what I was doing when I had stolen and lied my way about the country. I knew I would be punished, yet it didn't matter. I wanted money, wealth, the good things in life. I was greedy, inconsiderate and destructive. The kid-glove treatment I had received in Borstal hadn't done me any good. A short, sharp, strict sentence might have straightened me out.

If I had had the guts to face up to my wife, perhaps it would have stabilised me in normal society (according to what society likes to think of as normality). My children, given from my body, I had just let go.

Was my homosexuality to blame, or just a feeble excuse for copping out? And was I really gay, or was there more to it? My feminine mince and gestures were easily blamed on my homosexual streak, and I emphasised my whole lifestyle. 'Glad to be gay' was the motto on everyone's lips. But was my homosexuality to blame for my putting on outrageous women's clothes? Or was Sandy the real me? She always raised her head and spoke out when I was in trouble. I always hid behind her skirts for sanctuary, and she brought me an uncanny peace inside. Nothing she did was wrong. She was never violent, rarely lied and was always happy – such a nice person. When she disappeared I felt lonely. She made friends that George could never mix with. Sandy was more artistic, more determined, more realistic. Why was she always there deep inside me? Why wouldn't she go away? She was getting too strong – more uncontrollable every day. She'd never been like this in the past. Why now, when I was trying to make the decisions on my future that mattered so much.

George was slowly losing his grip on me. As Sandy, I was far stronger and more determined to survive. I knew that if I could leave George and all his problems behind, then I would succeed. All that was left of George was a shell: his body. My heart and mind belonged to the woman that was trapped inside this shell. That woman was me. George was not prepared to fight or struggle, the battle had really been won years before. I laid him to rest, at peace with himself and quite prepared to let me change his body. A new shape was needed in order to release the real me. Both Sandy and George discovered peace then. George was gone and I had my freedom. I had life and I could start to live.

As George, I had enquired, and tried to see a doctor about having sex-change surgery without much success. I had not really come to terms with my true identity. I had not realised that the real problem was trapped inside me. I only knew that I had been rejected. George had been pained, yet he had let me out to help him cope with life, as he had done whenever he had been in trouble and unable to face it. I was the stronger of the two of us and always had been. I had just had to wait for the right opportunities.

I had to find out what people's responses would be to me. George had always been friendly with the chaplain at Coldingley. I met him and explained how I felt: that I wanted to get rid of George's body. He looked at me, bewildered. Then scorn crossed his face. He must have thought the devil was within me and had been sent to test him. His attitude was standoffish. He told me to pray to God and ask for guidance. Guidance for what? God had given George the wrong body. We all make mistakes. The chaplain and I parted with the understanding that I must really consider what I was doing before I made a mistake.

The welfare officer was just as bad. When I told her she laughed nervously and said it was just a passing fantasy. No one understood me or even tried to. These people were lost when put in a situation where they really had to help. They were lost – but I wasn't. I could at least start where George had left off: at Charing Cross Hospital. Surely the doctors there would be able to see I needed help straight away?

When I told Johnny about my troubles, he thought the idea was great. Starting a new life with a new body, leaving all the old worries and problems behind – what more could anyone want? At least I had something to hang on to. I was going to have a sex-change the minute I got out of prison, or at least put the wheels in motion.

So I just had to get out. I pulled every string in the book. I had a good record in the prison and I intended to keep it that way. I worked more overtime than I had done before; I was determined to get parole once I had completed a year inside. But, to convince the parole board, I had to have something to go out to, and I had nothing; no home, no work.

My nights weren't sleepless any more. I spent hours of spare time working on a kitchen designer's course, designing and planning industrial kitchens. Costing and accounting. At the end of each hard day's work I was exhausted, and time was flying by. With the governor's consent I was able to buy a copy of the *Caterer and Hotel Keeper*.

I applied to hundreds of companies, using up a daily allowance of six letters, to ask for the break I really needed. I appealed from the heart, and with a prison letter-heading I could only tell the truth. I explained my offences and acknowledged the fact that I would have to start back down the ladder until I proved myself. I only wanted the chance.

As I began to receive replies, I became despondent. Each one apologised, making some feeble excuse. I had plenty of qualifications. If I had applied for any of the posts from Civvy Street I would have been snapped up.

No one seemed willing to give me even a trial – until I got an interesting letter and application form from the district catering manager of the Kensington, Chelsea and Westminster Area Health Authority. Although I had a criminal record, I was going to be offered a chance. I filled in the form and within a week received confirmation that I had been appointed a kitchen superintendent. My welfare officer was delighted. She now had a stronger case for getting me out.

Ten months into my sentence, and I was on tenterhooks. I had met a man from the parole board. He'd asked me many irrelevant questions about my discharge. I gave him the answers I knew he wanted to hear. I tried to explain that I was a changed person and had no intention of committing further offences. What use was it keeping me in prison another year when I was ready right now to conform and play the game?

As the days ticked away, I became restless. Mr M was very kind to me; he continually advised me to be grateful even if I got only six months' parole. But I wanted the year. I became unhappy in the laundry, and when a position became vacant for a cook in the officers' mess outside the gate, I applied for it. I got the job with the help of Mr M and two other officers, who were on the officers' mess committee. The governor allowed me out to work, and walking through that gate on a cold frosty morning was pure heaven. For ten and a half months I had been deprived of seeing the outside world. The grass was still green, the sky was blue, and there were still cars on the road, yet it was different. The birds chirped in the trees, dogs chased about on the lawns, but it was still different. I had never really looked at nature and life before – George hadn't let me. Oh, it was good to be alive! I didn't mind the body-searches as we left and entered the big steel gates every day; for me it was the start of my freedom.

Work in the officers' mess was easy and, along with the other two cons, I had a ball. During the afternoon we were able to relax and occasionally play the fruit-machine. The mornings were hard graft, scrubbing down and running around after lazy officers, cleaning out the single guys' rooms – and occasionally having a peep at the odd officer as he stripped off and had a shower. There was a utility cupboard at the side of the bathroom; the thin plaster wall soon gave in as I poked a minute hole with a nail at the right level to get an eyeful if the officer was standing in the right position. Several good-looking, unsuspecting officers washed and soaped themselves, much to my delight. Yet the male body, too, was different; I didn't find it attractive for the same reasons as George had. It had a new meaning for me. It was sensual. Once I had changed my body to its right form, I intended to please and delight men – not for gain but for self satisfaction. Hundreds of men had corrupted George, and I was going to get my own back; give them a little, then let them beg for the rest until I was ready.

My first year's date was four days away. I was nervous because I hadn't heard from the parole board; and when Mr M called into the office late one night I could tell by his face that I had been turned down. Instead, I could get out six months earlier; he said it was better than nothing. But nothing was what I had now. I was sure the position I had been offered wouldn't be available. Everything had gone wrong. The hours I had spent trying to please everyone – all wasted. I felt depressed. If I had to do another six months, I might as well forget everything. I had no intention of conforming any longer. I would be unruly. They had to let me out sometime. I was sure my outspokenness about having a sex-change had gone against me.

It was pointless for anyone to try to comfort me. I went into a blazing rage like a spoilt little child. In a matter of minutes I destroyed everything I had been working on. I ripped up all my theory papers, and analysis charges and kitchen designs were torn off the wall and destroyed. One officer who had followed my studies over the past year opened the cell door. He didn't say anything, but slowly shook his head. I knew I had been foolish; but so what? I wasn't being given a chance. What difference would six months make? I wanted to go straight.

However, careful planning soon changed my situation. I wrote a pitiful letter to my future employer telling him that I was sorry to have wasted his time; I would no longer be available to start work, and, although I only had six months to do before parole release, I intended to refuse it and finish another year.

I posted the letter and waited for the uproar. All mail is censored by wing officers. Sure enough, at ten a.m. two officers collected me from the mess and took me back on the wing. Mr M asked me what I was playing at. I stubbornly stood there and told him that the parole board could stick their six months where the money stuffs his nuts. I intended to do my full sentence. He could see it was no use talking to me, but the letter was held back and at lunchtime I was let out of my cell to see the senior governor.

I gave him the same story. If the parole board weren't trusting me all the way, but only halfway, then tough. I'd stay on until my time was up. I stipulated that I wanted the letter to be sent, and the Home Office to confirm that I had rejected the six months parole. The governor had been kind to me, and I felt sorry for putting him in such a compromising position. It was the first time an inmate had ever refused a parole board ruling. But I was adamant, and he agreed to contact the Home Office. That was it – or so I thought.

After a few days I realised I had been rather hasty, and that six months was better than nothing; but I wouldn't admit that to anyone. Most of the cons thought I was stupid, but I braved it out. I had nothing to go out to except my change. I had George in control, and I could wait.

About two weeks after refusing the parole board's decision, I was called to the chaplain's office late one evening. I only ever saw the chaplain when I made a morning application. When I entered his office I felt quite confused. The governor, the chaplain and my wing welfare officer were all there, with two other gentlemen who were apparently representatives of the parole board. The Home Office had ruled that my case should be reassessed. I was asked the same old questions I had been asked three months earlier, and gave the same answers. I was talked about as if I wasn't really there, and when my past records and history had been sorted out I was returned to the wing while they made a decision.

I heard nothing for several days. Then Mrs S, my wing welfare officer, came rushing into the officer's mess to tell me the Home Office had decided to release me the following week. The only condition was that I should stay in a hostel until I found suitable accommodation. My heart began racing. I could hardly believe it. By being pig-headed I had fooled the parole board. I had one hundred and ninety-two bloody hours left before I could walk out of the gate a free woman. Johnny and the gang on the wing wouldn't believe me that evening, but two days later I was on my home leave for three days. They all called me a jammy bastard, but I wasn't jammy – I was a good con-girl. It was one of George's traits I was glad I had kept.

The three days were spent at a grotty little reception centre for ex-offenders in Clapham, facing the common. I had to sleep in a large room with an assortment of alcoholics and bums. Yet it was comforting – no bars on the windows, no stink of urine wafting down the hall. It was heaven.

I had to be in by eleven o'clock each evening, but still managed to get over to the Elephant for a drink. However, Chas had left and the pub had gone to pot. I went round to his flat in Wimbledon, and he was very pleased to see me. I borrowed a suit and shirt and tie – they looked a lot better for an interview than the rubbish the prison had provided me with.

The interview at the Middlesex Hospital went well, and I was appointed as a 'periphery superintendent' in charge of a one hundred-and-twenty-bedded hospital in Muswell Hill called St Luke's. The catering manager was a decent enough chap, ex-RAF. I was grateful for the chance to prove myself, and he led me to believe that, if I could, the world was mine. He needed some good men.

On my last day I was at a loss for something to do; I had completed all that was expected of me. Then I remembered Sue, an old friend. I phoned her and went straight to the office she managed and we sat talking for hours. I hadn't let anyone but Chas know where I was – visits in prison only upset me; I was always better if I faced a sentence alone. But Sue couldn't do enough for me. She had just bought a new flat, and when I told her about the hostel she wouldn't hear of it. She called my probation officer in Clapham and volunteered to let me have a room at her place.

The probation officer was a very understanding guy. When he visited Sue's that evening he was delighted with the flat, and decided that I would have a far better start from there than from a grotty hostel. That was it, I returned to Coldingley the following morning with only three days left to do.

I was so excited I couldn't sleep. I spent a lot of time with Johnny. I knew he would be lost again when I left, but I promised to write and keep in touch with him. He only had a few years to do now. The last twelve hours were the worst; every time I looked at my watch only two minutes had ticked away. Then my time came. I was called down to the wing office, then marched over to reception. I signed an agreement not to hold firearms in my possession for five years; then, after my discharge grant of £28 had been paid over, I was marched to the gate, where George William Roberts F30901 for ever ceased to exist.

I stepped on to the train at Bisley a new woman – determined to survive, determined to win a new way of life. Nothing was going to stop me. Authority wouldn't hold me back. I had made the decision. George's old body must go for good.

Chapter 22
Operation Julia

I travelled down to Chichester to pick up my old belongings. They had been stored in the probation office there because Bognor Regis had no storage space. My trunks, not surprisingly had disappeared, and so had my most expensive clothing and make-up. All that was left in the huge black plastic bags was rubbish.

I was given a room in which to sort things out. Dirty washing had been mixed in with stage clothes, and the whole lot stank to high heaven. I sorted out all the drag, keeping everything feminine and dumping the men's wear. I ended up with eight bags of rubbish and four of clothes suitable for re-use. I didn't throw my old stage clothes away. They bore fond memories – not like the old suits and trousers; they were meaningless.

I struggled to the railway station with my black bags, cursing the girls in Bognor. It was only lunchtime; I would be in London for two o'clock. But Sue didn't finish work until six, and I didn't want to walk the streets with these heavy bags. So I took a chance and telephoned David and Stella's. After telling me off because I hadn't let them know where I was, they arranged to meet me at Victoria station.

It was great to see them all on the platform as the train pulled in.

They looked genuinely pleased to see me. The kids were on half-term and ran around us as we tried to carry the bags out. I was quieter than normal, and super-sensitive David knew that something was bothering me, but he left it until we were relaxing in their lounge. Then, when he asked what was wrong, I told him. He laughed nervously at first and said I must be joking. My face remained impassive. He knew I didn't joke about things of importance. Stella told him to shut up, threw her arms around me and in her chirpy English manner told me not to worry, mate. If that's what I wanted, then she'd help.

David sat bewildered for a while until the true meaning of what we had been talking about sank in. Then he interrupted, 'Hey, do you mean they'll cut your cock off?'

I nodded.

He just fell back in the chair and said, 'Jesus Christ.'

Over the next few hours we talked about life and why I had made my decision, and by the time I left that evening they were converted. They may not have understood why I was doing it, but they could see it was what I wanted, and they offered all I needed from them – support.

That was the first barrier over. I had to tell Sue next; that would be more difficult. That evening we talked well into the early hours, but by the time the lights went out in the lounge I don't think she was any the wiser. She didn't agree with what I wanted to do. She thought I shouldn't tamper with nature. But she said that, if it was what I really wanted, then fair enough. As long as I was sure.

The following morning I visited the Middlesex, and was taken over to St Luke's to be introduced to my staff and meet the rest of the hospital management. I spent a pleasant day chatting and looking round. Surprisingly enough, I only had one English girl on my whole staff, and she was of a very nervous disposition and shouldn't have been allowed to work there. The rest of the staff had all started as kitchen porters and over time had worked their way up to being cooks; but they still cooked like kitchen porters.

The hospital management team welcomed me with open arms. The kitchen was their sore point. It had been without a superintendent for nearly a year and was in a disgraceful state. Paying residents were always complaining. If I could improve the food and standard of hygiene, I would help them immensely.

The main kitchen had to cook and supply food for six wards, two day centres, the nurses' home and a staff canteen. In my first few days at St Luke's I reconstructed the weekly menus. Looking back through the records, I found that the same two-week menu had been used for sixteen years. Staff rotas were changed and overtime was scrapped – there was no need for it. The hospital catered for psychiatric patients, so special diets were very rarely needed, but I had to keep a tight control over portions. The catering staff had no idea when it came to quantities. I considered my job to be one that a woman should perform, so I was at home.

Within two weeks I had the place running smoothly. A weekly saving of four hundred pounds was made on wages alone. The district catering manager was very impressed and talked about offering me a job as a periphery manager, looking after five hospitals. I was very pleased, for since my release I had tried hard to prove myself. At last things were going well.

For me George had ceased to exist, but his old friends wouldn't let him go, and I didn't know whether they were talking to me or trying to get through to my old self. Many of the stories they re-collected were puzzling – I hardly remembered them; my past was very vague.

I tried to explain to people that I wasn't George any more. Their reactions were various. Most thought that the prison sentence had sent me doolally tap. Others felt sorry for me; they thought I must have been very confused. But I wasn't. Many showed disgust. They didn't understand my problem, and they didn't want to understand it. It was the kind of thing you read about in the *News of the World*. It's too much to comprehend when it hits you at close quarters. All my gay friends thought I was copping out. I didn't really want a sex change, they told me. I just wanted more cock, legally. It upset me to think that people could be so callous.

One guy even suggested that I go to church to pray to God to cast out the devil from within me. I had never been a religious person, but during my nights of torment in prison I had turned and spoken to God, asking for help as all people do when they're in trouble. I didn't get an answer. I had to make my own decision.

Some people were openly rude to my face; others were hypocrites and talked behind my back, and that upset me more. That first month of trying to gain recognition was the hardest. Then, in-credibly, I was given an opportunity to explain it better to everyone. The chance of a lifetime in a two-minute phone call.

I was sitting in my office, stock-sheets and order-books piled high on the desk, when the phone rang out. I picked up the receiver and a rather unsure voice said, 'Is that George Roberts?' I acknow-ledged that it was, and the voice rumbled on, still uncertainly, 'Is it true that you're going to have a sex change?' Again I said yes; then I asked who was speaking.

David Pearson was a news director with the BBC. He had just joined the 'Inside Story' team under the watchful eye of Roger

Mills, an executive producer. He had to make a fifty-minute film about a topical subject and someone had telephoned the Beeb and given my name and address as a contact. David had already approached Roger about the same subject, and he will openly admit that it was a million-to-one chance when my details landed on his desk.

We couldn't say much more on the phone; David wanted to meet me and talk. I agreed to meet, wondering what I would be letting myself in for. Once he reassured me he would be by himself, I felt more confident.

My first impressions of David haven't really changed. I thought him good-looking, very sure of himself and definitely middle-class. I also thought him possibly gay, but that thought dispelled itself straight away. In the first hour he must have told me fifty times that he had a girlfriend. So he was straight.

David sat as far away as possible, keeping his eye on his cup and saucer and looking up only when asking questions. I teased him a little, but answered all his questions honestly. He seemed amazed at my frankness, and by the end of the afternoon he was all for making the film. He had to talk to his bosses, so we arranged to meet the following evening.

David must have called me three times the next day to make sure I was still available. I decided that I would meet him as a woman, so I left work early and bought myself a new dress and shoes. Sue was at home when I arrived; she let it be known that she wasn't too happy about the BBC becoming involved. I told her nothing was confirmed, but she wouldn't have it, and went out in a bad temper before David arrived. I slowly made up my face, taking care not to overdo it. By the time I was ready, I was nervous as hell. I was worried about David's reaction. My make-up didn't feel right. When the doorbell rang I went to pieces, and flew to the bathroom mirror to check my hair. But, as I looked at my image, I changed. I felt my body relaxing. I looked good. If he didn't like me, tough. When I opened the door the surprised look on his face was enough to tell me I was all right. For the first few minutes all he could say was that he couldn't believe it.

An hour later Roger Mills arrived. We talked again for several hours. I felt that neither of them understood my problem, but they were sympathetic and showed interest. Roger wanted to know how far I had actually gone. I told him that I was in the process of visiting Charing Cross Hospital again. He was delighted and gave David the go-ahead. I wanted the films to educate the public and give other transsexuals confidence.

Once Roger and David were sure that I was a suitable subject, film schedules were set up and the process of going to see the doctor at Charing Cross started. It was well known that he had flatly refused to let any film crews near his unit. Several producers and directors had tried, but to no avail. I sent my letter, and David visited him and buttered him up. I was very surprised when David told me that the doctor had agreed to the first lot of filming.

David invited me to the Television Centre one lunchtime, where, from glass galleries high above the lighting structures, I was able to watch programmes being made. It was an exhilarating experience. David was gaining my confidence, preparing me for the first time I would have to appear in front of a camera myself. Sue, however, still wasn't happy about the filming, and refused to let a film crew into the flat. To make matters easier, I moved into residential accommodation at St. Luke's. I had a small room in the building that housed all the single sisters. I was one of the girls – little did they know. But I was treated as an outsider, for it was unprecedented for a male to live in female quarters.

Once my appointment at Charing Cross Hospital had been confirmed, I phoned David and we arranged to do some filming the following week. I was so nervous. I didn't know what to expect. My first session was to be as a man; then I had to do my make-up. David arrived early and calmed me down, but my heart was racing again once the crew arrived. There were so many. The cameraman and his assistant, David's assistant, the sound-recordist and the lighting man: although there were never more than three present at any one time. It wasn't very funny. Then I had to face the camera and talk about my past. Things that I really wanted to forget all came rushing back, and I was confidently telling them in front of all these strangers. Rita, David's assistant, was very considerate and soon found out that a constant supply of Mars bars kept me happy. The crews were all fascinated by the subject and I soon got used to the idea of having them around – although when they were changed I had to answer the same old questions time and time again.

Having the BBC around caused problems for me straight away. One of the sisters complained that equipment had been left all over the hall, and the hospital secretary and senior sisters came over and demanded to know what was going on. As I entered the secretary's office, she sat upright, a proper authoritarian. I sat in front of her desk like a little schoolboy. When I told her the BBC were filming my sex-change operation she nearly fell off her chair. She was nearly at retiring age and I couldn't possibly expect her to accept what I was doing. She started to speak, then stopped, composed herself and started again. It was unheard of. She was sure Area Health would object.

Luckily David stepped in and explained that we were making a long-term programme. This must have mollified the regional office, because they agreed to let the filming continue. Nevertheless, they advised me to see my district catering manager to tell him what was happening.

During the night some sleazy bastard telephoned the hospital and asked for several extension numbers and then told staff members that I was going to have a sex-change. One of my staff from the kitchen came over and told me about the crank calls. I was furious. David turned up the following morning and we went to storm the Middlesex. I was in a terrible mood. My boss was ready for me, the film crew had followed me up to the door of the hospital and a large crowd had gathered. It was the first time I had filmed in public, and I could hear people asking who I was. It was a satisfying experience.

Once I reached the district catering manager's office, my confidence hit an all-time high. He gave me a letter congratulating me and confirming my position as periphery manager if I completed a ten-week course at the Middlesex. I folded the letter and locked it in my briefcase. Then we got down to the matter in hand. My boss knew something was wrong, and had heard rumours from St Luke's about the BBC. I found it awkward to talk to him. He asked me if I was homosexual, and said that, if that was what was worrying me, I must forget it. Homosexuality was well accepted. But, when I explained that I was going to have a sex-change, he thought it preposterous. I was a man and I shouldn't interfere with nature. It was shameful. He sat quietly for a short while, then asked me to give him his letter back. I refused. He turned scarlet with rage. He wanted to sack me on the spot, and as he held back I realised that it was an advantage to have the BBC around.

The catering manager stamped out of his office, and when he returned he informed me that I would have to see the district medical team for a medical opinion as to whether or not I was a transsexual. I slammed out of the office myself. What a nerve! A medical team that weren't specially trained were to pass an opinion on my condition. As I left, his voice sounded behind me, telling me he wished he'd never employed me.

It was dark when I left the main door of the hospital, but the whole of the car park lit up as I stepped into the cold night air. Nurses and patients were all at the windows. I stood in front of the camera as rain drizzled down. I tried to explain what had happened, but all the people crowding round put me off, so we stopped filming and moved into a small café, where I showed the letter to David and explained a little about the Sex Discrimination Act. If my bosses refused to let me work as a woman I intended to take them to court. There was no law saying I couldn't wear women's clothes one day and men's the next.

The following day all hell broke loose. The area administrator had seen the BBC, and an enquiry was launched. I was told I would have to see the senior nursing officer that evening. The BBC were around all day, waiting to see what the outcome would be. I expected to see just one woman, but when I turned up in her office several senior administrators were present. I was grilled for over an hour. But they only really wanted to know how deeply involved the BBC were, and by the end of the day it was agreed that I could start work the following March as a woman.

I had got over one hurdle – I had been accepted by my bosses, if only because of the BBC. Now I had to face the doctor at Charing Cross. On the day of my appointment the BBC crew turned up at nine a.m. and filmed me getting ready. I talked about my doubts and fears, knowing full well what a swine the doctor could be. I carefully chose clothes that I felt good in. Then I set off for Charing Cross Hospital with my heart in my mouth. Today was the most important of my life. If the doctor didn't accept me as a National Health patient, I didn't stand a chance of surgery, for I would never be able to pay for it.

Sitting outside the doctor's office while the BBC set up their equipment was the most nerve-racking experience I have ever been through. Rita came out and told me that the doctor had three students in with him. That made me even worse.

Eventually I was called into the office to face the almighty. The chubby effigy that grunted at me looked a swine. If all the rumours I had heard were true, I would get into trouble. The doctor liked his girls to be seen and not heard. They must be conservative and do as they were told, when they were told. I wasn't a conformist.

The letter of reference I had paid a private doctor for was handed over, then my name established. I was to be called George Roberts until the day I had surgery – if and when the doctor recommended it. I sat facing the old man (whose balding head was covered with a few stray white hairs), trying to look as feminine as possible. Then he asked, 'Well, what's your problem?'

I could have laughed. That was the last question I had expected. I briefly sketched my family history. I couldn't lie – David knew the full story from our many conversations. Yes, I had been a male prostitute. The doctor informed me that that would go against me when he made his decision, as many transsexuals turn to prostitution to support themselves after surgery.

For ten minutes I was treated like a lump of shit, and endured questions that seemed totally irrelevant to my problem. No, I hadn't contracted VD. No, I hadn't wet the bed as a child. Yes, I did try to be tidy and clean. Ah? The doctor confirmed that most trans-sexuals were.

I then upset the doctor for the first time. I admitted to being on hormone tablets that I had bought on the black market. He stuttered into his microphone, then agreed to give me a prescription. I had been on six five-milligram Stilboestrol tablets daily. He prescribed me three 2.5-milligram tablets. That would just about stop me feeling horny, and with any luck I would develop a bust in ten years.

When the doctor asked me how I felt, I told him I felt like a woman. I was a woman. When he asked me to explain how a woman felt, I couldn't. It just felt like being me. Then he asked the young female student who was present what it felt like to be a woman. She answered that it felt like being her.

The whole interview made the doctor look unsympathetic. I was accepted as a National Health patient, and the date was recorded. I was to live as a woman for one year following a legal precedent. The doctor told me that after one year he would consider me for surgery, but not before. I had to prove myself first.

As the interview ended, he warned me that it was my own responsibility that I cross-dressed, and that I would be liable to the civil authorities if I tried to marry. It was illegal. He could make my body into a woman's body with the help of a surgeon, but I would never have the right to participate in the service of marriage that means so much to all women.

After standing by the door so that the doctor could take a photograph to add to his collection of thousands, I was dismissed. David questioned the doctor as to my chances. The doctor thought I was a classic case and had the symptoms of a transsexual – whatever those are.

Once the film crew had finished in the doctor's office, I made an appointment for eight weeks ahead, and got my prescription dispensed. We then did some filming as I left the hospital. I was feeling quite bewildered. I hadn't really learned anything in the interview, and hadn't been given any advice. I presumed I had to make my own way, hoping I did the right things. All the film crew thought the doctor a pompous old sod. We then gratefully retired to the nearest pub for a drink. I needed one more than anyone.

During the interview I had been asked if I wanted to be cured of my illness. What illness? I thought. No, I was quite happy – and that was it. I had no tests, no hormone counts to see if my body was more feminine; not even a blood or urine test.

That evening I returned to Muswell Hill feeling a little more settled in mind. I had taken the first steps, ready to transform this old body into something that I would be able to use. I confidently took my Premarin tablets (they were acknowledged to be far better than Stilboestrol), then drifted off to sleep, praying that my tits would hurry up and grow.

Chapter 23
From George to Julia Overnight

My life-style was now changing drastically. I was very happy working at St Luke's hospital. I got on well with my staff and felt more secure than I ever had done before. Through being involved with the BBC I had found many new friends who supported me in my bid for freedom.

I only had a few weeks to live as George, and there was much to do in the way of preparation for the big day, my first full day as a woman at work: new clothes to buy, my family to tell. I couldn't just go ahead and change my sex without telling them. I didn't owe them anything, yet I did not want them to read the story in the newspapers or see the film on television without some explanation.

I mentioned to David at one of our frequent meetings that I intended to go up north for the day to see my family. Typical producer, he dived on the idea, and we agreed that I'd tell my mother and sisters in front of a camera if they agreed. David could talk anyone into assisting, even if only for the sake of art.

We arranged a preview visit the following week for a day. We went to Preston, where David hired a car, and we travelled around Fleetwood viewing all the houses I had lived in, the toilets I had had illicit sex in and the pubs that my mother usually frequented. David was full of ideas for locations and shots, and, when he suggested that we came down for three days' filming, I knew full well he was going to rake up a lot of the past I wanted to forget.

David convinced me that, if he filmed me standing in a boy's public toilet telling of my shadowy past, it would give people a better insight. He insisted they would be more sympathetic. So the filming was agreed, and I set about making plans for the visit. It had seemed funny driving past all the houses I had lived in. We had driven past fifteen years of my life in about twenty minutes: memories came flooding back.

The following day I met Paul, another producer. He was totally fascinated about my past life and told me I should write a book. He knew an agent that might be interested. I was very keen. I couldn't really write; but, as Paul said, if the agent thought I had a good enough story he might be able to find me a ghost-writer. I mentioned it to David, and through Paul a meeting was arranged with Caradoc King, literary agent with A. P. Watt in Bedford Row, London. David had written many short stories, so he was a likely candidate to ghost the book.

Caradoc, young and energetic, talked about the filming with deep interest. He thought that I had a good story to tell and said that he would like to handle it. He showed great enthusiasm from the start, and many of his ideas inspired me. He thought it a good idea for David and myself to work together. Then he asked me the crucial question. 'What are you going to call yourself?'

Sandy wasn't a very good name to be labelled with for the rest of my life, so we agreed David and I would talk about it later over a drink. We were told to write up a synopsis and then return, possibly even with a draft chapter. I was very excited by the idea, and, if Caradoc was able to sell a publisher the story-line, I would have the finance to help me through.

That evening David and I sat in a pub in Holborn and discussed my future name. I had already decided to change my surname from Roberts to Grant. Grant was the surname of a beautiful girl I fell in love with at junior school. She was so pretty and wore the most exquisite dresses, but I think I loved the dresses more than I did her. I just needed a suitable Christian name. We went through lists of names and decided I was never to be a Mary or a Joan, and Elsie and Alice were definitely out. We gradually got down to three possibles, of which I favoured Julia. We wrote the three on slips of paper and drew lots. As luck would have it, Julia came out twice, and from that day on I was known to David solely as Julia.

Even before I had changed into my female role he had accepted me. On several occasions I took him and some of the film crew into gay pubs or clubs. It was a whole new world to them, but they enjoyed the pubs where you could see a good drag show. David had become more of a friend than a producer, and we got on very well. Occasionally while filming I would get upset or annoyed, and he either quietened me down or gave as good as he got. We never let it get in the way of the film, though. It was the most important thing to both of us. I wanted people to understand me, and David just had to tell the story so people would understand it. If things started to go wrong we talked about it, and, all in all, we survived.

A freelance film crew had been booked for the Fleetwood filming. They were a northern-based crew, so we met them at an hotel in

Blackpool. We spent the first day getting to know each other. David explained his ideas and plans to the cameraman, and while they whiled away the hours talking about planned shots I nattered to the assistants. Everyone seemed totally fascinated by the subject, as had all the previous crews we had filmed with. After a good meal and a late-night drink we bedded down for the night; at seven a.m. we were to start filming on the dockside in Fleetwood.

David couldn't have picked a colder day. We didn't arrive at the quayside till about eight, and we all looked the worse for the previous night's booze. It had affected the sound-recordist so much that he'd left all his equipment behind at the hotel. He then had to take the car back to Blackpool while we slowly froze. I hate cold weather at the best of times, and as the minutes ticked into an hour my temper got the better of me. I blamed David, even though it wasn't his fault, and he quietly took my volleying until the sound-recordist returned. I then had to walk along the same piece of dockside several times before the film crew got it right; and, when I eventually saw the film weeks later, I (if no one else) could understand why I was looking so bad-tempered. David then wanted me to talk about my family connections with the docks. That took a further two hours, and while the crew took other wildtrack shots I stamped off into the cold like a spoilt schoolchild. I had caused a bad atmosphere and I knew it. After a while I returned to the location, where all the men, including David, sat huddled in their cars, freezing to death. It was a good excuse for a lunch-break, where I eventually apologised for my rudeness.

I wasn't looking forward to the following day's filming at all. How does anyone tell his mother that he's going to change his sex? The film crew didn't envy my task one little bit, and were as surprised as I was at my mother's reaction. I had written and told her in advance about my planned arrival, but it wasn't until she was in the pub with me that she knew about the filming. She agreed to let David film as long as he waited for her to nip home and change. She was delighted that the BBC were making a film about my life.

Once the cameras were rolling, I mentioned that I had told her years earlier that I was homosexual. She explained how she felt and her reactions. Then came the crunch. I said that I was going to change my sex. She sat looking at me from behind her dark glasses. I could see her blinking back the tears. She held my hand and said that, if that was what I wanted. I must do it – as long as I was going to be happy. Then she said she'd brought me into the world as a son, but she would love me just as much if I were a daughter. We talked about my past; she couldn't see where I had gone wrong, and blamed herself for not seeing the truth beforehand.

I couldn't wait to get into the fresh air. Her reaction had choked me. David had pushed her into answering questions that pointed a finger at her. Her sickly attitude had been good in front of the camera, but she really was worried about my future. I could tell the truth from the tangle of lies that lay in the past, so after slipping her some money for a drink and promising to come again soon, we slipped away.

Rita was the first to notice how hurt I really was. As tears flowed, Rita tried to comfort me. I didn't even know whether I still loved my mother or not. Once David realised something was wrong we split up from the rest of the crew for a while to talk about it. I thought the whole thing had been false on my mother's part.

The rest of the afternoon was spent in the toilets at Memorial Park, where so many indiscretions had taken place when I was a child. I talked of my shady past and stressed the fact that no one had ever told me at the time that what I was doing was wrong. When the film was eventually pieced together I thought it a very powerful piece. My sordid life-style as a child was skipped over, and it was left to the viewer to decide just what I had been up to.

I was glad to get to bed. It had been a nightmarish day, raking up all the past I so desperately wanted to forget. I slept little as I worried about my sister's reaction. Even though I hadn't seen them for over six years, I knew they still thought of me as a big brother, and their reaction was far more important than my mother's. I had bags under my eyes when I joined the rest of the crew at the breakfast table the following morning. I telephoned my sisters and told them that I would be arriving just after lunch. They had all assembled for the big reunion; they knew nothing of the film crew's existence until David knocked on the door and left me outside while he explained that I had something to tell them and he wanted to film it. Out of sheer curiosity, I'm sure, they agreed. When at last I entered the front door, I was whisked into the kitchen, where child after child was thrown into my arms. My sister had given me a great many nephews and nieces that I never knew existed.

Once the big welcome was over and I had met my younger brothers for the first time in eight years, we settled down to the matter in hand. I thought it better to talk to just the older girls, so Lesley and Julie stayed behind. I explained in the gentlest way possible – and their reaction floored me as well as the film crew. Lesley said, 'Well, it's your life, good on yer,' and Julie confirmed that I had made them good hot-pots as a child.

I left totally bewildered. It was as if they had known all along that I was going to change my sex. They had assured me that I would be accepted as a sister whenever I had surgery. Their reaction encouraged me to go on. My sisters were normal, hard-working northern mothers. If they accepted it with such ease, perhaps my change wouldn't be so bad. Unfortunately, however, the fact was that because my sisters had been through bad times like myself they were ready for a surprise like the one I had sprung on them. Other people were to reject me as quickly as the girls had accepted me.

Life back in London took its normal course. I felt it only right to warn my staff of my plans. I was their boss, and if they resented my plans I could face a bad time with the unions. I rang the union branch secretary and told him. He accepted it as if I was confirming the day's date. Moreover, he told me that the union would support me if any problems arose during my changeover period.

I called a special staff meeting in the kitchen two days after my return. My staff, all sixteen of them, sat around waiting to hear what I had to say. As usual, they clung to every word I uttered. Firstly I told them of the successful month's figures. We had made many cutbacks. The management had rejected some of my early proposals but, once St Luke's had started to climb from the bottom of the league in terms of the hospitals' monthly figures, they had followed my policies. Now we had saved more money than any other hospital and were near the top of the list. Just a few more cuts would have us in the lead.

Once the business side had been dealt with, I told them about my personal problems. They all sat and listened intently. They had wondered why the BBC had been in, filming. All but one of my staff agreed to accept me as the boss, even though I would be wearing women's clothes. The only person to reject what I was doing was the only English girl who worked for me. She thought I was perverted and the change was disgusting. She let her views be known in front of everyone, then stomped off back to her labours. The rest of us talked the problem over in more detail. I tried to explain how I felt and they tried to understand. For that I was grateful. At least they were now prepared for the first day I would walk into work as a woman.

The night staff, too, had heard rumours about my planned change, and had left messages under my door asking me to contact them. They all showed a lot of interest. To them I was another set of case notes; they'd never met a real transsexual before. But many an hour was spent talking about the operation, cures and treatments.

As the days slowly ticked away, I at last reached my last day wearing male clothing – the day George was to cease in everyone's minds and Julia was to take over. That last day was important to me. As the evening drew to a close I slowly packed up all George's old clothing. The film crew were huddled in my room. It was an exciting moment. Once the last shirt had been levered under the lid, that was it. George was gone. I couldn't stand to have his things around, and just before midnight I left the box that contained my past in an egg-box outside the local Oxfam shop.

The following morning I had to be up an hour earlier than usual. I had to shave, make up and do my hair, and today was a special day: my first full day as a woman. Ray Rough, my local hairdresser had agreed to let the BBC film my first hairdo. In a short period he transformed my locks of hair from an unruly mass to the most beautiful raised style that I could have asked for. He also highlighted my hair, and as I viewed the finished product I felt much happier. It made me look far more feminine than my old style. Slight alterations were still needed in my make-up to change my facial shape, but Ray's wife helped, and by the time I left Ray's salon I looked and felt terrific.

This was the day I would always remember. But that afternoon, when I sat in front of the doctor at Charing Cross, my new hairstyle and clothes finishing off my full transformation, he said little although he looked impressed. As usual, his three students looked on; I answered his questions, was patted on the head, given another prescription and left his office having learnt no more than I'd known when I entered. The doctor had drained me of information but given me no advice.

Most of the nursing staff that bumped into me were shocked at the change. They had all been warned, yet were still not prepared for the sight that met them. I was sick of having to explain myself to everyone; the questions were always the same. Some people were very inconsiderate, and there were sly remarks that hurt me. I had to face up to it: people just didn't understand. They thought they did until they were actually faced with it. My first day at work as a woman was, for David, the end of the first film. For me it was the beginning of twelve weeks' hell.

On my second day I got a phone call from my boss. I had to travel to the Middlesex to see him straight away. I thought he just wanted to see how I looked as a female. The atmosphere was tense when I arrived. Everyone had been told about the queer at St Luke's, and people were peering around corners and pointing. Even the office staff giggled nervously as I walked to the catering office.

My boss told me that he had good news for me. I was no longer going to work at St Luke's as a supervisor; I was to be transferred to the Middlesex as a night cook. That was a demotion of eight places. I was insulted, and went to see the union secretary. He was behind me straight away and had a meeting called between management and union officials. There had to be a war, and until the rift was sorted out I was suspended on full pay.

I was worried about my future, and returned with David to see Caradoc. We had worked on a synopsis and a draft chapter; my rough copy had been transformed into better English by David. Caradoc read through both manuscripts. My work wasn't good enough, David's was too polished, and between the two the feeling had been lost. It was decided that I should keep trying to go it alone. While I was suspended I had plenty of spare time; and, when I presented Caradoc two weeks later with four chapters and an altered synopsis, he was amazed and decided we had found the right formula. Only by spending long hours talking to Caradoc, though, could I judge just what was needed from me; but that way I was able to add more description to my work.

The Greater London Council had taken pity on my plight at the hospital and offered me a flat near the Caledonian Road. It was a beautiful flat and I moved in straight away. Although I had very little there, not even curtains at the windows. I felt happier than I had done since changing over to St Luke's. My own staff had stood loyally behind me. The management, however, tried their best to move me, and after a twelve-week fight the case ended up in the Area Health appeal offices. They upheld the management's decision, and I had either to accept the transfer or take my case to ACAS, the arbitration service. The fight had worn me out, and I just couldn't go on; so, to the union's disappointment, I resigned.

Trying to find another job was going to prove difficult. Most transsexuals find it difficult to keep the job they were doing before surgery. I had already seen how others had fared and I didn't want to end up like many already had, as a prostitute. Only the girls who had been self-employed seemed to be surviving but I knew I would find a way – I was a fighter.

It wasn't long before the press started sniffing around. They had got part of the story from the BBC. The *Sunday People* wanted to do an exclusive on me, and I agreed to meet their journalist and photographer. I gave them only as much as I wanted to give; and I wouldn't yield to their probings for sensation, and I refused to pose in a sexy position for them. They eventually left the flat defeated. They didn't have the story they had come for; but they thought that what they had was good enough.

The interview had been on a Friday. On the Saturday night I was bopping away at a party in Leyton with two friends. Everyone knew that I was going to be in Sunday's paper. I telephoned the *Sunday People* and asked what page the story was on, and what was said. The night editor refused to tell me, so a gang of us decided to ride into the West End to get early copies from Leicester Square.

As we pulled into the square I dived out of the car. I had orders for ten copies. I ran up to the vendor and asked for ten *Peoples*. She looked up at me and said, 'Ere, love, you're on the front page.' I could hardly believe it. 'SHOCK SEX-CHANGE ON TV' was the headline, with a large photo. I half-ran, half-stumbled back to the waiting mass in the car. Everyone eagerly grabbed copies and started to read. Catcalls and whistles shot through the car and the driver read out the story. It wasn't as sensational as the heading. In fact the reporter had been very good to me. I cheered up a little, and when I returned to the party I was a celebrity. Front-page news. Everything was blown out of proportion. I telephoned David and everyone else concerned with the film, so that they could buy copies.

Caradoc decided to make the most of the publicity, and sent copies of the manuscript to about six different publishers, along with the synopsis. The date of the film had been set, and the publishers were advised to watch it. I saw it with ten of my friends from the Black Cap; an interviewer from Radio 4 turned up to get my reaction, and the following day I was on the early-morning news.

The following day Caradoc and I visited five publishers that were still interested in buying the book, so that they could meet me and form their own opinions. Three of them wanted to make drastic changes to the book's outline – only New English Library thought that its raw form had selling potential. They made a good offer for the book rights, and I thought they were far more suitable to handle the book than the other publishers I had met. Nick, the editorial director, was as enthusiastic as Caradoc and thought I had a good story to tell. Within ten days contracts were exchanged, and I was financially secure for at least a year.

The press had been good to me; all the local papers and national dailies carried photos, and plenty of space was dedicated to my story. The TV critics thought the film had been good. Everyone was talking about sex-changes, just as I had hoped. It had sparked off the first stages of understanding.

I did an hour's phone-in programme with Adrian Love of Capital Radio. The audience's reaction was fascinating. I talked as freely on the air as I had on the film. The switchboards were jammed, and only one person criticised me for having a sex-change. He said I was interfering with nature and God's laws. A Jesus freak preaching at me! I told the unfortunate chap that I had had a long talk with God and that even He sometimes made mistakes. Adrian Love was able to deal with any other irritating callers.

For days afterwards I could see people pointing me out in the street, and a member of the local tenant's association slipped a letter through my door, offering help whenever I needed it. It was a nice gesture; but even they couldn't stop the horror that I was to face the following week.

All my friends accepted me, and many new acquaintances praised me for my bravery in making the film. I was lulled into a false sense of security. Everyone had been so nice to me. I didn't expect anyone to deliberately try to hurt me. I hadn't wanted to hurt anyone else. I only wanted to help others. But someone, somewhere, took exception.

I had invested a little of my money in a company of my own. It was only a small office in Covent Garden, but I planned to arrange several fashion shows. One night as I left my office, dressed as a female, I was attacked by four men. They pushed me to the floor and started kicking and punching me. Several passers-by came to my aid and the offenders ran off. One of my saviours pushed me into a taxi once they were sure I wasn't too badly hurt.

I returned home badly shaken and phoned Gus, a loyal friend, who came straight round and tried to comfort me. It was difficult for him, because we had so little in common. We were opposites. He had his own life-style; I had mine. I needed someone to lean on and he was able to cheer me up. Little did we know that things were to get worse.

I received several abusive phone-calls the following day. Every time Gus rang from work to see if I was O.K., I was worse. I left to to go my office at lunchtime. When I arrived, the sight that greeted me made me feel very unbalanced. Someone had broken in and smashed everything up. The phone had been ripped from the wall, and paint had been thrown all over the new carpet and furniture. There was nothing left to salvage — all the files had been destroyed. Hours of work, up in smoke. I had nothing left. As I left the office, a car swerved and just missed me. I don't know whether that was planned or whether fate had put me in the wrong place at the wrong time. Feeling totally destroyed inside, I returned home. I phoned Gus again. He was very upset and promised to come round straight after work.

I sat around and watched television for a short while. Every time the phone rang, I ignored it. My nerves were all on edge. I had been home for about an hour when I smelt smoke. I didn't take much notice of it at first. As the smell got stronger I checked the kitchen; I was sure I hadn't left the cooker on. Then I checked outside. I thought it might be my imagination. I tried to settle down again, but the smell got worse.

Suddenly smoke started billowing in from the front door. I was panic-stricken. I didn't know what to do! I pulled open the door and could hardly see for the smoke. All I could make out were flames licking up the front door. It was the only way out of the flat. I ran into the kitchen and filled a bowl full of water. It didn't affect the flames when I threw it, but the smoke seemed to thicken. Several more bowls, however, had the flames out, and I opened all the windows. The smoke billowed out into the fresh air. I hung out of the window, gasping for air. I was shaking uncontrollably.

I phoned the police and they asked me to go round to the station. They didn't seem at all interested. It was three hours before one of their forensic experts came to check the cause of the fire.

Petrol soaked rags had been stuck through the letterbox and set alight. Why was someone trying to kill me? I phoned David and Gus. A film crew were soon round to film the damage, and Gus was able to calm me down. I felt as though I couldn't go on. Then came the last phone-call.

The voice at the other end of the line told me they hadn't got me this time, but they would next. I was terrified. I couldn't spend another moment in the flat – not alone. Gus had no intention of letting me. I packed several dresses, smelling of smoke, and make-up into a bag, and, as soon as the BBC had gone, I left the flat. Whoever was trying to get me had made a good job of destroying my self-confidence.

Chapter 24
True Love at Last

I was lucky to have Gus as a friend. He wasted no time in helping me. He didn't stop to think of what people would say about him. He dragged me down to Manchester for a weekend. The break did me good, and we talked for hours about my future.

On our journey back to London, Gus asked me to stay at his place in East Finchley. He knew that if I returned to my flat I would only be inviting more trouble. At that time he was the only person to show concern. I agreed reluctantly; I didn't want to be a burden to anyone. The BBC thought that I had been through enough, and left me alone for a short period. For that I was grateful. I needed time to think. I knew where I was eventually going, and I didn't want to rush it. Gus was guiding me slowly back to the right road.

I stayed in East Finchley for three weeks. I felt confident enough by that time to go away by myself for a week. Gus thought Blackpool would be good for me, and I set off on my first holiday as a female. It was inevitable that I should end up in Lucy's Bar. I had no choice but to mix on the gay scene; at least I was safe there and didn't have to commit myself. If I went into a straight bar, inevitably a guy would ask to buy me a drink, and drinks would lead to other things. There was a limit to how much I could get away with. Rather than provoke trouble, I stayed away from it. Once I had had the operation, things would be different. I would be able to compete on the straight scene instead of hiding from it.

The sea air cleared my brain, and by the time I returned to London I was more determined than ever to go ahead. Next I contacted the Greater London Council and explained my predicament. I was worried about all the old people that lived in the new block where my flat was. If another petrol-bomb attempt was made, a lot of damage could be caused. They, too, were worried, and I suggested they give me an older flat in the same area. This should have taken months to arrange, but with the GLC's northern office's help I had one within days.

That flat was very old and it wanted a lot of work done to it, but at least I would be safe there. I spent several days redecorating it. Once everything was sorted out, I was able to leave East Finchley to restart my life. The first few nights were very lonely, but it was something I knew I must get used to.

My third interview with the doctor was rather hair-raising. He refused to let the BBC in, and preached to me like a naughty little boy. I shouldn't have allowed the press to write stories about me. As if I could have stopped them! He told me that if I got my name in the paper once more he'd cross me off his books. I had to do what he said, when he said it. If not, my operation was at stake. I knew that the doctor wasn't one to mess around. If one didn't behave as a respectable conservative lady, one didn't stand a chance. One must not wear a wig, and slacks were definitely out.

David and Caradoc, however, were pleased to see me back on form. I had neglected my writing, and David was ready to start filming again; we had a lot of gaps to fill and little time to do it in.

I had been doing my regular tour of gay pubs and clubs in the West End, and I met a friend who took me down to the opening night of Scandals, a gay disco in Wardour Street. It was supposed to be the biggest and best on offer to the gay community, and my first visit there was a great success.

The first thing that everyone noticed as they stepped into the doorway was the doorman. Standing erect, over six feet tall, he looked beautiful. He had a neatly cut beard and 'tache and was very

Arab-looking. I would have been more than willing to have his shoes under my bed. The receptionist was an old friend and, because of all the publicity I had had, he gave me an honorary membership. As I turned to enter the disco bar I couldn't help but notice that the doorman had come down to reception and was watching me. After buying a drink I dragged David onto the dance-floor, and as we danced away I spotted the doorman peeping through the door at me. He was interested. There was no doubt about that.

I eventually got around to talking to Danny on reception. Amer, the doorman, had told him he thought I was a lovely woman and couldn't understand why I was the only girl in the club. When Amer next came downstairs Danny introduced us. We both smiled at each other nervously but said little. Amer was as shy as I was.

During the next few weeks I visited the club every night, totally fascinated by Amer. I spent nearly an hour talking to him on the door before I even entered. There was no doubt in my mind that he was straight. He constantly had to parry the advances made by the gays who frequented the place. They constantly worried him; he was too much of a gentleman to hit them, so he just quietly pushed their probing hands away and told them he was straight.

He was always courteous to me, and on several evenings he walked me to my cab. On one of these occasions he bent and kissed me goodnight. My whole body was set alight. I was tingling from head to foot. I knew that I loved him, even though we hadn't had any sexual contact. I craved for him – but I craved for him as a woman. I wanted him for his male body, but only when I could offer him everything a woman has to offer. I slept little that night.

The following evening I arrived at the club earlier than usual. I couldn't wait to see Amer again; but as I entered the club he just turned and ignored me. I felt very hurt. I couldn't understand why he had suddenly changed. Danny soon confirmed the worst. Amer had excitedly told him that he'd kissed me goodnight. Danny had then teased him about his not being queer. When Amer had realised that I hadn't had surgery, he had gone berserk. He was annoyed because he had kissed a man. I tried to talk to him but he didn't want to know. He thought I had deceived him.

It was something we hadn't even talked about. I had been sure he knew I was a transsexual – I hadn't hidden the fact. I left the club that evening feeling very low. I would never meet anyone like him again. If only I had had the operation, everything would have been fine. I didn't know what to do or where to turn. It was all my fault. I didn't visit the club so frequently after that, and, every time I did, Amer ignored me. I desperately wanted to talk to him and Danny faithfully passed messages between us. Yet we didn't get together and talk about our problems.

I changed my name officially to Julia Anne Grant with the help of my solicitor, and set about changing all my legal papers. New bank accounts were opened, and my passport now carries my feminine identity. My medical card proved the most difficult to change, but after a few challenging solicitor's letters the DHSS soon made the necessary changes, and my card arrived in order.

I went ahead in my normal life-style, making visits to the hair-dressers and so on; and, as usual when I felt depressed, I went out to buy some new clothes. I missed Amer very much; there was so much I wanted to explain to him. I couldn't force myself to stay away from Scandals. I had tried other clubs but, without seeing Amer's warm friendly smile, life meant nothing. Gus and all my friends knew that I was infatuated with him, and understood the problems that stood in my way, but they were powerless to help.

One day I met Victor Spinetti, the film producer. I had arranged to have tea with him to discuss the chances of his producing a new cabaret show for me. He proved a very likeable man, and I ended up staying many more hours than I had planned. During the course of conversation I mentioned Amer, and Victor gave me some advice that I will forever be grateful for. He said that, if I loved the guy so much, I should go out and get him before someone else did.

I went down to Scandals that evening, Victor's warning ringing in my ears. I had had quite a bit of drink – in fact, I was plastered; but the booze gave me the courage I needed. I made it to the top of the stairs, where Amer stood talking to two of his friends. He could see that I was the worse for drink. As I slipped, he grabbed me and stopped me falling back down to the reception area. His arms felt warm around me, and as he held me close to him I could feel my whole body coming alive again.

He sat me on an old chair in a little passage by the door, and asked me why I had got myself into such a state. I told him it was all his fault. He got rid of his friends, and for the first time in weeks we were able to talk. We didn't say all that much, but at least we broke the barriers. I gave him a copy of my front-door key and told him that he was welcome at any time. I didn't want to use him. Then I gave him my address, stumbled down the stairs, collected my coat and made to leave. As I half-fell into Wardour Street, Amer grabbed my arm and told me to be careful. I could see the tenderness in his eyes.

I had been home about an hour when the phone rang. Still in a drunken stupor, I picked up the receiver. It was Amer. I sobered up instantly. He wanted to know if I had reached home safely. Then he cautiously asked me if I was alone. I told him I was. All he said was, 'Good. I'll see you tomorrow night.'

The following night, however, Amer offered me back my key. He thought I had only given it to him because I was drunk. I assured him he could keep it and use it when he thought he was ready.

Amer had an older brother working in the club and a younger brother who visited him each night. They were Muslims, and sex outside marriage was against their religion. Amer, however, had lived with a Scottish girl for six months, so according to his brothers he was beyond saving. They warned me off Amer; they didn't want him to get mixed up with someone like me. That made me more determined to get him. When at last they realised that I wasn't forcing Amer into anything, they gave him their blessing. He apparently spent hours explaining to them how I would eventually be a woman. They were totally bewildered.

One night, about ten weeks after our first meeting, Amer told me that he was going to come home with me. Even then he nearly changed his mind, and on the way home I could sense the fear within him. He was taking a big step for me, and didn't really know what was expected of him. I suggested we stop and get some Kentucky Fried Chicken; at least that would give us something to do when we got home, instead of making the slow advances towards the bedroom straight away.

We went straight into the lounge. Amer settled into one of the comfy couches while I adjusted the bright central ceiling lighting to that of a more suitable atmosphere. I put on a quiet record and we ate our way through Colonel Sanders's delicious recipe. Once that was out of the way I offered Amer a drink. Silly me – Muslims don't drink alcohol. We both settled for a Coca-Cola.

We sat for an hour holding hands, talking about each other. It was getting us nowhere, and I slowly leant over and kissed him. He pulled away at first, but then responded with furious passion. We sat kissing and cuddling for ages. I suggested we made a move towards the bedroom; he resisted, but I assured him he was safe, and we slowly entered the hallowed portals.

I thought it better to leave off the light. Slowly, in the darkness, we undressed. I cautiously left on my pants and crept between the sheets. Hesitantly, Amer joined me. He too still had on his pants. I was pleased I had been cautious. If he had felt my full naked torso by his side he would probably have been disconcerted.

The hormone tablets had had some effect on my bustline, and as he slowly caressed my body it was those two spots his hand made for. He slowly kissed me, then moved down so the he could kiss my nipples. It was almost too much for me. I could feel he had an erection. I didn't want to make a grab for it, so I just let him get used to the idea that at least my body was changing. We then cuddled up together and fell fast asleep.

The following day I expected Amer to excuse himself and make a bolt for it; after all, he had always seen me immaculately groomed from head to toe. In the morning I even shocked myself when I looked in the mirror; but Amer didn't seem to mind even the smudged make-up. I had dived into bed so quickly I had forgotten all about my make-up removal and usual night-cream treatment.

I made coffee and toast and returned to Amer in the warm bed. We spent most of the day there. One question he did ask me was why I hadn't insisted on his making love to me. I told him that I didn't want that kind of relationship. I wanted someone to love me as a woman and not treat me as a homosexual male. If that was what he wanted he could have his choice of men at the club. He hurriedly apologised and told me that he wanted only me, and that if he had to wait, wait he would.

Every evening after that Amer returned home with me, and we had some wonderful times together. Some of the boys who worked in the club took the piss out of us both. They had all tried to make it with him, and as he constantly refused their offers they became more and more jealous of our relationship. A couple of them even asked me if I was paying him for his services. I always said yes, just to let them believe what they wanted.

Yet Amer and I knew we had found something special together that no words could express. At that time we were truly in love, but I was later to discover that even he would not be there when I really needed him. He turned out to be just like everyone else in my life, but back then I was greatly relieved on the day he moved his personal belongings in. I knew then that I had him for always. I had succeeded in finding the perfect partner.

Yet it wasn't always a bed of roses for us. It was some time before Amer realised that I was still making two more films for the BBC and even longer before he discovered I was writing a book.

During our courtship I had tended to let things slide. I had made several excuses to Caradoc and David, and they had seemed to understand. But now I had love and happiness, and the sooner I got my transformation over the better. Soon I was writing this book with undue haste. The film schedules too became tighter and tighter, and I was totally exhausting myself. I was trying to keep every side of my life active at once. Amer couldn't keep up with my day-to-day appointments and busy schedule, and thought at times that I was neglecting him. I decided that I should go to the club every night, but Amer considered that to be a waste of time and money. So, when the owners offered me a job, it solved many of our problems.

I started behind the bars but was also to work in the bistro when things were busy. The cash-flow into the bank was also good. I liked to keep enough by so that, if the chance came for me to have private surgery, I could take it. Amer was pleased to see that I was actually doing a decent job instead of galivanting around filming all the time.

One Sunday night, however, I was standing by the bar in Scandals when the music suddenly went dead and the house lights were turned up full. It was a police raid. About five hundred gays stood around talking in whispers while the policemen slowly started taking everyone's name and address. I had had a little too much to drink, and I couldn't stand police harassment. The crowd in Scandals were quietly enjoying themselves, doing no one any harm, and these pigs had to come and ruin a bloody good night. I went mental.

The dance-floor was clear, and I stroke into the middle and quietly viewed the scene. They all looked like frightened rats unable to run; they watched me expectantly. After all, I was a cult figure; I had become a leader in the minority world because I'd let the BBC make a film about me. I was disgusted. I shouted out, 'I wonder how long you queens are going to stand around and be pushed about by the pigs.' There was a stirring in the crowd, but little was said. I turned upon the nearest copper and asked in a loud voice if the raid was official. A hush descended over the club. The policeman ignored me.

I didn't like being ignored. I had the full floor; no one else was going to make a move. I shouted for the DJ to put on a record, but as he made to do it a policeman stopped him. People started booing, and when things eventually quietened down I shouted out, 'Who needs music anyway?' and started dancing around the floor.

A policeman strode over and grabbed me by the arm. I told him, so that everyone could hear – It was amazing what a deathly silence there was in that club – that if he didn't remove his hand from my body I'd give him something to nick me for. Not very nice words for someone dressed up as I was, in a full-length silver evening-dress with a diamanté collar.

Suddenly I was surrounded by four policemen. I was helpless. Not one person had spoken out to help me. But, as I stood there trapped, at the top of my voice I began to sing 'Land of Hope and Glory'. To my amazement others joined in, and by the end of the first verse the whole club was singing. An inspector who was standing by the door signalled the men to get out, and they quietly left. Everyone could see them going, and as soon as we finished singing I called for three cheers for the police. The crowd cheered on; then suddenly the music began pulsing away, and people started dancing again as though nothing had happened.

We heard later that we hadn't been the only club to get raided. The police had raided every gay club in the West End – and only in Scandals had they met any resistance. The owners were delighted. Amer was annoyed because I had made an exhibition of myself, but I was given a bottle of champagne by a secret admirer, who also hated the police but who hadn't had the gumption to stand up for his own rights without the help of a transsexual.

On my next visit to the Gender Identification Unit at Charing Cross I was determined to ask the doctor to take me as a private patient. I couldn't bear the thought of having to wait nearly three years for the operation on the National Health. I told David of my plans, and proved to him that the doctor had a private practice in which he and a surgeon carried out hundreds of operations.

I kept my cool during the early part of the interview; then I put my question. The doctor refused point-blank to discuss it. He told me that I could buy the operation but not his medical opinion, which was that I should first have lived for a year as a woman. On that he was adamant, I then threw a few brickbats in front of the cameras to make the show look good. But the doctor kept control and refused to comment further. He then promptly ended the interview and told me to go away for twelve weeks. I knew that I had touched a raw nerve, but he deserved it. Why should I have a hard time just because the BBC were filming? It was then that I realised that, although the BBC had helped so far, they were now proving a bit of a hindrance – although the last thing that David wanted to do was get in the way of my operation.

I returned home that evening feeling very depressed. Amer tried to comfort me, but it was no use. The longer I delayed the operation the worse our relationship would get. It disturbed Amer that I got an erection when we were in bed together. At first the tablets had cooled my urges; now they had no effect. Although Amer said little about it and never complained, I knew that deep down it was worrying him. I tried to talk it out of him – and, when we did have a row, it was one of the first things he would throw back at me: the fact that I didn't have a real woman's body. That used to hurt me very much. He always regretted it afterwards but, although I accepted his apologies, his taunts were engraved deep in my heart. Only by having my penis removed would my depression be lifted.

I found my writing even harder to face. It didn't inspire me any more. Caradoc urged me on. It was the knowledge that, if I didn't write, I wouldn't have the extra finance I so desperately needed that kept me going.

I was having other problems too. The hormone tablets were having terrible side-effects. My hair was getting very fine and falling out every time I brushed it, and I constantly felt weak. An hour after taking each tablet I felt depressed, and even Amer's jovialities meant nothing. My bust had stopped growing as well, and I was putting on weight. Nothing seemed to be going well for me.

I had heard about a surgeon in Hove who had done a bust operation on a friend of mine. It was a marvellous job, very realistic – not like the hard falsies I had seen come out of some London clinics. I telephoned the surgeon and asked for an appointment. My doctor at Charing Cross had said that I had too many problems with the tablets I could always have a bust operation later!

I telephoned David and told him that I was going to see Mr P in Hove. It didn't take David long to phone him and arrange to film the first interview. I was a little nervous at first about having surgery, but once I stepped into the surgeon's office all that disappeared. I sat and talked about the treatment I had received from Charing Cross. The surgeon examined me, then told me exactly what he could do for me. Because I had only a small bust development it was more difficult and there were limits to what he could do. But at least he was honest about it all. He showed me a replica of the bag he would be inserting inside me and told me how it worked. The crew filmed on, totally fascinated by his revelations. He then went on to explain all the side-effects that could happen. He was so openly honest that it was touching.

He then assured me that he'd done operations both here and in the States and hadn't had one failure. That was enough for me. I wanted the operation. We discussed finances. It was to cost me between £650 and £700 – a lot cheaper than many London clinics, and that included a three-day stay. Many of the London clinics kept you in for only eight hours.

I returned to Amer in London feeling very happy. The first thing I did was to throw all my tablets in the bin. He thought I was going crazy but, when I told him that ten days later I was going into hospital and would come home with a full bust, he was as delighted as I was.

At last things were moving. In a year my body shape had changed little; and yet in just a one-hour interview with the surgeon in Hove I had been given a new lease of life. I was ready to start the transformation I had waited so many years for. I could prove at last that I was a woman.

Chapter 25

Operations

As I packed my bag for the journey down to Hove the cameraman followed my every action. In two days I was to have my first operation. I had expected to be nervous and had asked David to leave his filming until the last minute. It looked better anyway when what was being filmed was actuality. Somehow the quality of film was always better.

I didn't pack any tight-fitting dresses; I knew I would not be throwing my arms around for a while. But inside I felt nothing. I was neither excited nor worried. I had convinced myself that it was all just a formality.

I travelled down with David in his car. He could hardly believe that things were actually happening. He had been very involved with the filming for over fourteen months, and knew more about my struggle than anyone else. Little was said on the journey; we had said it all before. His encouraging boyish grins were enough. I could see that he was excited. He was going to be filming his first operation. As always, he was totally absorbed in his work. He had seen the operating theatre and knew where the surgeon would be standing, and he was working out the best shots. He knew full well that there was a limit to how much his bosses at the Television Centre would let him show; but he had broken several barriers with the first film, and I knew that he intended to put as much of the operation in the next film as possible.

The crew were all assembled by the town hall when we arrived. The film operations manager who was working on our films had gone to great lengths to secure a crew I had worked with before. For me it was an emotional time, and I wanted only people around me who knew the full story, so I had little explaining to do. I had given David and Mary hell. Film crews had to be booked months in advance, but for our filming it was impossible to know when the next day was going to be. David knew that if he turned up with a new crew I would stamp about and be damnably rude.

When I booked into the clinic I was taken to my private room where several telegrams and a bouquet of flowers were waiting for me. The room was quite unlike the usual hospital room; it had a comfy chair and colour television. I had my own private toilet, too. The film crew set about filming me being booked in and signing the consent forms for the operation.

Just before six p.m. there was an almighty rush. The surgeon hadn't reminded me to bring a special bra. I dived back into a dress. The matron showed me what type of bra I would need, and David drove me at an illegal speed to a local store. We got there just as it was closing. It was Sunday the following day; but luckily they let me in after I gave them some tall story about my unfortunate sister who had been rushed to hospital and that I needed a bra for her. The manager of the store even helped me to find the right size.

I had imagined that I would be swathed from head to foot in bandages, and was very surprised when matron explained that when I woke up all I would have on would be my bra. I was going from a 36B to a 40C cup overnight, which would give Amer something to get hold of – but he'd have to wait six weeks, as I couldn't take the bra off before then.

The following morning the film crew burst into my room at the crack of dawn; but I was ready for them. I wasn't allowed to wear make-up, so I had groomed my hair immaculately and used plenty of face cream to give me a shine. The operation was to be at 9.30 a.m. The anaesthetist popped in at eight and checked that I still wanted to go ahead.

Then, at 8.30, the night nurse strode in with her silver tray in hand. I slipped into my white medical gown and aimed my bum in the direction of the nurse. The cameras rolled and the needles went in. I could hardly feel them, but the penicillin one seemed to go on forever. I wasn't allowed out of bed from that moment on. David turned the camera towards me and asked how I felt. I just replied, 'Great! How should I feel? I'm going to wake up singing, "Gee, but it's good to be here."'

The needles were taking effect by the time the anaesthetist and the operating-theatre sister came to collect me. They looked like two little green gnomes in their theatre gowns, but I didn't tell them. The cameras followed me from my room to the lift. Then the film crew dashed up the stairs.

All I remember in the lift was taking out my teeth and giving them to the sister, making her solemnly promise to put them in before they filmed me waking up. She promised, and slipped them into her pocket. Soon I was outside the theatre.

The anaesthetist picked up my hand, patted it several times so that the vein stood out and then inserted the needle. He told me that I would soon drift off. I lay awake, waiting for the big moment. All I was conscious of was the sister holding my hand and the damn camera whirring away by my right earhole. The last conscious thought I had was, Bloody BBC. Then I was gone.

The next thing I remember is opening my eyes and being back in my small room. A nurse was holding my hand, and the first thing I asked her was, 'Are my teeth in?' She just smiled and said yes. I was lying flat and my white robe was just covering me. I looked down and I could see the two bra cups, full; not full – overflowing. The operation was over. I had done it.

Soon the door opened. It was the film crew with their bloody camera again. The nurse said I would be round again in a minute. I flickered my eyelids, the camera rolled and David asked me how I felt.

My chest felt as though it had been through an assault course. It was very tight; the 40C cup bra I had on was far too small. Yes, I was happy. Yes, I was glad it was all over. Yes, I just wanted to go back to sleep. My eyelids flickered once more and I was gone again.

Many people will be wondering what went on in the operating theatre. I will tell them.

Once the anaesthetist had fitted on my mask I was breathing normally, the surgeon and theatre sister re-positioned my body so that it was symmetrical. The surgeon then spent half an hour measuring up, ready for the incisions. I had a natural bust crease six centimetres from the nipple; the prosthesis was thirteen centimetres, so it had to be positioned accordingly.

Once all the lines had been drawn on my chest, the surgeon inserted a needle above each nipple. The syringe contained a solution of adrenalin and saline, which apparently reduces bleeding, and also helps to dissect up the tissue planes that form the chest.

Once the solution had done its job the surgeon started making the first incision. He talked about taking care over the first cuts, so that the skin is easier to re-sew afterwards. Then the incisions were deepened down to the muscular wall of the chest. The surgeon commented that it was 'a long way down to this patient'. If that wasn't a hint to go on a diet, I don't know what is.

He then set about making a pocket for the prosthesis between the breast tissue and the chest wall. There seemed to be a little struggle – the hole wasn't big enough to take the large boobs I had ordered, and slightly bigger incisions were made. Then the cavity was dusted with an antibiotic powder. The prosthesis had four fixation patches on the back of it, and it was hoped that eventually they would stick to the muscle wall of the chest. Once everything was safely in place, I was stitched up.

The next thing I remember is waking up and finding Amer sitting patiently by my bedside. I reached out for him, but my arms ached. He had brought me two bunches of flowers. It was so good to see him. I still felt rather drowsy, but every time I drifted off I awoke to find him still there. He was as chuffed as I was and, when the nurse came in the room to sit me up, I couldn't help catching a glint in his eye as he spotted my well-loaded bra. We both started laughing, though he seemed slightly put out that he had to wait to play with them.

I couldn't help but touch them. They felt quite firm, and that worried me; but when the surgeon visited me again that evening he explained that it would take several weeks for the skin tissues to give and the prosthesis to heat to body temperature. I believed him, and I could see Amer was well pleased. He asked me how big they were, and, when I told him they measured forty inches he gasped. The Scots girl he had lived with had only been able to offer him two hard-boiled eggs. Like most men, Amer wanted something to get hold of.

The surgeon eventually released me at five p.m. the next day, and, after writing out the cheque, I hobbled to the car – dreading the ride back to London in David's bumpy Diana. That car must have found every pot-hole between Brighton and London, and David didn't help matters when he nearly knocked one of my boobs straight off with his elbow as he clambered back into the car after buying petrol. I cursed and swore all the way back, and only quietened down once I was back safely in Amer's arms at home.

It took several days to get over the operation. Once I felt better, David arranged another hectic film schedule. We were travelling up to Preston and Fleetwood to get more family-reaction shots. For all the family it would be the first time they had seen me as a woman.

I wasn't looking forward to the reunions at all, but everything went better than I could have dreamed. My sisters were totally overcome by my appearance. They admired my taste in clothes and shoes, and thought my new hairstyle and make-up made me look pretty – better-looking than any of them. That cheered me up. At least I had been accepted fully. Then I suddenly realised I was being called a sister and an auntie, such was the transformation.

The meeting with my mother the following day was far more dramatic. We hadn't told her that we would be arriving. We waited in the local pub for her regular visit. Maureen, the landlady, greeted me and happily nattered away in front of the camera. My uncle Sid came into the lounge bar and Maureen called him over. He was totally oblivious of the cameras. She introduced us, then asked him if he knew who I was. He replied in the negative; when she told him, he turned ashen. He couldn't believe it. He walked back to the bar and ordered himself a large Scotch.

It was getting late, and it looked as if mother wasn't going to arrive. Maureen ran across to the flat and told her that there was a long-distance phone-call for her. We all watched them both run back to the pub. Maureen offered to buy my mother a drink, and it wasn't until that was ordered that she became aware of the cameras. She knew that could only mean one thing. She spotted me and threw her arms around my neck in tears, crying, 'Me daughter, me daughter, she's come home.' I felt very embarrassed; the whole pub was watching. All I did register was that I was now a daughter. Three new roles in life; I only hoped I could live up to them.

The following week we had to travel down to see the surgeon to check that the operation had been a success. When I had to remove my bra I became very aware of the film crew, and I wanted to cover and protect myself. David was one of the first to realise it, and restricted the shots. Being shy and coy weren't in my character, but I was becoming both. I didn't want to show my boobs to anyone but Amer.

The surgeon was soon finished, and I mentioned to him that I was worried about waiting two years for my next operation if my own doctor wouldn't take me on as a private patient. Did he know any urologists that might be willing? Mr P said that he did, and that if I got into problems with the Health Service I had only to ring him. In the meantime he would mention my case to Mr R. I left his office feeling more relaxed.

I had an interview at Charing Cross the following day, and I anticipated a bad time, even though I only had five weeks to go before I had completed my first year as a woman. The psychiatrist there demanded to know who had given me permission to have the bust surgery. He was talking down at me as though I were an animal. I told him in no uncertain terms that I had done it to prove to him that I was sincere and to show that I was willing to take permanent steps to secure my castration operation.

He told me that I had no right to do anything without his permission. His surgeon, the almighty, preferred to do the castration service before bust surgery. I couldn't see the sense in that, and told him so. Surely it was better to leave the worst surgery till last? At least if I wanted to change my mind at this stage I could. Anyway, it was my money.

Then we had a furious row, and the doctor asked me to leave his office. I did, nearly taking the door with me. David and the film crew were out too within seconds – he wanted to get me on film while I was still in a bad mood. I flared up. The surgeon hadn't told me not to have bust surgery. He had just criticised everything I did. I wasn't going to stand for it like all his other patients. He could go to hell. If I couldn't get surgery anywhere else in England, I intended to fly over to Casablanca on 10 March. I knew that could complicate things for the Beeb and the book and that I also stood a good chance of being butchered, but even that was better than having to put up with what I'd had from Charing Cross.

I felt terribly depressed for the next few days. Then the letter came from Charing Cross that was to break my links with the hospital for good. The psychiatrist told me that, if I didn't write within ten days and give him the name of the GP that had recommended me to Mr P., all my treatment would have to be suspended.

I didn't wait – I didn't want to give him the satisfaction. I wrote him a very civil letter asking him to cross me off his books as I thought I could get better treatment elsewhere.

I telephoned my bust surgeon and told him of the problems I had been having. Mr R., the urologist he had recommended, had agreed to see me, and an appointment was made to coincide with my next check-up in Hove with Mr P. At least there was the chance he would help me – but what he needed in the way of assurance that I was serious about castration I just didn't know. I couldn't face another year of cross-dressing just to prove myself.

We had decided to make it an overnight stay at Brighton. David had been introduced to a female-to-male transsexual, and he wanted us to meet so that we could compare notes about former identities. I didn't know what I was letting myself in for, and Steve really shocked me.

David had arranged a drinks session the evening before filming was to take place, so that Steven, Sara – his beautiful girlfriend – and myself could get acquainted. The following morning the three of us chatted away in front of the camera. No one in the neighbourhood knew of Steven's past; he was coming out as much as I had done. He knew of the struggles that transsexuals had to face. He had been through four years of hell before getting surgery. To look at Steve, no one would guess his secret. He was small and had a swarthy beard. He had had his bust removed and had undergone a hysterectomy to remove his womb and other non-essential female organs. Yet I found it hard to believe he could do no more even to this day, surgeons have not fully developed a technique for building a false penis. Some think it could happen very soon though. Steven helped run a transsexual society called the Gender Research Foundation, based in London; he was also a leading contact for most gay and 'befriending' organisations. If they had an enquiry that they couldn't deal with, it ended up on Steven's plate.

Money is desperately short for all gay advice groups, and none more than Steve's. But he has also formed a group of transsexuals who run a shop in the Manchester area. The profits go to help other transsexuals who have problems. Steve's dedication left me thinking that I should be doing more for my brothers and sisters; but I was already loaded down with work.

I felt good after meeting Steve. I wasn't half as worried as I had been about seeing the surgeon. The interview was held in the same office as Mr P. had used. The urologist was a lot younger than I had imagined he would be. The usual formalities took place while the BBC set up their equipment. It had already been agreed that the doctors' faces wouldn't be shown, and that their names wouldn't be mentioned. It all had to look formal, and not as though they were advertising their services – which I personally think is a shame. They both helped me to find a new life, and they could help many others if only people knew where to contact them. But no doubt the grapevine will spread their names all over the country and they will succeed in helping many.

The urologist treated me in the same way as the bust surgeon. I had first to tell him just what I wanted. Then he told me what he could do. He was honest, and we discussed the complications and side-effects. He was able to offer me a vagina with a depth of approximately six inches. The clitoris and vagina lips would also be matched up. Until he opened me up he didn't know the position on lubrication.

He then told me he had assisted on several similar operations, but hadn't done one alone. I would be his first. I wanted to be his first, and accepted his offer. He insisted, however, that I saw a psychiatrist who worked both locally and in Harley Street. He didn't doubt my sincerity; he just wanted the medical sanction that I was sane and that I knew my own mind.

I agreed straight away, and he picked up the phone and arranged for an interview that very evening in the same office. The film crew had had a long day but they were willing to stay on. They, too, wanted to hear the magic words.

The psychiatrist turned out to be as likeable as the two surgeons. We settled down to discuss my past. He hadn't dealt with a similar case before and became totally absorbed in my revelations. The interview went on for nearly two hours. At times he pressed me for answers I just wasn't willing to give, and he surrendered. I was totally sane – more sane than anyone else he had met. His wife had been watching all the filming; she too was absorbed.

While the BBC packed up the equipment we had a fascinating conversation about Charing Cross.

The following day David confirmed that the surgeon had agreed to do the operation on 9 March at midday. I was thrilled. So was David. The surgeon had agreed to let them film, and the bust surgeon was so fascinated that he had agreed to assist Mr. R. That cheered me up beyond all doubt. I was in the hands of two of Britain's best surgeons. A month ago nothing had been going right. Now I only had days to go before the complete transformation.

Amer was delighted. We now both had a date to work for. Mine was 9 March. His was six weeks later than that, when he knew I would be in full operational order and ready for action!

The last few days at home were hell. David wanted to film, but I wouldn't let him. I uttered the famous line, 'I want to be alone.' I needed the last few days to compose myself. It was a big step I was taking. I had no doubts about my actions; I just didn't want to listen to people asking me if I was nervous.

Our journey down to Brighton was anything but quiet this time. I felt relaxed, but David was as nervous as hell. He wasn't sure whether he could cope with watching the operation. This time there were two cameramen, and David was going to watch the operation on two videos in another room. David dropped me outside Steve's with all my stuff. I'd decided to spend my last night with people like myself, who understood.

Everyone at Steve's expected me to be nervous. Steve had been before the operation. Thank God I was a cool lady; I was a little bit shaky inside, bit I kept a cool image. I took Steve and Sara on a pub crawl – the last time I could ever do that. Then we returned to the house and talked until the early hours about anything but sex-change surgery.

The following day the crew were assembled outside the clinic. It was a bright Sunday morning. During the first hour I made two arrivals at the clinic, while the cameraman filmed me struggling across the road with my heavy baggage. He just couldn't get the shot right. But at last I was signed in, and happily sat watching television and doing a little sewing.

Then the nurse came in and ruined my day. She told me that I had to have an enema straight away, and later, in the evening, a bowel wash-out. The film crew started slowly turning green. David saved their day by telling them that it didn't need filming. There were sighs of relief all round – none bigger than mine and the poor nurses'.

I was also banned from eating for the next seven days. I couldn't go without food for seven days – I'd waste away; so I was offered the odd bowl of consommé and a special mixed liquid meal that was full of vitamins. That just happened to taste like sawdust and milk. With that the nurse took me in the bathroom and whipped the pre-packed enema up my back passage, and within five minutes I was to make the first of what seemed like a thousand visits in two days.

The irrigations were even more unpleasant. Two nurses marched in with a gallon jug of water, a funnel and a length of garden hose. The garden hose reached home and the water flowed freely; the nurses were amazed how quickly it emerged. Then the smell came. It was terrible. I could hear the poor nurses retching. If one of them threw up, I didn't stand a chance. This service was performed three times the following day, by which time the water re-appeared as clear as it had gone in. The nurses called it bowel preparation. I called it sadism.

On that last day before the operation I had to have a blood test. I hated blood tests, but it went off without my passing out. Three pints of blood were ordered for the following morning in case I needed them.

I had faithfully promised Caradoc to keep a diary through the operation period, so here is an extract covering that last night.

'*Saturday 8 March 1980: 11.00 p.m.* Today has been my last full day with it! Tomorrow it is coming off. I don't feel bad about it. I'm quite pleased, in fact. We have had our hard times. We have been in some unspeakable places. We have been friends for years. We've always been able to make a stand together. There have been times when we have both miserably failed each other. We can joke together now, because tomorrow we both know we will both have peace of mind – even though one of us ends up in a bucket.'

I don't know if that's what he really wanted in my diary, but that's how I felt. Relieved at last. I had been tortured inside for years, and I was being given a new lease on life.

The following morning the surgeon came in to see me for about half an hour, just to check I still wanted the operation. He tried to dissuade me right up to the last minute. I was sitting up in bed when the crew arrived. Every one of them looked the colour of a gooseberry. They all stood about my room nervously, none wanting to be the first to speak. I broke the silence, and joked that I would be asleep by noon, when for them the horror of filming the operation would only just be beginning.

I had remained calm in front of them and intended to stay that way. But I was grateful when at last the anaesthetist called in and my first injections were administered. They were a lot stronger than the ones I'd had in January. They took effect immediately and I began to doze off. However, the crew stayed round my bed until about twenty minutes before I was due in theatre, taking photos of us all together for the *Radio Times* and the BBC internal paper *Ariel*.

Here is another extract from my diary.

'*Sunday 9 March: 9.00 a.m.* Only two hours left to go. I feel calm, even though I slept little last night and have terrible butterflies. Thank God my pains will soon be over. If anything goes wrong, tell Amer I loved him to the end.'

The long journey to the operating theatre wasn't so long this time, and my teeth were being well looked after by the nurse who held my hand all the way up in the lift. This time, too, the camera came in. But the needle was the same, and again I could hear the camera whirring away in my right ear. Then I heard Mary shout, 'Good luck.'

The surgeon had to draw a diagram around my genitals showing where he was going to cut and which areas of skin from the testicles and penis he was going to use to create the vagina. Once all the pre-parations were done he made the incisions and the penis and testicles were removed just leaving the skin. The surgeon had to re-position my urethra and then the skin was folded back inside to create the vaginal walls. Once he was happy with his work, I was stitched up and packing was inserted.

It was six and a half hours later when I first opened my eyes. Mary was by the bed, and her first words were, 'Congratulations, it's all over.'

I was aware of others standing around my bed, and it's hard to describe how I felt at that moment. I felt a wave sweep through my body, washing everything away. I had been freed from the night-mare that had trapped me for twenty-five years. I was free. I was a woman at last.

I felt no pain. I tried to speak, but said little. I just slept on. Every time I opened my eyes that night, Mary and David were there. I knew Amer wouldn't be round till the following day; but I slept peacefully in the knowledge that two friends were close at hand.

Chapter 26

Convalescence

I cannot recall what time David and Mary left my bedside, but at two a.m. I was able to hold a conversation with the night nurse on duty. I was constantly having my blood pressure and temperature taken. I slept little, and at eight the night staff were able to sit me up. I felt a little drowsy, but not as bad as I had feared I might. I could feel no pain or discomfort; I had a constant flow of pain-killing injections pumped into my body to relieve that.

I knew that the BBC would be in by nine, so I slowly made up my face and re-arranged my hair. I looked better and it gave me the inner lift I needed. When Mary stuck her head around the curtain, she looked astonished. Everyone had imagined that I would still be gaga after the anaesthetic. It was a pleasant surprise to them. I felt on good form and asked them if they had all enjoyed their dinners the previous evening. Most of them hadn't eaten and they had all slept little as they re-lived the horror of the operation.

They had all been in control of their stomachs for the first five hours. Then, at the last moment, when the penis was actually cut off, the filming stopped, and Mary, who had been taking stills for the surgeon, just could not raise her camera. The theatre sister had received the offending article from the surgeon, but the cameraman did not film its journey to see where it eventually ended up.

After doing a little filming the BBC left me for a while. Amer was expected to arrive at noon, and they wanted to ask him how he felt. They caught him arriving, and when he eventually peered around my door he said little. The cameraman was following him. His every move was being recorded, so he held back a little. Once David had all the film he needed, they quietly left the room, and Amer and I were alone together for the first time.

We smiled at each other, and Amer moved in closer. He was fascinated with all the drips and needles that were embedded in my body. He did not want to knock me, so he leaned over the bed and tenderly kissed me. I wanted more, but he pulled away. Something was worrying him, I could tell, and I just had to find out what it was.

I finally got it out of him. He thought that, now I had been through the surgery, I no longer needed him. How wrong he was! I loved him more than ever at that moment. He had had the guts to accept me as a woman when we had first met, even though I had still had a male body. He had stood by me and shielded me from harm. He had given me the strength to face all the surgeons and the will to fight on until the end.

I had to reassure him constantly to lift him out of the depression he had worked himself into. He stayed all day by my bedside, and when I occasionally dropped off to sleep he sat silently waiting, ready to pick up our conversation the minute I was able.

The next five days nearly killed me. I was still not allowed any food, just liquids. I must have had a gallon of water a day forced down me, just to keep my waterworks in order, and weight was dropping off me. But I knew it was all for the best.

The following Monday morning the surgeon arrived to take out the packing that had been thrust up me after surgery. I was given two injections, and lay back ready to take the agony. I did not feel a thing. Once the packing had been removed and the assisting nurse had cleaned me up, the surgeon prepared me for my first dilating session. He produced two offensive-looking glass objects, one slightly larger than the other. The largest one was lubricated and inserted into the vaginal cavity; this had to be done three times a day for five minutes until I was ready to start having intercourse.

I did not feel a thing during the first session – I had had too many painkillers flowing through my system. But, when matron returned that evening, I could feel her every movement. Although my legs were flying in the air, I lay on my back and watched her. She covered the dilator firstly with an antibiotic cream and then with lubricating jelly. I felt every inch of the dilator entering me, and down below I felt I was on fire. I broke out into a sweat, and when I had my temperature taken two hours later it was still two points up.

The following morning two nurses came into my room to help me. I was propped up in bed and all the necessary equipment was laid out around me. A mirror was placed so that I could see what I was doing. I don't think the nurse realised that it was the first time I had seen myself down below. I was badly bruised and very swollen; yet I stared into the mirror, fascinated. It was a sculptured masterpiece. Although it was in its early stages, I could see just what it was going to look like after the swelling and bruising had disappeared. I lubricated the dilator just as I had been shown. Then I aimed it down below – but I did not know where to put it. The two nurses made suggestions; but I didn't want to take any chances, so I chickened out until the surgeon arrived. He sat me up and showed me exactly what to do and why. From that day on I managed by myself – although two nurses always stood by my bedside to ensure that I endured my stretching for the full five minutes.

I had made a remarkable recovery, and couldn't wait to get home. I spent very little time out of bed, and when I did get up I hobbled around like a penguin.

Ten days after surgery, the surgeon said I could leave. I noted thankfully that everything was going according to schedule. The BBC turned up to film me being discharged; then I hobbled out to David's car. It was tough going, but I was ready to endure anything as long as I could get home to Amer. It took me quite a while to get to the car, and even longer to get into it. I needed pillows to prop up my legs, so that my butt was suspended above the seat. Painful – but worthwhile.

Once I was settled at the flat, the crew left. Amer sat beside me, and I just could not help myself from falling into his arms, sobbing. He didn't understand, and thought that something was wrong; but I was deliriously happy. Happier than I had ever been. I told him that I loved him, and we kissed as we had never kissed before.

For the next few days Amer had to help me in and out of bed, cook for me and run around seeing to my every whim. I could not have managed without him. Even though I was in a little pain, he sat and encouraged me to write the last few chapters of this book. He did, however, have to go off to work each evening, and only days after my arrival home I thought disaster had struck.

I had continued to dilate as the surgeon had shown me, taking every care and precaution. I always waited till Amer was at work before doing the last session. Then I could relax, without having to worry about him walking into the room. I was sure that he would pass out if he caught sight of the operation before it had healed.

I was just cleaning up the mess when I suddenly started to bleed. I tried to swab it down, but it flowed fast and freely. The phone, as usual, was out of order. I had not mixed with my new neighbours, for I could not afford to risk exposing my identity. I was trapped. The local phone-box was usually vandalised, and in any case I dared not take the risk of trying to get there in one piece.

I tried to keep calm, and stumbled to the bathroom. I ran the bath full of cold water and say myself in it. I was freezing cold; tears of pain ran down my face. Even the dog sat at the side of the bath: he knew that something was wrong. The water turned pink, then slowly darkened. I was absolutely terrified. I let it run out, then turned the cold shower on to myself. I could not think straight.

I slowly packed up the bleeding area with cottonwool. Eventually the bleeding stopped. Two blood clots were left on the cottonwool, and I washed them down the plughole. I sat in the empty bath for a long while, frightened of moving. I eventually made my way back to the bedroom, cleaned up the mess and lay, shaking, with the bed-covers wrapped around me.

When Amer returned, he was furious, and very nearly pulled the phone out of its socket. He felt hurt that he had not been around to help me when I needed it most.

A week after that unfortunate night the swelling had gone down, and when I viewed myself in the mirror I felt comforted, to know that in four weeks' time the surgeon would give me the go-ahead to have my first sexual experience as a woman. It would be a very tender moment for Amer and myself. At the end of it all, only we would know if the operation had been a success or not. For the next couple of weeks I was deliriously happy, even though I was in pain. Having the surgery and becoming the woman I wanted to be was at last a reality and the pain was all worth it. I would have had fifty operations to feel as I did then. I was floating on a cloud, my dream had come true. There would be no more nightmares and no more doubts.

But life can be so cruel, as it was to me, just six weeks after surgery.

Chapter 27
My Darkest Secret

I was sitting by the lounge window, looking out at the garden when the pain struck me. It literally threw me to the floor. I lay there doubled up in sheer agony, gasping for breath. The pain between my legs and in the pit of my stomach was unbearable and I could not understand what was happening to me. It was completely out of the blue – I had had no pain for three or four weeks and had felt a lot better in myself. It had only been a bit uncomfortable down below when I had to dilate.

I do not know how long I lay there, but it seemed like hours and the pain was increasing all the time. I had always thought I had quite a high pain threshold, but I had never experienced anything as painful as this. It felt as though a knife had been thrust inside my stomach and was slowly being dragged through my lower body.

I knew I had to get help, so I grabbed my keys and stumbled out on to the main road. I must have looked a pitiful sight, bent double and trying to move forward with tears streaming down my face. I remember seeing two old ladies running towards me, one with a look of horror on her face. I looked down and saw that I was covered with blood. A trail was visible from my house to the road. I began to feel sick and dizzy, and then everything just went black.

I kept drifting in and out of consciousness; I could not open my eyes but I could hear voices shouting for help. I heard a car screech to a stop beside me and a voice shouting for someone to call an ambulance. I could hear the sound of the ambulance's siren as it approached, but the closer the sound seemed to get, the further away I seemed to be drifting. Hands started grabbing at my feet and shoulders and I knew I was being lifted into the ambulance. I could still hear the voices, but I could no longer understand what they were saying.

The ambulance pulled away and I could hear the siren screaming overhead. I tried to speak, but my throat was constricted and nothing would come out. I heard the voice of a man. He was sitting beside me, but talking to the driver and he said, 'The stupid bitch. Looks like she's tried to abort herself, she's in such a mess.' Then there was silence, as the blackness totally surrounded me again.

I came round again to excruciating pain. I tried to curl myself into a ball, but many hands pulled me back. I felt a strap being tightened across my chest and my legs being pulled up into the air. As I opened my eyes I was blinded by a big shining light right above my head. Voices were all around me but nothing seemed to make sense. Voices kept saying why? . . . why has she done it? . . . what's your name? . . . abortion . . . miscarriage . . . abortion . . . The words kept ringing in my ears. 'Silly fuckers,' I wanted to scream, ' I can't get pregnant.' Then I felt something like a cold steel tube being pushed into me. There was more pain and then blackness returned, but this time there was a warm glow in the blackness and I could see a hand stretching out towards me. A voice kept saying it was there to help. It was so peaceful for a moment, but then the bright light and the panic returned. I kept drifting from one to the other, the twisted faces looming over me and that warm peaceful hand. The faces were so hard and cruel: I could see their mouths moving, but could hear nothing.

I wanted to tell them that I knew what was wrong, that they were hurting me, not helping. I tried to struggle, but big hands held me down and then I saw a man with a syringe and all I remembered after that was the warm light and that tender hand.

Gradually I began to feel very warm, there was no pain and I could hear voices talking. I opened my eyes and a nurse at the side of my bed said 'she is awake, doctor.' I touched my legs. They were still there, even though I could not feel them. I felt as though I was in the middle of a bad dream. The doctor came into my line of vision and I can remember him saying to me he was so very sorry. He sat on the side of my bed and explained what had happened. I had been rushed into casualty and treated as if I were a genetic female. Their first thoughts were that I had miscarried or tried to abort an unwanted child. They thought that the internal damage they could see was self-inflicted. They tried to insert a probe that was supposed to close up the neck of the womb and slow down the bleeding. However, not being a genetic female, I had no womb, and in inserting the probe they had ripped apart and totally damaged the surgery I had had only six weeks earlier.

The doctors said that it was too late by the time they realised what had happened. The damage had already been done so they just stitched me back up. I had fifty-eight stitches and there was nothing more he could do. He told me I should go back to see my surgeon as soon as possible and he said he would give me a letter explaining what had happened and what he had done. I was told not to dilate until the stitches had dissolved and even then it might not be possible. He assured me that my surgeon would sort things out for me and again he apologised. I still owed him my life – if he had not stopped the bleeding when he did, I might have died – but I could not look him in the face any longer and I turned away. He patted my arm and said he would look in on me later – he needed to get some details from me, but he never even asked my name and I never asked him his.

To this day I feel no malice towards the doctor that treated me, even though he destroyed the dream I had always believed in. I can still see his face today: he looked so tired, and the frown lines on his forehead aged him past his young years.

After he left the room I realised with some panic that I could not go back to see my surgeon because I could not afford any more treatment. I had spent all I had on having the operation in the first place. The films were due to go out in a couple of months. The press would have a field-day with this twist in the tale. I could see the headlines: they would destroy me and all that I stood for. I would become a laughing stock, I just could not take the lies and criticism.

After all, there were so many people that looked up to me. I had given them the faith that they needed to carry on with their own paths of discovery. Yet my own life was destroyed. I could not put any doubt in others' minds. I knew the films would help so many people, and the press must not be allowed to destroy all the good the films would achieve. All I needed was a little time and when the publicity had died down and I had saved the cash I would sort things out. No-one need ever know my secret. It was mine alone and I would deal with it when the time was right.

A nurse came into my room. I closed my eyes but she saw my tears and sat at the side of my bed. She stroked my hair and told me not to worry – everything would be all right. She needed some personal details but she would come back later so she gave me a couple of painkillers and left the room. I then realised that she did not know my name either. It was then I realised that no one must know. I could not take the risk and reveal my identity. I had to protect myself.

I tried to get out of bed, but my legs felt numb and I could not move. I panicked every time I heard the door handle move so I closed my eyes and feigned sleep. I decided I must not talk to anyone until I had the strength to move. I drifted in and out of sleep. I hadn't a clue how long I had been there but it was dark outside. I knew I must try to move. I could see my clothes in a plastic bag on a chair in the corner and was able to swing my legs off the bed. I tried to get my balance but my legs were like jelly, so I sat back on the bed. To try and walk now would be stupid – I would cause myself even more damage than had already been done so I lay back on the bed for what seemed like ages. I kept trying to stand, but it was only when I could get my balance and hobble without falling over that I attempted to get dressed. The hospital was deathly quiet. All the lights in the corridors were dimmed, so I had to move very slowly and follow the fire exit signs to a staircase. Thank God I was only on the first floor – I could not have managed many more stairs. It took me a long time to get home and when I got there I realised my clothes were still covered in blood: even my keys had blood on them.

As I closed the front door I caught sight of my reflection in the hall mirror. My skin was grey, my eyes were red and the bags under them looked like coal scuttles. I looked like something from a freak show. I leaned against the front door, exhausted, then slid down to the floor, overcome with emotion and in so much pain. I crawled over to my bed and clambered in.

I woke to find Amer standing above me looking concerned. He wanted to know where I had been as I had been missing for nearly three days. He took me to the bathroom and helped me clean myself up. The next morning he went to the chemist to get me some painkillers and over the next few days he went back and forth between my house and the chemist. I tried everything available to dull the pain.

Amer tried to comfort me as much as he could. He had been so supportive to me all the way through surgery, but the only thing he could do when I was upset was hold me tight. I remember sobbing into his chest but to him life was all so simple: I had had surgery and I was now a woman. No questions. No moral dilemmas. I was his and only his and with his support I knew that I could overcome my fears.

He moved his lips close to my ear and whispered, 'Just a few more days and then I can finally make love to you. I can show you that my love is true.' I felt myself go rigid. That was the last thing I needed to hear right now, but it was like a countdown for him. We had kissed, petted and even had oral sex before but he would not make love to me because in his eyes that would not be the right thing to do.

I did not even try to explain to him what had happened at the hospital. I would not have been able to cope with his rejection as well. I needed love and support. It was then that I realised it was going to be a long, painful journey back to my surgeons.

I tried to go to sleep but my mind was restless. I just kept asking, why me? What had I done that was so wrong? Please God, let me be strong. I prayed that He would help me. Surely if there was a God, He would not let me suffer like this for long. I had a sleepless night due to the pain and when I woke the next morning, Amer was looking at me with concern on his face. I had been crying and talking in my sleep all night and he wanted to know what was wrong. But I could not tell him. I just asked him to trust me and I told him that I did not feel very well but that I needed him more than I had ever done before. He smiled and said, 'I will always be here for you. You must know that?'

The pain had become unbearable so I was taking four pain-killers every hour. I decided that I did not want Amer to see me going through this hell. But there was one person I could turn to who would ask no questions and look for no explanations: Gus. I telephoned him and told him that I needed to get away for a few days. His mum and dad owned a caravan in Hemsby, near Great Yarmouth so he arranged to pick me up and take me there as soon as he finished work.

I told Amer that I needed a few days away to work on my book. He never questioned me but bought me more pain-killers to take with me.

Gus collected me from home about seven in the evening and we arrived in Hemsby at about half-past ten. We had driven in near silence. Gus told me I looked a mess and asked me whether what I was doing was the right thing. I knew he was just concerned but I did not want to discuss my problems with him yet. There would be plenty of time for that and he would be the first person that I would tell. He left me in the caravan and I lay back on the bed. It was cold and dark outside, rain lashed down on the tin roof of the caravan and I felt so desperately alone. My happiness had turned to tragedy and I started sobbing from my heart. I had been through some shit in my life but those few days in the caravan were the longest and worst I had ever been through.

After a couple of days I ventured out of the caravan and went to walk on the beach. There was not a soul around and I walked for hours. Anyone passing by would have thought I looked a sad sight. Gradually day turned to night – I watched the sun set and the moon rise, listening to the waves lapping against the shore. I found it hard to comprehend why things had gone so desperately wrong: only six weeks ago I had been the happiest person on earth and now I felt like the saddest. The operations, the pain and the years of planning had all been for nothing.

During the next few days I had to prepare myself to face the outside world. I had convinced myself that nothing could be done for me so I had to face up to my new life as a woman with a dark secret. I could not tell anyone about what had happened. During those few days in the caravan I cried all my tears: I slept, I cried, I took painkillers, I cried, I reasoned with myself, I cried and slept again. After six days there was no emotion or self-pity left. I felt as though I had a heart of stone.

I telephoned Gus and asked him to collect me. I had dressed and made-up my face, so that I looked better, even if I did not feel better. When Gus arrived we went for a walk on the beach. He put his arm around me and told me that whatever the problem was, he would always be there to talk whenever I needed him. I loved Gus dearly with a special kind of love, that you only ever experience once in your life.

It was then that I realised that even in those desperate moments, with my hand on my heart, I can honestly say that I still did not regret having surgery, even if my happiness was short lived. I also knew that I had to go back and face everything.

When the films went out on television and my book was first published, the press had a field day. Everywhere I turned the press were there, but people were relying on me and needed my support so I could not let them discover my secret. I was held in high esteem by many people. They thought I was so brave for letting the films be made and for going ahead with what I believed in. Everyone wanted to talk about the operation and what they really wanted to know was just how successful it had been. If only they knew the intolerable pain I felt and the anguish I went through while meeting the press and dealing with all the publicity.

I did not want people to feel sorry for me because it had all gone wrong so I had to live a lie until I could get help. Gradually the pain went away, taking with it my feelings and my heart. I became a living, breathing shell with no heart but survival was the name of the game. I never for one moment thought that weeks would turn into months and months into years before I would have the strength to face up to my problems.

Life was beginning to get back to normal when Amer started asking me why we had not made love. I kept telling him that the surgeon had asked me to wait a while because he needed to do another small operation. I could see the disappointment on Amer's face and I knew he thought that intercourse was the only thing he could do to prove his love for me.

One night, while standing in the club where we both worked someone asked him what it was like, 'Did it feel like a real woman when he made love to me?' He smiled and said 'Of course it does.' But in his eyes I saw his despair and suffering. He had waited nearly two and a half years and was still waiting. I knew I had to do something . . . but what?

Chapter 28
Into the Gutter

To shake off the press, I left London and moved to Halifax in West Yorkshire. I tried to settle into a new home and job and I had left Amer behind in London where he had employment until the end of the year. He was then going to join me. We had found him a small bedsit in West London and I had taken a one-bedroomed flat in Halifax. We left our home in Hackney feeling no regrets. I had told Amer that there was more work for me in the north and he did not seem to mind me moving. After all, he was to visit me as often as possible and I promised to spend every other weekend with him.

But it did not take the press very long to track me down and when they did, they made my life a misery. One national Sunday paper journalist offered me £5,000 to go with him to the Netherlands, where he would provide me with a willing partner who would marry me. They wanted photographs of us together during and after the wedding ceremony and a photo of the wedding certificate. They would even pay for any legal expenses I would incur. I could not believe that they would stoop so low. They would do anything for cheap headlines.

After a few months I realised that I must start to try and get things sorted out and the best thing to do was explain everything to Amer. Together we would be able to plan what to do about it. So I travelled to London without phoning Amer to tell him I was on my way. As I got to the top of the street where he lived, I was stunned to see Amer walking down the opposite way with a young girl on his arm and it was obvious from the way that they were acting that they were more than just friends. I stood back slightly so that they could not see me, not that they were aware of anything that was going on around them. Another door in my life had suddenly slammed shut. I had had no idea that anything had been going on, but I felt that I could not blame him. I had messed him around by not telling the truth. I could not give him what he wanted – he was human and he had cravings like any other man. I no longer wanted him to be involved in my life so I never ever spoke to him again. I did what I always did when faced with a crisis – I ran away from it. I had nothing to hold me back now.

Within a week I was sitting on a train heading for Amsterdam. I had several gay friends that lived there and they were always asking me to go and spend some time with them. I also knew two guys who sold poppers (amyl nitrate) in the UK and they wanted someone to sell them in the Netherlands. I planned to open a branch for them. When I arrived I found that we did not operate from a shop, but that we just had a small stall, which we set up in four big night clubs on different nights of the week. We also stocked leather goods, t-shirts and sex-toys. It was just like a portable sex shop really. I knew a lot of English people in Amsterdam so I found it quite easy to settle down and be accepted into the gay community there. Within days of my arrival I was known for being totally outrageous and screaming my way round all the bars. I soon had a good clientele and I was selling poppers cheaper than the bars and local sex shops.

Before very long I was sucked into the seedy side of the Dutch gay scene. I found a small flat at the top of a warehouse, just outside the red-light district. I slept all day and partied and worked a little at night. Gradually the partying became more important than the work, but I just could not keep up with everyone else. With partying twelve hours a day every day, I was exhausted.

One night, one of my new Dutch friends, Bob, slipped me a tablet. He told me it would cheer me up and within an hour I felt great. I danced and boogied all night and I still wanted to carry on, when everyone else was ready to go home. I didn't sleep very well that night and when I woke up I felt like shit. The following night I gladly took another tablet from Bob. I wanted anything to make me feel better and before very long I needed two tablets to get me through the night. I was becoming as hooked as my friends and all that seemed to matter was drugs and booze. I even started selling joints in the clubs along with tablets to boost business.

Life no longer seemed real. What money I made I spent on drugs. I just could not stop myself. I had always taken a pride in my appearance but within two months I just could not give a damn. I had no respect for anything and finally I lost my pitch in two of the clubs which made money even harder to come by. The Amsterdam 'mafia' were not very happy with me either. I had had several run-ins with them and they warned me off. I took the occasional thumping and lost stock but I always survived.

The drugs were getting heavier the longer I stayed in Amsterdam. I always told myself that I could give them up at any time and I really believed that I could, but I would do anything for the money to buy them. I degraded myself beyond belief in those few months.

Then one morning, I returned to my flat to find everything I owned had been destroyed. My stock was smashed and ripped to shreds and the only things I had left were the clothes that I stood up in. But I was as high as a kite on drugs at the time. I went round to Bob's, but I couldn't tell him what had happened for laughing so he gave me more of what I wanted and I stumbled out into the early evening. I remember being in a bar at around midnight, but after that it all gets a little hazy.

I woke up in a garden by the old riverboats on the Kirkenstrasse. As I opened my eyes, I saw three faces looking down at me. My dress was around my neck and my knickers around my ankles and I was bleeding. I struggled to my feet and ran blindly through the streets. What had I done? where had I been? I just did not know. What the hell was happening to me?

I went back to Bob's but there was no reply. I knew how to get in the back way so I searched the place for some speed or anything. All I could find was a little cash and that would not get me very far. I cleaned myself up, pulled a big baggy jumper out of the wardrobe and put it on. I left the way I had entered and walked the streets for hours. As I sat down by a flower market, watching everyone going on with their business, I realised that this was not what life was meant to be about. If I was going to do anything about it, I must do it now, before it was too late. I didn't want to end up in an obituary column, known only as an old druggy. I had seen too many people laid up against park railings with syringes hanging out of their arms. I didn't want to end up like that. My life would have had no meaning whatsoever.

I decided to return to the UK but I could not afford the fare. I had the sense to phone the British Consulate. I had to surrender my passport in return for a rail ticket home. When they asked me what part of the UK I was returning to, I automatically said Preston, where my family were. I needed to feel part of a family just then. I am so glad I caught that train home. If I hadn't I would have died on the streets of Amsterdam.

But going back to Preston was a big mistake. Although I thought a lot of my family, I did not feel part of it any more. They all had a bond that kept them close together but I always felt like an outsider. I could not come to terms with family life. It took me some time to adjust back to living in the real world. I went through a bad time while withdrawing from all the drugs I had been on, but I soon decided it was time to move on.

I was lucky, I found it easy to get work. I moved to Southport where I worked as an entertainer during the evening. I also got involved with a hotel chain doing their promotion and advertising during the day. I found this job rewarding because if there were results from a promotion it was due to my hard work. I became obsessed with work. I felt I had to achieve; I had to prove to myself that I could get on alone. Material things became important to me: I felt I had to look successful to be successful. I moved from one company to another and I carried my knowledge with me. I had some good teachers in those early years and I was soon teaching others how to be successful.

One night, while working in Southport, I was approached by the managing director of the largest leisure company in the north-west of England. His company owned over thirty different venues in and around the Liverpool area and he had heard of my reputation for pulling in big crowds, so a few days later we visited all the largest venues he owned and I was told to pick which one I wanted. The choice was completely mine. He wanted me to open their first fun bar.

I chose a venue that had been a large French restaurant called Le Jardin. It was ideal for a fun bar but the directors didn't have the same confidence as I had. We opened within two weeks and within four it was the most successful bar on Merseyside. Many people eventually tried to imitate the bar, but were never completely successful. The company and the brewery were delighted and I was encouraged to take several more bars under my wing. I turned one of their small clubs into a high class gay venue, and I also looked after a new housing project the company set up.

But Le Jardin was my baby. Outrageous bar shows and blue humour pulled customers in from miles around. At one stage we had eight entertainers dancing and performing every night. We did our own comedy adaptations from all the top West End shows at the time, including the Rocky Horror Show. Liverpool is the home of so many top comedians and they were often in the crowd. It was there that I learnt to manipulate a crowd. It felt great: I had them by the bollocks and that's where I kept them.

To everyone who worked for the company I was their contact with senior management. I had a reputation for being a tough cookie to do business with but I always tried to be compassionate towards my colleagues. The brewery took a big interest in my career at that time. All the venues I operated sold their beers and the barrelage was extraordinarily high. The brewery made me several offers to go and work for them, but I knew I would not have the same independence in a national company, I would only be a cog in the machinery. I would not have the power and respect that I had in Liverpool so I decided against their offers.

While I was in Liverpool, I met a guy who I became very fond of. James was a typical scouser: he enjoyed his booze and was fun to have around. I didn't see a great deal of him as I worked day and night, but he was always there when I got home. He said that he understood my problem. I had told him that I had to go back to see my surgeon and I was just waiting for a bed before I had more surgery, and he believed that. While I was out at work, he dedicated his life to drinking. He slept all day and drank all night.

It was the night I came home early because I felt so ill that destroyed our relationship. I came back to find him screwing one of my barmaids, on my couch, in my lounge. I totally flipped: I threw her out and then turned on him with a vengeful rage, lashing out at him. He just stood there screaming at me 'I'm only human. You're to blame for what I've done. I can't get sex from you so what am I supposed to do? You're not a real woman anyway – you're a freak.' At that point I had had enough. He hit the door and his clothes followed in a taxi to his mother's house the following day. I had vowed before that I wouldn't let another man hurt me and humiliate me and I had let it happen again. I decided then that I would rather be alone and unhappy than have to go through that again.

While I was in Liverpool David Pearson contacted me and came to visit. It was nearly six years since the films were shown and he had lost touch with me when I left London. It was so nice to talk to him and catch up on the old days but I did not discuss my problems with him. I gave him the impression that I was happy and successful, which I was in my own way. But if I had told him about my problems I am sure he would have tried to help and support me through my trials – he was that kind of guy.

One night a private detective approached me in Liverpool, representing a wealthy American family who wanted to meet me. They had read my book and wanted to discuss a personal matter with me. I met the family – father, mother and daughter – in their hotel suite in Liverpool the following day. Their daughter was a petite, beautiful girl of around eighteen years old.

They wanted to discuss my operation: had it been successful? Was I happy with the results? Would I recommend the surgeon? Did I know of any other surgeons? The questions were endless so I asked why they were so interested. They pointed to Emily, their daughter, and said that they wanted her to have surgery. You could have knocked me down with a feather, I had no idea whatsoever that she was a boy! I could normally sense if someone was a transsexual, but I had really thought that Emily was a young girl.

The meeting was quite formal, but they wanted as much information as they could get. I discussed all the different surgeons that I knew of: two in England, and also surgeons in France, the Netherlands, and Casablanca, in Morocco. I told them about the different criteria for doing the surgery.

I was invited back that evening to have dinner with the family and I wasn't working, so I agreed. I was rather intrigued by the young girl as she never spoke and her eyes seemed distant. I arrived at their suite that evening and Emily answered the door. She thrust a note into my hand, written on a piece of hotel letterheaded paper. It said:

> You must help me, please. I must talk to you alone but I do not know how to contact you. Please, please help me.

I read the note when I slipped out to the loo before we went down to the restaurant for dinner. I was quite alarmed and did not know how to handle the problem. I could slip her my phone number but would she get the chance to phone me! But I knew something was wrong, I just had no idea what. I suggested to her parents that as I was going to Manchester the following day, Emily could join me if she wanted. I was going on a shopping trip to buy new clothes and Emily got really excited at the prospect. She begged her mother to let her go with me, but at first they would not agree to it. Emily's parents were both in their sixties and I discovered that Emily was their only child. Maybe that was the reason they seemed so over-protective. Eventually though, Emily's father agreed, but her mother was still not happy about it at all. We finally arranged that I would collect Emily from the hotel at 9.00 a.m. and I was to have her back by 5.00 p.m.

I was completely shocked by the conversation I had with Emily on the train. Emily had been born in Illinois, a perfectly healthy boy. Emily's mother had wanted a girl, so had registered the baby at birth as female, and had not even told her husband, at that stage, that his child was really a boy. He did not find out until the daughter he loved so dearly was due to start school. They then could not let Emily go to normal school in case the secret was discovered so they provided private tutors at home.

But Emily was a boy and wanted to be a boy. He had fallen in love with a girl who lived down his street but he could never tell her and he was heartbroken. He did not want to have an operation to become a girl, but he was frightened of his mother, and his father was just as involved in keeping the secret. I was used to sorting out dilemmas, but this was a situation I had never been in before. Should I go to the authorities and tell them? Would they help or would I just be stirring up a hornet's nest that would make Emily's life even more complicated?

We walked around the shops for a couple of hours and went to one of my favourite restaurants for lunch. Just talking to my new friend convinced me that I had to do something to help him. I asked him what he would call himself if he was living as a boy and he said he liked the name Peter, so Peter it was to be. I phoned his parents and told them that I was now aware of what had been done. His mother went absolutely mental on the phone and demanded that I return 'Emily' to her immediately, or she would phone the police. I slammed the phone down: I wasn't going to be threatened by her. I suggested a plan to Peter, and he was prepared to go along with it. We then went around a couple of stores and bought some boy's clothes and shoes for him.

I booked into a hotel and Peter changed into his new clothes there. He removed all his make-up and then we visited a good hairdresser. He had his long blond hair cut into the most masculine cut I have ever seen. The transformation was unbelievable: he became a very good-looking young man, and his smile spread from ear to ear. We went back to the hotel, and I phoned his parents again. His mother was still steaming with rage because I wouldn't tell her where I had her child. She would not talk sense, so I intended to make her sweat. I told her I was going to go to the police and at this point her husband interjected and asked if he could meet me in private. I told him that I would think about it and phone him later.

Peter and I stayed in Manchester that night and spent a memorable evening together. For the first time in his young life he was able to be himself. He was walking on air and was so proud. In a couple of the bars we visited it wasn't very long before he was chatting all the young ladies up. I knew then that what I had done was right, no matter what the consequences. I was prepared to do anything to help Peter.

I spoke to Peter's father the following morning. He wanted to meet us both, straight away. His wife was sedated and he said he needed to talk to me to explain what had happened. I thought we should meet on neutral ground, so he travelled to Manchester and we met at Victoria Station. I spoke to him by the bookstall, while Peter waited by one of the platforms. His father was obviously distressed by the whole situation. He told me that he had not been able to stop his wife and he could not afford to get the police involved. He had decided now that he would help his son even if it meant leaving his wife to do so.

I believed him, so I signalled for Peter to join us. The look on his father's face was enough: he could not believe what he was seeing walking towards him. They then ran towards one another and threw their arms around each other. Even I had to hold back the tears. Peter's father promised his son that nothing would be done to him that he didn't want. He told me that his wife had done what she had because she had lost three daughters at birth and when he had discovered Emily was really a boy he felt powerless to do anything about it. Peter's father thought that he would have been in trouble himself with the authorities in America for registering the wrong birth details, but he had decided now to go to the American Embassy and make sure that his son was helped.

Peter had entered the UK with a female passport. How they were going to explain this away was beyond me. I went with them for lunch and that afternoon they set off for the American Embassy in London. I have no idea whether they got things sorted out, but before they left I took Peter to one side and said to him that if anything went wrong he must wait until he was going through American customs or near a policeman and he must scream and shout and break away from his parents and tell the truth to anyone that would listen.

Peter was not the only boy I was to meet in that situation. I have met two others in the UK. In each situation I have done what I thought best, but I never found out what happened to Peter. I hope he survived the clutches of a mother who smothered him, and that his father finally stood up to his wife.

Chapter 29

Goodbye to Family and Friends

I was in bed when the phone rang. It was Gus's mum, ringing to tell me that Gus had died an hour earlier. I was devastated. He had been ill for several months and I had visited him only two days before. He had asked to see me knowing he only had a few hours left. We had talked so openly to each other. He told me that if things had been different he would have spent the rest of his life with me. I told him finally all about my problems and he made me promise that one day I would sort things out. There he was, lying in bed dying, and he was still able to shed a tear for me. They were tender moments that I will have with me for the rest of my life – no-one can ever take them away from me even though they took him away. I would not go to the funeral. His parents knew that I was devastated by his death and they understood. Even now we meet and talk about the good times we all spent together.

A few days after Gus's death I went on holiday to Tenerife. It had been booked months before and I was looking forward to a break. I always spent my holidays alone, sleeping all day and enjoying myself in the bars at night, but this time it turned out differently. I sat in Jim's bar in Porto de la Cruz on my first night and in strolled Richard and Graham. They sat at the bar on the two stools at either side of me. Richard was loud but Graham was the total opposite. Within minutes we were gabbing like old friends. Richard loved the bright lights and fun whereas Graham was much more serious and intense. I was attracted to both of them as they were so much like me. Graham was like the big brother that I had always wanted and Richard liked the big sister I could giggle with. My whole life changed that week. My final night on Tenerife was spent blubbering at the bar with the two boys because I did not want to go home.

My flight home was uneventful – all I looked forward to was calling the boys as soon as they got back home the following week. Within two days of their return I was up in London having dinner with them. Graham could see into my soul and we had many deep and meaningful conversations. When there have been problems he has helped me pull myself through. I hope at times when he has needed my support, it has been enough to help him.

I wanted to put things to rights with the world. I wanted to help people that had problems with their sexuality. The Salvation Army and Samaritans had my number so that if they had a transexual client they could not help, they could phone me. I had learned how to counsel and talk to people with problems and I discreetly set up a helpline where people could contact me direct twenty-four hours a day if they needed help.

On my return from Tenerife I realised that all the problems I had had with James had soured Liverpool a bit for me. When the brewery made me another offer, I considered making a move. I knew it would be a gamble, but my whole life was a gamble. It was time to move on to pastures new. I needed a new challenge, another ladder and more rungs to climb.

For several months I opened new fun bars for the brewery as a consultant. I also worked as a private consultant to several leisure chains. Eventually, I decided to settle with a new company in the Sheffield area. They only had three venues, but they did have an enterprising, smooth-talking managing director who seemed to know where he was going. I liked his ideas and his plans for the future. I wanted to be part of them.

One of my first jobs with the new company was the launch of a night-club in Mansfield. When the doors opened we had the most successful night-club the area had ever seen. The club was sold a year to the day of opening, and showed a huge profit.

I had a good position as entertainment and promotion manager and worked day and night, seven days a week. I also worked with the managing director on the development side and I eventually held the title of development manager as well. I spent what little spare time I had travelling around the country looking for new sites. The company's clubs eventually spread as far afield as Newcastle in the north and Mansfield in the south. We had venues throughout the south-west and north of Yorkshire and also seven venues in the Greater Manchester Area.

I had a nice home in Mansfield, not that I saw a great deal of it, but I was proud of my achievement. I had an excellent job where I was respected for who I was, not what I was and my position within the company gave me a standing that I had never had before in my career. If I wanted to disappear for a few days to France and get away from everything and everybody I could now just fly off, and hire a car when I got there. France was a land that I so desperately loved. Every time I travelled there it was like going home. There I was unknown, a nobody. I loved Paris and the Auvergne and I tried to stay off the tourist tracks. I got to the heart of France and France worked its way into my heart. It was worth all the hard work, just to snatch those few days of French freedom. It was such an enterprising time for me and finally I felt ready to face up to my problems and get things sorted out. I needed someone special to help me to get through it, but there was no-one special in my life at the time – I only had my friends.

One of the good things about my new job was that I could now provide more for my mother. I had always hoped there would come a day when I could give her a better life than she had ever had before, but I knew I would have problems trying to control her drinking.

She had had eight children by the time she was twenty-seven and a husband that beat her black and blue every time he got drunk. She had lost her children to the courts so she had nothing left in the world except her bottle of booze. She had even tried to help herself, but early electric-shock treatment had scrambled her brain so much she never really stood a chance. Whenever I had visited her, I did all that I could but I knew that if I gave her money she would rush down to the off-licence the minute I left to buy more booze. If I bought her something new for herself or the flat, she would sell it and spend the money on drink. Even when I replaced everything for her after a fire at her flat, the next time I visited, half of it had gone. She had either given it away or sold it.

I wanted to do something to make up for all her suffering, so one night I arrived at her flat just after midnight. She was already in bed and slightly the worse due to the dreaded bottle. I asked her if she wanted to come and stay with me and she agreed to come, so I packed her few clothes into a couple of bin-bags and moved her and her dogs back to my home in Mansfield.

However, it only lasted a few days. One night, when I returned home from work she was sitting on the doorstep with her bin-bags packed. She wanted to go back to her own flat. She had raided the drinks cupboard and ploughed her way through it. She looked so sad, sitting there, but she would not listen to me – if I did not take her home she would walk, she said. I couldn't let her do that, so I agreed to take her home.

As I drove, I kept checking the rear-view mirror. I could see her with a bottle to her lips. I asked her to wait until she got home, but she started crying and told me not to pick on her. She drank most of the way home and I was getting more and more annoyed with her. She dropped an open bottle of whisky and the stench filled the car. I angrily told her to put the bloody bottle away. I was sick of seeing her destroying herself. She screamed back at me that she only drank because none of us loved her, no-one cared and we never visited her. I asked her what she expected her children to do – they dared not take their children to see her in case she was drunk when they got there. We rowed for a good hour until she fell into a drunken sleep. I had not wanted to row with her, but a few home truths came out that disturbed me and must have hurt her.

When we arrived in Fleetwood I had to nearly carry her out of the car. I put the dogs in the bathroom, her straight into her bed and went back to the car to get her things. I could hardly lift one of the bin-bags for the bottles that were inside: she had raided my cellar good and proper. I tipped the contents of every bottle that she had taken down the sink and left the bottles draining. She would find them when she woke and would know what I had done with them.

Then I started hanging her clothes up in the wardrobe and I found my roll of jewellery, which she must have taken from my bedroom. I was totally gutted and as I left her that night in her flat I had a very sad heart. I realised that I could do no more and I vowed that I would never try to help her again.

As I drove home I remembered my childhood. There didn't seem to be any happy moments. All I could remember was her suicide attempts and the cooking, cleaning and ironing I had done as a child. I was pleased that I had broken free and made my own way in life.

A week later I received a letter from her which asked me to forgive her for what she had done to me, especially after I had tried to help her. I read the letter with a cold heart, then screwed it up and threw it in the bin. I thought I would eventually come to terms with what had happened and then I would contact her. I always had done in the past.

I never did reply to that letter and a week later, my sister phoned to tell me that my mother had died the night before. I felt so guilty for ignoring her letter and, even worse, I had thrown the letter away. I had treated the letter as rubbish, as I had treated her. I felt disgusted with myself. She was my mother, I should have tried harder than I did. I kept asking myself questions. Why had I given up on her so easily? If I had forced her to stay with me in Mansfield, would she still be alive today? She had been visiting one of her neighbours on the night she died. She had had a little to drink, and around midnight, had set off to go home. When she got to the front gate she collapsed and had a heart attack. The neighbours had done all that they could to help her, but they all complained that the ambulance had taken so long to get to her. If it had arrived sooner maybe things would have been different.

The next day I travelled down to meet Shirley and we went to make the funeral arrangements. I intended to give my mother a good send-off. All her family and her children were to attend, so I ordered three funeral cars. I am sure she would have been pleased at the turn-out but I felt sad that they could come to the funeral but not be there for her when she was alive and needed them most.

As I stood by the hearse, waiting for the guests to arrive, the neighbour my mother had spent her last few hours with came over to speak to me. She asked me if I would call and see her after the funeral. Once the family had all dispersed, I went back to Fleet-wood. I had the keys to my mother's flat so I let myself in. My family had already removed all her furniture and personal belong-ings, but on the window-sill in the lounge stood a silk flower display that I had bought her for mother's day about eight years before. No-one had dared to move it, they knew how much she had loved it.

I had kept my dignity at the funeral, keeping my head high and trying to be the head of the family, but those few minutes in the flat were my time for grief. A time for me to say goodbye in my own way. I knew she would forgive me for not replying to her letter and in some way I felt relieved that she was gone – she would not suffer any more pain or heartache. She had always believed in God, even though she could not understand why He treated her so cruelly. She had always told me that she would be at peace when she got to heaven and I hope she got there.

I called in at the neighbour's house before I left Fleetwood. She gave me an envelope and in it was a ring that she said my mother had been wearing when she died. My mother had asked the lady to make sure I got it. She then told me of the many nights my mother had spent with her, talking about her children and her life. She said that my mother had been so proud of me. She had always thought of me as her little snowball, her number one. That neighbour had obviously spent many hours with my mother. She knew everything about the family and she knew all my mother's fears and feelings. If only I could have got that close to her. I felt so sad that I had not taken the time to be as close as a stranger had become, but it was comforting to know that she had a good friend.

It had taken a stranger to put things back into perspective for me. I put the ring on a chain around my neck so that I have a part of her with me at all times. It's sometimes comforting to think that she is watching over me, that she has become my guardian angel. I truly believe that she is there.

A year to the day after my mother's funeral, my father died. I was in France at the time. I rushed back to the UK not because he had died, but because I felt it was only right to support my family as they grieved. I did not pay him my last respects. I just wanted to be there at the cremation to make sure that he had really gone. I know it may sound callous, but there is no way I can forgive him for what he did to me. My brothers and sisters did love him as a father should be loved, but I could not pretend, or hide all the pain he had caused me during my life. He had never been a proper father to me.

I could not forget that he had abused my mother and me, and had helped destroy the family I had grown up with. I had to live with the memories. As I watched the curtains close in the crematorium, I realised that I was glad to think that he was gone. He was gone for good.

By this time the company I worked for in Sheffield had gone from strength to strength. A three-year plan was drawn up that involved more investment in the company, with it growing to approximately 200 venues before being floated on the Stock Exchange. Suddenly, due to mismanagement and the recession, the company plummetted into receivership.

Everything I owned was tied into my work and even my beautiful home was repossessed by the bank. They had been so willing to lend, lend, lend during the good times, but when things got a little rough they wanted all their loans repaid more quickly than I could manage. Just two days after the bank repossessed my home, the law was changed to stop lenders taking such drastic action, but for me it was too late. The Baillifs had taken most of my furniture away, but the bank still wanted more. They threatened to make me bankrupt, but there would be no point, I had nothing more to give, they had completely wiped me clean.

I was determined not to let it get me down. It had taken me ten years to get where I had and I wasn't going to let this pull me into the gutter again. I had toughened myself up over the last ten years and now I could take the knocks. I had already been to Hell and back and I wasn't going back to Hell again.

Chapter 30

New Beginnings

My good friends stood by me during those difficult months. I moved in to the Manhattan pub in Chesterfield where Keith the owner let me have a free room and gave me a couple of nights work a week. I made sure that the audiences I entertained had no idea what I was going through. There were two girls who also lived above the pub, but I always felt as though I was intruding into their lives, so I kept myself to myself when I could. I needed my own space at that time.

Barbara, my former neighbour and friend, made the clothes that I needed for work. She also made sure I was fed and watered. Graham and Richard in London provided the sanity. They talked me through the worst times. The people that I had worked with for years just dumped me, even after all the loyalty that I had shown them. It was only about eighteen months later that they contacted me, saying that I could rejoin the company.

Gary, Michael and Paul also proved themselves to be true friends – they helped give me back my self respect. A lover had never materialised, my material dreams had been destroyed and my personal dreams had never really got started. They had always been just that little bit too far out of my grasp.

One day, while driving down the A17, I noticed a rocking-horse at the side of the road. A sign pointed to the Fulbeck Heath Craft Centre. I drove down a country lane that led me to a whole new way of life. At the centre I met Charles and Betty Lemmon, a couple in their late fifties. Charles made rocking-horses and Betty taught hobby ceramics. As I got to know them I began to spend more time there. They had a little studio where I spent many happy hours learning how to teach the techniques of ceramics.

I absorbed everything Betty and Charles had to say about the business: the pitfalls that they had encountered and the pleasure teaching gave them. I was as hooked as all the other students seemed to be and I would proudly show all the pieces that I made to Barbara and Graham. Through my new hobby I discovered a new me. I found that I could be creative with my hands. I absorbed knowledge quickly.

Then I decided to turn my hobby into my new profession. With financial support from Graham and Barbara, Wonderland Ceramics was created. With the knowledge from my days in the leisure industry I was able to promote it to the full and all the skills I had learnt from Betty were put to good use when students visited our small unit. My friends are the directors of the company and I work night and day to make it work. I don't have a large salary but I have proved that I can bounce back. I enjoy working in the environment I have created and I enjoy passing on what I have learnt to others. It is so rewarding to see the look on someone's face when they finish a figurine or a vase. They are so proud of what they have achieved and I am proud that I have helped them.

Things had got back to normal when, one Sunday evening, a friend telephoned me to say that there was an advert in a paper, someone was looking for me or information about my where-abouts. I dialled the number with a little trepidation, wondering what the hell was going to go wrong now. I was shocked to find that it was David Pearson, from the BBC, who had placed the advert. He had had a research team looking for me but they had come to the conclusion that I was either dead, (they had been told that I had committed suicide in Liverpool years earlier) or that I had changed back to my former gender role and was living and working as a man, somewhere in the Midlands. I put his fears to rest and told him that I was well and living in Chesterfield and was still the same old Julia. We arranged to meet the following day.

When we met, we talked for hours about what I had been up to. He was fascinated by my new career in ceramics and of course it was not long before he broached the subject of the films. He was amazed that fourteen years on, people still remembered them and they still asked him how I was, and were disappointed when he could not give them an answer. We talked endlessly about how things had changed in the transexual world. Although I was not associated with it, except for working on the helpline, I still had my finger discreetly on the pulse of what was happening out there. I told him about young Peter, the American boy and he couldn't believe that such a thing could happen in this day and age.

David suggested making another film. It would not necessarily be about me, but it would be based on a journey through the transexual world, showing how things had changed, in the past fourteen years. I thought it was a good idea, particularly as I wouldn't have to be too personally involved. I spent a couple of weeks doing some research myself and was quite shocked at my findings. I telephoned all the helplines that I knew and asked them to summarise the problems that they had to deal with and asked them what kind of things they would like to see changed. If I was going to speak on behalf of the transexual community, I though I had better get their support and advice. The same problems were happening all around the country and I was soon assured that a new film would help people to identify with some of the problems.

But I was also aware that a new film would once again highlight me in the media, and the press would start sniffing around. I still had a dark secret that would make sensational headlines, but I wanted it to come out the way I wanted it to and not as a headline in a tabloid that I could not control.

I arranged to meet David again. After I had told him about my research I thought it only right to tell him about my own problems so that he knew what he was about to let himself in for. David was totally shocked by my revelations. I think he understood why I had kept it all quiet at the time because he too had discovered how vile the press could be. It's hard to explain, but everyone who had worked on the last films was affected by them. There was an emotional link between us. I had broken away from that chain, but the others still felt it all those years on. So we decided that the new film would be a journey through the transexual world and would also reveal my problems. Somewhere along the line I knew I would have to meet my surgeon and after fourteen years it wasn't going to be easy. I told David that I might not even get that far, he would just have to see how things worked out. I did not cherish the thought of everyone knowing the truth about me. I did not want people to feel sorry for me and I certainly did not want people to make fun of me – the few times that it had happened had hurt me deeply.

Chapter 31

The Journey

It took David about six months to get the go-ahead for the new films. During that time I noticed that I was drinking day and night, but I could never quench my thirst. I visited my GP several times, and blood tests showed that I was diabetic and had been for quite some time. I had put on a lot of weight and while I was being weighed one day, the nurse asked if she could measure my height. I told her I was 5' 10½". She just laughed and said that I must be shrinking because I was only 5' 6½". I did not believe her at first, because I had been the same height since the age of fifteen, when I joined the Navy, but I had lost four inches in height and it concerned me. I mentioned it to my doctor, but he told me not to worry and explained that it was probably due to being overweight.

Not long after this, we started filming in France. I was delighted to be there again and at least I would be relaxed. It was nice to talk with old members of the film crew and catch up with what they had been doing. We spent a couple of days in Paris. I did not want to go back to Amsterdam as it was too difficult for me to relive my time there. Paris had the same atmosphere, particularly around the Pigalle, as parts of Amsterdam. There was also a large community of French transexuals, who worked the streets as prostitutes. Paris, for me, holds the excitement that London did in the late 'seventies. I found it quite difficult talking on film about my experiences in Amsterdam. God knows how I would react when I had to talk about my personal problems.

Back in the UK, I met several transexuals I had not known about in the past. The research team had worked hard to find other transexuals who would contribute to the film. The Gender Trust had also agreed to become involved: they are a charitable organisation, run by transexuals for transexuals. Although I had admired their work, I had never approached them to see if there was anything I could do to help. I met Angela Price, their publicity officer and we had discussions, both in front of the camera and privately. They were very frank and open. Afterwards I found out that Angela had been a little worried about our first meeting as she had heard so many rumours about me. She left with a very different impression, and I am glad to say that she is now a friend.

I had never had any hormone treatment since my surgery, although I had made several attempts to get it. My doctors had told me that it was not necessary for me, so in the end I gave up.

It was through Angela I discovered that my height loss was part of a more serious problem. Angela was alarmed that I wasn't on hormone treatment, and said that the height loss I had suffered could only mean one thing: I was a likely candidate for osteoporosis. She advised me to see a bone specialist and endocrinologist as soon as possible before any more damage was done.

The guys at the Beeb soon got that in hand. I got a new GP, who soon referred me to a leading bone specialist at the Royal Hallamshire Hospital in Sheffield, where I had tests done for my bone density and calcium scans. Within minutes the results were through. If I had been a genetic female, my results would just have been safe, but I was a genetic male at birth, which made my results look totally different. They were dangerously low, so I was rushed down for spinal and hand x-rays. The specialist looked at my results and the x-rays, and confirmed that although osteoporosis had not taken hold, the x-rays showed that my bones were brittle and thin and that arthritis had set into my spine. Although it does not cause me too many problems at the moment, it will in the future. In laymen's terms, what had happened to me was simple. A genetic female, as she goes through the menopause, ceases to produce the female sex hormone, oestrogen. As a result of my surgery, I had ceased to produce the male sex hormone, testosterone. In both sexes, these hormones promote the replacement of bone tissue, so my sudden drop in testosterone production had an effect similar to the female menopause. I had the skeletal frame of a woman twenty years older, and I would have to take care of myself. My bones could be as brittle as those of an old-age pensioner. It also accounted for my height loss, as bones in my spinal column were wearing away. To reduce the strain on my spine, weight reduction would now have to play a major part in my life.

The endocrinologist was not so helpful. I had no hormones being produced in my body, I had brittle bones, so what? Only hormone replacement therapy could have helped, but I had never had any, and now the damage was done. As I have had no illnesses or felt unwell, apart from the diabetes, I would not have been alerted to these problems if I had not started making this new film. If you are transsexual, or if you know anyone who is, tell them to get their bones checked. It could have a devastating effect on them in later life if they don't do it straight away. Now I'm on the treatment I need. I will still have problems in the future, but they won't be as bad as they could have been.

After I had had my original surgery there was nowhere for me to turn; no aftercare service was available. It is shocking to think that fifteen years on there is still nothing. The minute your surgery is complete you are on your own and if you haven't prepared yourself for your future, tough.

One thing I honestly believe is that taking the step and having a sex-change operation is going to be tougher than you ever thought possible. Surgery does not suddenly change the way you think and handle situations, it doesn't make you more employable and it certainly doesn't make your life any easier.

Chapter 32
The Big Decision

I had decided to go back to my surgeon and my meeting with him was quite emotional. The night before, I didn't sleep a wink because he was going to tell me the next day what I had either feared or longed for, for years. What he would say to me would change the course of my life, and I knew that either way, my life would never be the same again. My great fear was that he would tell me nothing could be done and I would have to spend the rest of my life like this. I longed for him to tell me that everything would be all right and I had been worrying for nothing.

My living nightmare was no longer a closely guarded secret – I had already discussed it on film, and the more people I met and discussed it with, the more determined I was that the outcome of this meeting was going to be positive, but there was still that niggling, doubting fear in the back of my mind. I only hoped that if the result was bad, I would not go over the edge.

Anyone watching the films or reading this book will now know my secret and most people will probably feel compassion for me and wish me well. Others, however, will use it against me. I have already experienced the hatred that some people have for anything or anyone that is not normal and I know just how vindictive and unkind people can be. I am supposed to be a big strong girl and I should be able to take all the knocks in life, but sometimes it hurts deep down inside when someone calls you a freak, or a fat bastard. Surely they do realise that I can still be hurt and that I have feelings and emotions like anyone else.

I always try not to let people see that they have hurt me. I would not give them the satisfaction. But even now, when I feel low, I think about all that hurt and it can be quite disturbing. I would have no way of fighting back if I did not believe in myself and I was worried that if my surgeon said the wrong thing, I might lose that belief. I realised I was taking such a gamble as I sat down in front of the surgeon. I do not think the camera could pick up the anguish I felt at that time, thinking it wasn't too late, I could still get up and run like hell.

But I stayed – it was now or never. I explained to the surgeon what had happened to me. We had spoken on the phone a couple of days earlier, but I had not told him everything. Now, as I related the full story, I could see the compassion in his eyes. I know he felt sorry for me and I think he was as concerned as me about what he would find when he examined me.

He asked the film crew to leave the room before the examination. This was the first time a doctor had looked there since my visit to my local hospital on that awful night. He had problems with his examination because I had not dilated for fifteen years and had pro-lapsed. The examination was quite painful and he made me bleed a little, so I was glad when it was all over.

The film crew were hustled back into the room, and there was a nervous silence until the surgeon started to speak. Yes, the damage was serious, and if I had approached him two years earlier, there would have been nothing that he could have done for me. However, gender surgery had advanced a great deal over the last few years and there was a new surgical technique that could be performed. Colonplasty, the technique in question, has been performed in the United States for a few years now and was now being used in the UK. He said that if I wanted his help, he could do something for me. I can't explain the relief or emotion I felt at that moment. He asked to speak to me privately, without the film crew there.

The guys moved their equipment out as quickly as they could. We made small talk while they did and when we were left alone, he explained just what would have to be done. This operation would be far more complicated than the first. They would have to remove part of my intestine and use it to create a vagina. Everything from the first operation would have to be removed and I would need a little more cosmetic work done down below to give it a better appearance. In reality it meant I was to have another sex change operation and this time it would be far more complicated.

My surgeon then explained that the biggest problem I would have to face up to, was my weight. I would need to lose about seven stone before he would even consider doing the operation. He re-assured me that the colonplasty surgery already performed in the UK had been very successful but I would also have to be prepared to take about eight weeks to recover from the surgery and this he would insist on. When I left, I was floating on a cloud. I wanted to scream and shout. It was like being released from a cell, after being kept in the dark for fifteen years.

It is going to be an expensive operation, so that is to be another problem that I will have to resolve. Since that day my surgeon and I have spoken again and he has assured me that if I am going to go ahead and have the surgery then he will be there when the time is right.

The thought of having the surgery absolutely terrifies me. The first time round I would have done it myself, I wanted it so desperately, but the fear that something could go wrong again terrifies the hell out of me. I am going to have to overcome that fear more than anything else.

We had to rush off to meet Graham. He was the only person I wanted to discuss the surgeon's news with. I know he was waiting nervously for me and I only hoped now that I would not start blubbering. I wanted to be strong and show him I was able to handle the situation.

It was so easy to talk to Graham, even in front of the film crew. He knows me inside out and his compassion was felt by all present. As we discussed the implications of the surgeon's answers, I knew that he would be there to help whenever I needed it even without me telling him. He and Richard would help me convalesce and provide the support I would need. As Graham left me at the railway station that evening he knew I would sort things out in my own way. I always did. I just needed time. I sat alone on the train that night, heading north, and I cried most of the way back. The emotional strain was too much. I wrote five letters on that journey: to my surgeon, the film producer David Pearson, Graham and Richard my most loyal friends, to my mother and to my father even though they were both dead. I never sent those letters, they just express how I really felt at the time. Maybe you can understand how I felt during that journey. I know those people will understand my true feeling and hopes, and I know they will not mind you reading something that was meant to be personal to them.

Chapter 33

The End of the Journey

My journey has come to an end as far as the BBC is concerned, but my journey through life still goes on. I have had a few weeks to reflect on what my surgeon had to say and we have spoken several times on the phone. I have made the decision that, God willing, and finances being available, I will go ahead with the surgery option that was offered to me.

It is not going to be an easy path to that special day and I have at least a year to wait, maybe even two. It could take me that length of time to lose all the weight I need to shed. I am hoping that such drastic weight loss will not change my personality. I must eat more healthily and learn to control my eating habits. I will even plan an exercise programme that I can stick to. I really need to get my body back into shape and ready to face the trauma of surgery, but I also want to enjoy a more relaxed lifestyle and spend a little more time on myself. I still feel scared, but I will talk that over with a trained counsellor and shall learn to overcome that fear.

I set out on my original journey over fifteen years ago and I owe it to myself to complete that journey. I cannot ask for the years back that I have lost. I can only hope that I will put the years I have ahead of me to good use. I hope that somewhere, someone can be helped by my story or even by me personally and I will do all that I can to highlight and help solve the problems of transexuals everywhere in the world. We are human beings and not freaks; we have feelings and dreams as well and I hope those dreams are allowed to come true.

I am still looking for Mr Right and maybe one day he will knock on my door. Then I will be able to share my life with someone who really cares for me. If that never happens though, then it was never meant to happen and I won't be sad. If it does, then I deserve the right to marry, to make my bond with my lover, to join in wedlock, as normal people are allowed to do. Maybe the Church of England will practise what it preaches and love its neighbour, no matter what gender that neighbour was at birth.

I hope in years to come to spend more time in France. There are many country lanes there that I long to walk down and many mountains I wish to sit on and look out over the world. I feel as though it's my world there and nothing can take that away. Neither can anyone destroy the peace of mind that I now have. Life will be what I make it from now on. I am so glad that I have been given a second chance and I am going to take that chance for all that it is worth. I am going to live my life to the full.

There are friends who have gone now that I cannot share my joy with, but I will always remember them. Gus would have given his life for me, of that I am sure. I would have given my life for him.

There are several people who touched my life in the early days who have gone now. Many were taken so abruptly, and early in life, by AIDS. They must not have died in vain. People must learn to show others that they care. There is so much war in the world, so much pain and death but life is so precious. Live yours to the full.

Postscript

The new film highlights only part of my journey of discovery: fifty hours of film will have to be condensed into fifty minutes for transmission. Some of the people I have met, through the BBC and also through the helplines, have had some very interesting stories to tell. As I do not yet know exactly what the new film will contain, I would like to tell some of these stories here, as I feel they may help others.

Mandy was a young girl who had had her surgery done by an inexperienced gender surgeon. He had basically castrated her and created a hole for her to urinate through. She has had over seventeen major operations. Most have been in the UK but several have been in the USA. The operations had cost her and her lover a fortune and they still have to work day and night to pay for all her corrective surgery. The NHS wouldn't operate on her and her original surgeon refused to help her. I think she should have sued him and had him drummed out of practice. One of the surgeons I spoke to showed me pictures of Mandy's first surgery. It was shameful. It should never be allowed to happen again. I will be keeping my eye on the surgeon who did it and if I ever learn he has performed another sex-change operation and it goes wrong, I will make his name public.

Michelle had surgery two years ago and has suffered from internal bleeding every day since then. She spent what little money she had on getting the operation done in the first place, and has no way of raising the kind of money she would need for further surgery. Her local Area Health Authority will not approve her referral to Charing Cross Hospital for treatment on the NHS, presumably because gender surgery is not very high on their list of priorities. It seems ironic to me that the Health Service is prepared to spend so much on patients who may have smoked their way on to the cancer ward, but there is apparently no money available for Michelle. If she was a genetic female, she would have received treatment for her symptoms long ago.

Michelle's original surgeon agreed to operate on her again at his own expense but failed to stop the bleeding, and he has now washed his hands of her. His last words to her were to tell her to 'go and sit on a traffic cone'!

Karen is fifty-five years old and a transexual. She has lived and worked as a woman for twenty-five years. You could not wish to meet a nicer person. However, she cannot have surgery because she has a bad heart complaint. She wants to take the chance: she would rather die on the operating table in an attempt to fulfil her dream, but there is not a surgeon in the country that would take the risk and operate.

Kim is seventy-two years young. She had known she was a transexual for forty years and waited until her wife of fifty-one years passed away before having surgery, because she did not want to disgrace her. She had only had surgery four months earlier when I met her, but she was so happy and so content with her new life.

When the original programmes were broadcast in 1980, I must admit to feeling a little guilty at perhaps encouraging so many people to start on the path towards changing gender. So many suddenly identified themselves as transexuals, because of the films, causing a lot of distress to families and friends. I think if you do feel you have to change your sex, you should see someone to get help. I recommend that you approach the Gender Trust for help and information before making any major decisions. There is information from them at the back of this book, along with a list of other organisations which can help.

I have discovered many people who were unhappy after their surgery, some of whom did even commit suicide. It grieved me to think that no-one was there to help them when they so desperately needed it. I feel guilty that I could not share their pain and even now, years later, I still feel some of that guilt.

A lady once contacted me, on my helpline service, and asked if she could meet me. She was obviously distressed, so I travelled sixty-odd miles to see her. She told me that some time ago her husband had been treated at a private clinic in London for gender dysphoria, and had been given hormone treatment. She had had no idea that her husband had been having any kind of treatment, as for the past five years they had slept in separate bedrooms. About a month ago, he left to go to a seminar in Europe for three weeks. During that time away from home, her husband actually had a sex-change operation. Even when he returned home, tired and withdrawn, she did not realise what had happened, and thought that it was the seminar that had taken it out of him.

She finally discovered the truth when she found him dead in bed five days later. He had taken an overdose. He left her a note saying that the sex-change had all been a big mistake. He felt that he had been railroaded into surgery. No-one had ever tried to dissuade him and he had not known where to go for help in making his decision.

She had found a copy of my first book in his suitcase with the helpline number written in the back. Where he got the number from, I do not know. He may have been given it by another transexual. If only he had phoned me before he took his own life, I might have been able to help.

Through the filming and my own research I have found some very different places. I have discovered psychiatrists that you can go to privately and, if you give the right answers to the right questions, you can be put on hormone treatment the same day. There are also surgeons here in the UK who will perform sex-change surgery with no questions asked. This is just too easy. I spoke to one surgeon on the phone. I knew that he had performed about sixteen male-to-female operations in the early 'eighties; they had all gone drastically wrong, and most of his patients subsequently had to have corrective surgery elsewhere. Several of them have successfully sued him. This man did not know who I was when we spoke, and he agreed to meet me the following week. At our meeting, he told me that he could perform the surgery within a fortnight, no questions asked and no psychiatrist's report needed. All I would have to provide was £6,000 in cash.

During filming, we visited a chain of sex shops whose head office is in the Manchester area. The same organisation also owns a 'gender clinic', which I had been aware of for several years. Among the pornographic magazines and videos in one of the shops there were large signs advertising the clinic. I just couldn't fathom out why they were there: this was a sex shop that catered for transvestites, so why were they advertising a service for transexuals? I thought it would cause confusion as transvestites could easily be misled by the adverts, and accidentally guided on to a path that could have disastrous consequences.

The shop specialised in 'change away' services, where a transvestite could dress up as a maid, a tart, or even wear a bridal gown, for a four-hour period. They charged just £65. Different kinds of pills and potions were littered around the shelves, promising bust development, or even the feeling of suffering from premenstrual tension. Why the hell anyone would want to buy tablets to experience PMT is beyond me. Most women I know would gladly give theirs away, so to spend £40 a month on it seems crazy.

Among the bras and panties, munching on a meat pie sat a transexual called Wendy. She was quite happy to talk to me. She told me that she was waiting to go across to the gender clinic to see a doctor and pick up her hormone tablets. She only had one tablet left and had travelled nearly 200 miles for this appointment. She had to do this every eight weeks, and the expense of travelling to her appointments was crippling, but she had paid for a year's treatment in advance. It had cost her £1,200 but she was pleased with the arrangement because if she had paid for it on a monthly basis the treatment would have cost £300 more. For her money, she would see a nurse who would take her blood pressure and occasionally a urine sample. She would then see a doctor for about five minutes. She could also see a counsellor if she needed to. That day, I watched Wendy go into the clinic and leave within six minutes. She was happy as Larry because she had a prescription for hormone tablets. I was alarmed to learn from Wendy that this was actually her third year of treatment and she only had another three months to go. Her seventeen appointments over three years had cost her nearly £4,000. I asked what her psychiatrist had said, but she had never seen one. She thought that she was due to see one at the end of the three-year course and that then a doctor would automatically refer her for surgery. I just could not believe that she was being so misled. I recommended that she ask her GP for a referral to a NHS gender clinic, and then the truth came out. Her GP had refused to refer her three years ago, so she had turned to the private clinic after seeing it advertised in a national newspaper. The clinic had told her, when she phoned, that they would take on her case because no-one else would help her. I suggested that she should try and find another GP, and keep trying until she found one who would help her, instead of wasting her money. The poor thing was not even aware that she could change her GP.

I also met Tracy. I was later to find out that he was a male transvestite, although at first he told me he was a transexual. Tracy was due to start having treatment that very day, over at the clinic. He had been a regular customer on the 'change away' experience and had been told he was too pretty to be just a transvestite, he must be a transexual. I must admit he was very attractive as a female.

Tracy wanted to start hormone therapy. I asked if his family knew of his intention. He told me that his girlfriend knew that he was a transvestite, but no more. He had decided he would tell her later, when things were more established. I asked him how he thought his girlfriend would react when, after being on hormone treatment for a couple of months he couldn't get an erection. Tracy looked a little confused at that. He had not realised that by taking hormone tablets he was subjecting himself to a form of chemical castration and that he would no longer be able to have sex with his girlfriend.

Our conversation continued for another hour and in the end Tracy never did go for that appointment. I am still in touch with him and his girlfriend, who are going to get married in the summer of 1994. Tracy was grateful that someone had been truthful with him before it was too late.

Later that same day, I spoke to the owner of the sex shop chain. She claimed not to know how much the clinic charged for its services, something I found hard to believe, after all, she owns the place. She admitted to having over 1,000 patients registered with the clinic but knew full well that of those, only twelve would possibly go forward for surgery. Now that clinic is either doing a good job convincing people that they do not want surgery, or there are many confused transvestites receiving unsuitable and unnecessary hormone treatment, when what they really need is the help and services of a trained gender psychiatrist. Referral to gender identity clinics at the main teaching hospitals should be the first step for anyone with a gender problem, but those people have got to have the courage to approach their own GP first.

My long journey has taught me so many things about the system and has introduced me to some of the top surgeons and psychiatrists in Europe. They all believe that they bring happiness to the true transexual, but they are all aware that occasionally someone who is not truly transexual slips through the net. It is not for me to decide that the pre-operative 'waiting' period should be a minimum of three years, although I believe strongly that it should be. I think a social or welfare worker should be attached to every case during the pre-operative period to ensure that the patient is really living in their new gender role within society. It is actually very easy to lie, and say you are living and working in the opposite gender, but you should be made to prove it. It is so important that you find out for yourself because if you cannot survive your pre-operative period in your new role, you won't survive in your new gender after surgery. It is only your gender that will have changed and not your circumstances.

Other transexuals will say I am a bitch for stating such things, after all I have had my surgery, why the hell should I try to make it difficult for them? My answer to that will always be that I have been there and I do know what you are going through. I know from experience that if a little more time and thought goes into planning for the future, you can still succeed but you must be made aware of all the pitfalls that you will encounter along the way and you must be ready to take the knocks. It won't all be plain sailing but really, three years is no time to wait if your ultimate goal is achieved in the end.

The way the system works at the moment, for male-to-female surgery, you are more likely to have the main gender surgery before the breast surgery. I think this is wrong. I have met many transexuals who have been able to do it the other way round and have stopped after breast surgery, not taking it any further. Breast surgery can be reversed if you change your mind, genital surgery cannot.

I still say with my hand on my heart that I do not regret having surgery – I never have – but the best years of my life have now gone and I will never get them back. My only regret is that for so long I have lived a lie, letting people think I was happy when I was not. For others who are contemplating surgery, I hope I have made you aware of some of the problems and the need to think carefully before making a decision. If you know someone out there who is facing this dilemma, you must have the guts to stand by them all the way. They will need all your support until they can stand alone and proud.

Julia's Thanks

I would like to give my thanks to all the following people:

To David Pearson and all the film crew involved in making *A Change of Sex* in 1979/80 and 1993/94: you have helped to inform and change people's attitudes about a sensitive subject. On a personal level, thank you for being so understanding and compassionate when it was needed. You have helped me rediscover the right path.

To Mr Royale, my surgeon: for fifteen years I lived with the dread that if we met again you would tell me nothing could be done for me, and that I would be trapped in limbo for the rest of my life. Now, I have the courage to address my problems and face surgery again. I would never consider taking that step if you were not going to perform the operation. I had faith in you in 1979, and the problems I have had since then have done nothing to shake that faith. I now have a new goal in life: to go back to the operating table and to come away from it as the complete woman I set out to be all those years ago. When I do, I shall have you to thank for my new life.

To my mother: I only wish that you could be here to see me succeed. Thank you for always accepting me for what I was, first a loving son and later a loving daughter. You never questioned my sexuality.

To Richard and Graham, my dearest friends: you have both always been there when I needed you. I know you have both had problems in the past, and I hope I have always been able to help you when you needed it. You both deserve happiness.

I must also mention Amanda and Tim Bossom (Stoke), Alice and Angela (Gender Trust), Dayle and Mick (Arcadia), Steve and Phil (Wonderland), Keith (Manhattan), Michael and Chris (Lingard's), Gary (Crown and Anchor), Paul and Ian (French Retreat), Betty and Charles Lemmon (Fulbeck Heath), Barbara (Mansfield), Paul (Millionaires), Christine, Ray and Joanne (Northwich) and Ray and Brenda (Transnet). Thank you all for being there: you have all helped me shape my new life.

Finally, I would like to thank all my new friends at Boxtree.

The Gender Trust

Julia has asked me to write about the Gender Trust, explaining the work we do now, and what is needed for the future.

Essentially, we help individuals, their families, friends, employers, the professionals treating them, other agencies e.g. social services, the Samaritans, academic and research bodies, the media, in fact anybody who needs or wants to know something about gender dysphoria.

To do this we offer:

Confidential and impartial advice

Factual information

Befriending

A list of qualified counsellors with experience in gender problems

An interface between individuals and professional or other agencies

An information/research database

Our main aim is to help individuals to be at peace with themselves by coming to terms with their situation, and for them and their families to cope with the stresses and trauma that so often accompany gender problems.

We are non-judgmental and impartial, helping individuals to make informed choices rather than prescribing them. We believe in treatment which is tailored to the individual, and contributes towards an outcome of greater self-acceptance.

We believe people are more important than systems, so we want the system to be client-centred, and to have national Standards of Care to protect both clients and the professionals treating them.

We want to prevent isolation, because loneliness is a fatal disease. Affiliated to the Trust is the Gender Membership Society – GEMS: this is a self-help network for transexuals and other gender confused persons, with associate membership for those who have a genuine interest in the subject. Membership includes a confidential contact system, regular newsletters and local activities which are run through regional representatives.

We provide information and speakers to professional and voluntary agencies who may see gender-confused clients. We also run conferences, and publish information packs and handbooks. These are all ways in which we are attempting to reduce prejudice through education.

The number of persons requesting gender surgery is increasing. Many are mistaken or ill-advised and surgery is inappropriate for some. We are trying to reduce these tragedies through better, more accessible information and support, and lobbying for Standards of Care. We are needed more than ever.

We can help you: write to us at the address on the following page (please enclose a SAE), call or fax the information line 0305 269222.

You can help us, by joining GEMS, giving us your time, a special skill or a donation. All officers and trustees are unpaid volunteers.

ANGELA PRICE
Information Officer

Useful Addresses and Telephone Numbers

The Gender Trust, BM Gentrust, London WC1N 3XX
Helpline number 0305 269 222 (before 10.00p.m.)
Provides information for transexuals and professionals in the field of care

The Beaumont Trust, BM Box 3084, London WC1N 3XX
Information for transvestites and their partners

Transnet Central, Tel: 0246 551 100
A twenty-four hour helpline service, run by dedicated helpers.

Changes, Tel: 0850 799 026
Helpline service for transexuals run by a transexual

Northern Concord, Jenny Baker, PO Box 258, Manchester M60 1LN

The helplines listed below are operated by volunteers. If no-one is available, an answer-phone service is in operation.

Bristol	Karen	0934 838 527
Derby	Jed	0773 828 973
Leicester	Jo	0533 512 523
London	Joanne	081 346 3909
Sheffield	Andy and Julie	0742 588 167
Swindon	Karen	0793 420 212